3000 800053 41317

St. Louis Community College

D0204038

Meramec Library
St. Louis Community College
11333 Big Bend Blvd.
Kirkwood, MO 63122-5799
314-984-7797

JAPANESE AMERICAN INTERNMENT DURING WORLD WAR II

JAPANESE AMERICAN INTERNMENT DURING WORLD WAR II

A History and Reference Guide

Wendy Ng

St. Louis Community College
at Meramec
Library

GREENWOOD PRESS
Westport, Connecticut • London

Library of Congress Cataloging-in-Publication Data

Ng, Wendy L.
    Japanese American internment during World War II : a history and reference
guide / Wendy Ng.
        p.   cm.
    Includes bibliographical references and index.
    ISBN 0–313–31375–X (alk. paper)
    1. Japanese Americans—Evacuation and relocation, 1942–1945.   2. Japanese
Americans—Evacuation and relocation, 1942–1945—Bibliography.   3. Japanese
Americans—Evacuation and relocation, 1942–1945—Sources.   4. World War,
1939–1945—Reparations.   5. United States—History—1933–1945.   I. Title.
D769.8.A6N4   2002
940.53'17'0973—dc21   00–069128

British Library Cataloguing in Publication Data is available.

Copyright © 2002 by Wendy Ng

All rights reserved. No portion of this book may be
reproduced, by any process or technique, without
the express written consent of the publisher.

Library of Congress Catalog Card Number: 00–069128
ISBN: 0–313–31375–X

First published in 2002

Greenwood Press, 88 Post Road West, Westport, CT 06881
An imprint of Greenwood Publishing Group, Inc.
www.greenwood.com

Printed in the United States of America

The paper used in this book complies with the
Permanent Paper Standard issued by the National
Information Standards Organization (Z39.48–1984).

10 9 8 7 6 5 4 3 2 1

Copyright Acknowledgments

The author and publisher gratefully acknowledge permission to reprint the following material:

"Missing Pieces" by Ann T. Muto. Reprinted with permission of the author and Japanese American Resource Center/Museum.

Excerpts from "Okaasan" by Grace Shibata in Mei Nakano's *Japanese American Women: Three Generations, 1890–1990.* San Francisco: National Japanese American Historical Society, and Berkeley: Mina Press, 1990. Reprinted with permission of the author and the National Japanese American Historical Society.

Excerpts from *Suspended: Growing Up Asian in America* by Clifford I. Uyeda. San Francisco: National Japanese American Historical Society, 2000. Reprinted with permission of the author and the National Japanese American Historical Society.

Excerpts from the testimony of Warren Furutani as appears in "Rites of Passage: Commission Hearings 1981" *Amerasia Journal* 8(2), 1981. Reprinted with permission of Warren Furutani and the University of California.

Excerpts from *Manzanar Martyr: An Interview with Harry Y. Ueno* by Sue Kunitomi Embrey, Arthur A. Hansen, and Betty Kulberg Mitson. Fullerton, California: Oral History Program, California State University, Fullerton, 1986. Reprinted by permission of Arthur A. Hansen and The Oral History Program, California State University-Fullerton.

Excerpts from "Tom Kawaguchi" in John Tateishi's *And Justice for All: An Oral History of the Japanese American Detention Camps.* New York: Random House, 1984. Reprinted with permission of John Tateishi.

Contents

Preface

As the daughter of a former Japanese American internee, I never fully understood the significance of that period of my mother and her family's lives. Uprooted from their home in Berkeley, California, they lived for three years at Topaz Relocation Center in Utah. My mother attended junior high school at Topaz. She told me it was the place where she learned to ice skate on a pond of frozen water, was introduced to new foods such as apple butter and marmalade, and had to buy all of her clothes through the Sears and Roebuck catalog. Beyond the material possessions that she lost, her greatest loss was her oldest brother, who died in Italy while serving in the army with the 442nd Regimental Combat Team. Because she never revealed to me any more details of her camp experience, I have always thought of that time as one she did not want to remember. Her selective memory of the events stirred my interest in the subject. Researching the ordeal has brought about my deeper understanding of the significance and tragedy of the events as they occurred.

There is a wealth of material about the Japanese experience during World War II. This volume touches upon the significant events of the time period, as well as the developments that have taken place in the past twenty years in the study of Japanese Americans. Incarcerated as they were, they became an ideal population for social scientists to research. Those early studies conducted by non-Japanese social scientists bore the interpretations of the time period. Now, more than fifty years since, the topic of the camps still generates much questioning and interest. Today's historians and scholars have brought forth new interpretations of the wartime experience. This book contains materials designed to assist readers in learning about the internment experience: a chronology, a series of interpretive essays, primary source documents, brief biographies of key individuals, an annotated bibliography, and a glossary of terms. Although the focus is on the Japanese American internment experience, certain materials apply to the Japanese in Hawaii, who were not interned, but were still suspect in much the same way as mainland Japanese.

As a sociologist, my work has focused on the way that different generations of Japanese Americans have interpreted the wartime experience and have created a sense of memory and community from the event. The social and historical memory of what happened in the past has become intertwined with Japanese American identity and sense of the present day. The Japanese American experience during World War II has undergone much reinterpretation as social scientists within the past twenty years have begun to look at history in new ways. Rather than looking at Japanese Americans as passive participants in history, new interpretations look at the role of resistance and response to the evacuation and internment. This book would not have been possible without the work of scholars Roger Daniels, Yuji Ichioka, Gary Y. Okihiro, and Ron Takaki, community activists Michi Nishiura Weglyn, Bill Hosokawa, Mike Masaoka, Clifford Y. Uyeda, and many others. All of these individuals and many others have contributed to a better understanding of the Japanese American experience.

More than anything, the Japanese American community continues to undergo changes in an attempt to define itself as a part of American history and society. It has had to accept the differences that have divided the community in the past, and recognize the struggles of many individuals and groups to gain acknowledgment and recognition of the events of World War II. The issues of loyalty, resistance, and interpretations of the events are still being debated on every front, with new views and interpretations being brought forward all the time. Although one cannot be fully immune to particular biases and viewpoints, this book tries to provide many different options and avenues for exploring the different issues faced by Japanese Americans during World War II.

Japanese American Internment during World War II brings together numerous sources about the Japanese American internment experience. In the six thematic essays, I have relied on the extensive research done by historians and sociologists that has documented and analyzed the complexity of the event. Chapter 1 begins with an overview of Japanese immigration and communities before World War II, and the anti-Japanese movement. Chapter 2 details the U.S. government's decision to evacuate and detain the West Coast Japanese population, both citizen and noncitizen. Chapter 3 discusses the formation of the camps, the internal and external conditions, and life for the camps' residents. Chapter 4 discusses the issues surrounding loyalty and Japanese Americans, the formation of the all-Japanese American army unit, the 442nd Regimental Combat Team and 100th Battalion, and the challenges brought by draft resisters in the camps. Chapter 5 discusses the legal challenges to the curfew, evacuation, and internment orders in the Supreme Court cases of Fred Korematsu, Gordon Hirabayashi, Minoru Yasui, and Mitsuye Endo. Finally, Chapter 6 chronicles the immediate post–World War II period of resettlement through the redress and reparations movement of the 1980s, and the contemporary issues facing the Japanese American community today. The photographic essay is compiled from the more than 4,000 photographs that were taken by the War Relocation Authority. These images document the evacuation and internment and are a part of the public historic record. The primary documents include several government documents related to the internment, and personal memoirs by Grace Shibata, Clifford Uyeda, Tom Kawaguchi, and Warren Furutani. Their personal reflections highlight the individual circumstances of the more than 120,000 Japanese Americans who were caught in the turbulence of wartime.

ACKNOWLEDGMENTS

Many people have contributed, directly and indirectly, to the writing of this book. The time for writing this book was granted through a sabbatical leave from San Jose State University during the 1999–2000 academic year. Funds for research were provided by the College of Social Sciences Foundation Research Grant. The Women's Leadership Institute at Mills College in Oakland, California, provided office support for the year. Warm thanks goes to the scholars affiliated with the institute who listened to me and gave feedback to my ideas: Robin Balliger, Ellen Barry, Megan Boler, Yvonne Payne Daniel, Ilana DeBare, Susan Lyon; and especially lawyers Cynthia Lee and Lisa Ikemoto, who helped me wade through the legal cases, and the director of the institute, Edna Mitchell, who makes all things possible.

Several colleagues and friends have provided much needed information during this project: Frank Abe, Steven G. Doi, Art Hansen, Greg Marutani, Curtiss Takata Rooks, and Alexander Yamato. Barbara A. Rader at Greenwood Press patiently gave me critical feedback on the manuscript and kept me to my deadlines.

Very special thanks goes to two Nisei women who entered my life during the process of writing this book. Mary Kimoto Tomita came to a presentation I gave at Mills College, and asked if I were going to mention anything about the Japanese Americans who were in Japan during the war. She was one of several hundred Nisei trapped there at that time. Since this book focuses largely on internment in the United States, I was unable to include her story, but it is documented in her book, *Dear Miye:*

Letters Home from Japan 1939–1946 (Stanford, Calif.: Stanford University Press, 1995). Grace Eto Shibata and I share the same alma mater, and I am grateful for our Mills College connection. She kindly allowed her essay "Okaasan" to be reprinted in this book. Other personal thanks goes to Dr. Clifford Uyeda and Warren Furutani for allowing their powerful essays to be reprinted in this book and to John Tateishi, for permission to reprint Tom Kawaguchi's oral history.

Finally, very special thanks go to my immediate and extended family for their time and patience during the writing of this book: my husband, Roger Jue; my children Justin and Natalie Jue; my in-laws Will and Quannie Jue for providing the invaluable child care I needed during the year; my aunt Toshiko Yoshida for providing me important information just when I needed it, and my parents, Henry and Haru Ng, for always asking about what I was doing. Finally, I want to honor the dreams, struggles, and triumphs of my grandparents Tamejiro and Suye Sagimori. It is to their memory that I dedicate this book.

Note on Terminology

During the past fifty years since World War II, scholars have questioned the terminology used to describe the forced removal and incarceration of Japanese Americans. Although the title of this book is *Japanese American Internment during World War II*, it should be understood that *internment* and *relocation* were the terms used by the government to describe the overall removal and detainment program. There were different types of detention centers used to house people of Japanese ancestry during the war. The *assembly centers* were the first local, temporary, holding facility for the Japanese under the auspices of the U.S. military (Camp Harmony, Tanforan, Pomona, Santa Anita, etc.). The War Relocation Authority (WRA), operated under the Department of the Interior, ran the *relocation centers*, the ten so-called "camps" (e.g., Manzanar, Topaz, Poston, etc.). The term *internment camp* was used to refer to prisons operated by the Department of Justice that detained people of Japanese, Italian, and German ancestry (Crystal City, Bismarck, Missoula). A final type of center, the *citizen isolation camps*, detained U.S. citizens removed from the camps for safety and security reasons at Moab, Utah, and Leupp, Arizona.

Many scholars within and outside of the Japanese American community have called the term *relocation center* a euphemism—a term that covers up the real identity of the detention centers to which Japanese Americans were forced to move. One of the terms now favored by scholars is *concentration camp*. The government "relocation centers" can be viewed as part of a continuum of "concentration-style" camps. At one end there are milder types, in the middle there are slave labor camps, and the most extreme are camps where torture and execution are enforced among the inmates. The Japanese American relocation centers were a type of "concentration camp," albeit on the milder end of the scale (Drinnon, 1987; see also Lane Hirabayashi's explanation in Nishimoto, 1995: xxi–xxii). Historian Roger Daniels explains that the term *concentration camp* was widely used during World War II but as news of the Nazi death camps reached America, the term fell into disfavor. Thus, it is important to note that they were concentration camps, although not in the same sense as the Nazi death camps in Europe. Daniels feels that *concentration camp* is still the most appropriate term to describe the Japanese American relocation and internment camps (Daniels, 1993: 46).

It is always difficult to choose terminology that can be understood by everyone and that carries an accurate meaning and intention. I agree with other scholars that the camps were not just "relocation centers" but camps where people were not free to come and go as they wished. They were prisoners being detained against their will. However, for consistency's sake, I have chosen to use the terms that are used by the Commission on Wartime Relocation and Internment of Civilians, calling the camps *relocation centers* or *camps* and the camp residents as such, as well as *detainees*, or *internees*. Among former internees, the term *internment camp* or simply *camp* is still widely used and has become a standard part of the Japanese American vocabulary. It is not my intention to give the message that use of these terms is universally accepted or preferable among everyone who has studied the Japanese American internment experience, but to use the terminology that is best understood by the greatest number of people, while understanding their limitations.

Abbreviations

CWRIC	Commission on Wartime Relocation and Internment of Civilians
E.O.	Executive Order
JACL	Japanese American Citizens League
MIS	Military Intelligence Service
MISLS	Military Intelligence Service Language School
NJAHS	National Japanese American Historical Society
RCT	Regimental Combat Team
WCCA	Wartime Civil Control Administration
WDC	Western Defense Command
WRA	War Relocation Authority

Chronology of Events in Japanese American History

1868	Japanese immigrants arrive in Hawaii.
1869	Japanese immigrants arrive to the mainland United States and establish the Wakamatsu Colony in Gold Hill, California.
1882	Chinese Exclusion Act is passed, prohibiting immigration from China. It was enforced between 1882 and 1892 and brought about labor shortages in the West, resulting in an increased demand for Japanese laborers.
1893	The San Francisco School Board passes a regulation to send all Japanese children in the city to the segregated Chinese school. The Japanese government protests and the order is withdrawn.
1898	Hawaii becomes a U.S. territory. About 60,000 Japanese living in Hawaii can travel to the mainland United States without a foreign passport.
1906	The San Francisco School Board orders the segregation of ninety-three Japanese American students.
1907	The school board rescinds the segregation order after being ordered to do so by President Theodore Roosevelt. Anti-Japanese activity continues. Congress passes an immigration law banning Japanese laborers from entering the United States through Hawaii, Mexico, or Canada.

1908   The Japanese and U.S. governments negotiate the "Gentlemen's Agreement" whereby Japan agrees not to issue visas to laborers who want to emigrate.

1913   California passes the Alien Land Law, which denies "all aliens ineligible for citizenship" the right to own land in the state. Similar alien land laws are soon passed in Washington, Oregon, Idaho, Montana, Arizona, New Mexico, Texas, Kansas, Louisiana, Missouri, and Minnesota.

1920   A second Alien Land Law adopted in California forbids the leasing of lands to aliens "ineligible for citizenship." Under pressure from the United States, Japan stops issuing passports to "picture bride" Japanese women, effectively halting their immigration from Japan.

1922   The Supreme Court rules in the case of *Takeo Ozawa* v. *U.S.* that U.S. citizenship is limited to "free white persons and aliens of African ancestry," thus prohibiting people of Japanese ancestry from becoming naturalized citizens on the basis of race.
                         Congress passes the Cable Act. This law provides that anyone marrying an "alien ineligible for citizenship" will also lose their U.S. citizenship.

1923   The Immigration Act of 1924, the National Origins Act, bars all immigration from Japan.

1936   The Cable Act is repealed.

1941

October–November   Military Intelligence opens a language school under the Fourth Army at the Presidio of San Francisco. There are four Nisei language instructors with sixty students total, fifty-eight of whom are Japanese American.

November 7   Curtis Munson submits his report to the president, the State Department, and the secretary of war. His documentation corroborates years of surveillance of Japanese on the mainland and Hawaii and suggests no reason to suspect their loyalty to the United States.

December 7   Japan attacks Pearl Harbor.

December 8   U.S. Congress declares war on Japan. The U.S. Treasury Department seizes all Japanese banks and businesses.

December 9   Japanese language schools are closed.

December 11	United States declares war on Germany and Italy. FBI warns against possession of cameras or guns by suspected enemy aliens. More than 2,000 Issei leaders in Hawaii and the mainland United States are arrested and imprisoned by the U.S. government.
December 27	Attorney general orders all suspected enemy aliens on the West Coast to turn in shortwave radios and cameras.
December 30	California revokes liquor licenses held by noncitizen Japanese.

1942

January 14	President Roosevelt orders re-registration of all suspected enemy aliens in the Western states.
January 27	Los Angeles City and County discharges all Japanese on civil service lists.
January 29	U.S. Attorney General Francis Biddle issues the first orders establishing "strategic military areas" on the Pacific Coast requiring the removal of all suspected "enemy" aliens from those areas.
February 4	Attorney general establishes curfew zones in California.
February 14	Lieutenant General John DeWitt, commander of the Western Defense Command, sends a memorandum to secretary of war Henry L. Stimson recommending the removal of all "Japanese and other subversive persons" from the West Coast areas.
February 19	President Franklin D. Roosevelt signs Executive Order 9066, authorizing the secretary of war or other military commander designated by the secretary to establish "military areas" that would exclude "any or all persons" they felt needed to be excluded.
February 20	Secretary Stimson designates General DeWitt as military commander empowered to carry out an evacuation within his command per E.O. 9066.
February 21	The Tolan Committee meets in San Francisco and holds hearings on whether to incarcerate ethnic Japanese, citizen and alien.
March 2	General John DeWitt issues Public Proclamation 1. The order specifies Military Zones 1 and 2. Zone 1 encompasses the western portion of California, Washington, and Oregon, and the southern area of Arizona.

March 11   General DeWitt establishes the Wartime Civil Control
             Administration (WCCA). Colonel Karl R. Bendetsen is
             appointed as director of the evacuation program.

March 18   Executive Order 9102 creates the War Relocation
             Authority as the government division supervising the
             evacuated population. Milton S. Eisenhower is appointed
             as director.

March 21   President Roosevelt signs Public Law 503 (77th Congress)
             making it a federal offense to violate any order by a
             military commander under the authority of Executive
             Order 9066.

March 22   First large group of evacuees from Los Angeles arrives at
             the Manzanar Reception Center (later changed to the
             Manzanar Relocation Center) in eastern California.

March 23   General DeWitt issues Civilian Order 1. All people of
             Japanese descent are removed from Bainbridge Island
             (near Seattle) by March 30 to the Puyallup Assembly
             Center.

March 27   Proclamation 4 is issued forbidding any voluntary
             migration of people of Japanese descent from the West
             Coast to areas outside of the military zone.

March 28   Attorney Minoru Yasui decides to test the validity of the
             curfew orders and turns himself in at a Portland, Oregon,
             police station.

March 30   The War Department ceases to induct Japanese
             Americans into the armed forces on the West Coast.

April 3   Japanese from Los Angeles are ordered to evacuate to the
             Santa Anita Assembly Center.

April 28   Seattle Japanese are sent to the Puyallup fairgrounds,
             called Camp Harmony.

May 5   Gordon Hirabayashi refuses to follow the curfew and
             evacuation orders and turns himself in to be arrested.

May 7   The American Friends Service Committee helps to
             organize the National Japanese American Student
             Relocation Council to assist Nisei college students in
             continuing their education and relocating them to areas
             not within the restricted military zones.

May 30   Fred Korematsu is arrested in Oakland, California, for
             refusing to report for detention.

May 21	A group of evacuees from the Portland Assembly Center leave to work in seasonal agricultural work in eastern Oregon.
May 27	First group of evacuees arrive at Tule Lake in northern California.
June 17	Milton S. Eisenhower resigns as director of the WRA and Dillon S. Myer is appointed as his successor.
July 13	Mitsuye Endo files a writ of habeas corpus. Her petition asks that she be released from the relocation center.
July 20	WRA adopts a leave policy allowing Japanese American citizens (Nisei) to leave the camps to work in the Midwest. Evacuees from the Turlock Assembly Center arrive at Gila River Relocation Center in Arizona.
August 10	Minidoka Relocation Center (Idaho) opens with evacuees from the Puyallup Assembly Center.
August 12	Heart Mountain Relocation Center (Wyoming) opens with evacuees from the Pomona Assembly Center.
August 27	Granada Relocation Center (Colorado) opens with evacuees from the Merced Assembly Center.
September 11	Central Utah Relocation Center (Topaz) opens with residents coming from the Tanforan Assembly Center.
September 18	Rohwer (Arkansas) opens and receives residents from the Stockton Assembly Center.
October 6	Jerome (Arkansas) is the last center to open, with residents from the Fresno Assembly Center.
November 14	Community demonstration and strike is held at Poston (Arizona) in protest over the arrest of two residents accused of beating another resident.
December 6	Demonstration and protest at Manzanar (California) over the arrest of a resident, resulting in military control over the camp and the shooting death of one resident.

1943

January 28	The War Department announces plans for an all–Japanese American military unit within the army.
February 1	The 442nd Regimental Combat Team is officially activated by President Roosevelt.

February 8   The "loyalty questionnaire" (Application for Leave Clearance) is administered to all people over seventeen years of age at the camps. It is used for army recruitment, as well as for segregation and relocation of potentially "disloyal" internees.

April 20   More than 9,000 Japanese from Hawaii join a special combat team, which is later named the 100th Battalion.

May 6   Eleanor Roosevelt, wife of the president, visits the Gila River center in Arizona.

July 15   Tule Lake (California) is designated as an official segregation center for those who had unacceptable responses to the loyalty questionnaire. Residents of Tule Lake with "acceptable" responses are transferred to other camps.

November 1–4   Demonstrations and outbursts of violence occur at Tule Lake. The military is called in to control the disturbance, and the camp remains under military supervision until January 1944.

1944

February 16   The WRA is transferred to the Department of the Interior under Executive Order 9423.

May   The 442nd Regimental Combat Team is sent to Italy.

June 30   Jerome (Arkansas) is closed with remaining individuals transferred to other relocation centers.

July 1   President Roosevelt signs Public Law 405 (78th Congress) allowing U.S. citizens to renounce their citizenship.

December 17   The War Department revokes the mass exclusion orders (effective January 2, 1945), which affected all people of Japanese ancestry living on the West Coast.

December 18   The WRA announces that all internment camps will be closed before the end of 1945, and the WRA program closed by June 30, 1946.
The U.S. Supreme Court hands down its ruling in the case of *Korematsu* v. *United States*. They rule that the government detention orders are a valid use of "war powers" by the government. At the same time, in *Ex parte Endo* the court declares that the WRA has no authority to detain admittedly loyal American citizens in internment camps.

1945

April 29	522nd Field Artillery Battalion frees prisoners at the Dachau concentration camps in Germany.
May 8	V-E Day; Germany surrenders.
August 6	Atomic bomb is dropped on Hiroshima, Japan.
August 9	Atomic bomb is dropped on Nagasaki, Japan.
August 15	V-J Day.
September 2	Japan officially surrenders.
September 4	The Western Defense Command issues Public Proclamation 24. This revokes the individual exclusion orders and other military restrictions against people of Japanese ancestry.
October 15 to December 15	All WRA internment camps are closed, except for the Tule Lake Segregation Center.

1946

March 20	Tule Lake Segregation Center officially closed.
June 30	The War Relocation Authority program ends.
October 30	Japanese Americans from Latin America are released from the Crystal City (Texas) Detention Center.

1947

December	President Harry S. Truman grants a pardon to 257 Japanese American draft resisters.

1948

July 2	Congress passes the Evacuation Claims Act. Japanese Americans have until January 3, 1950, to file claims against the government for damages to or loss of real or personal property as a result of the evacuation. A total of $31 million is paid by the government for property lost by the internees. The total amount in claims paid was estimated at less than ten cents per dollar lost.

1952

April 17	California's Alien Land Laws are considered unenforceable by the California Supreme Court.
June 11	Congress passes the McCarran-Walter Immigration and Naturalization Act. It modifies the 1924 National Origins Act and allows Japanese and other Asian immigrants to apply for naturalized citizenship.

1956   California voters repeal the former Alien Land Laws by a two-to-one margin.

1959   Hawaii becomes the fiftieth state.

1965

October 3   The Immigration Law of 1965 eliminates the "national origins" quota systems used since 1924 and modified in 1952. A quota of 20,000 immigrants per year per Asian nation is granted.

1970   Nisei activist Edison Uno proposes redress for Japanese Americans, and it is adopted as a platform by the national JACL.

1974   The Seattle Evacuation Redress Committee and the Seattle area JACL propose a legislative plan for redress payments for all people interned during World War II, including Aleuts and Latin American Japanese.

1976

February 19   President Gerald R. Ford rescinds Executive Order 9066.

1978

July   The JACL National Council passes a resolution to seek redress. A national JACL Redress Committee is formed.

November 25   The first Day of Remembrance is held at the site of Camp Harmony at the Puyallup fairgrounds in Washington State.

1979

May   The National Council for Japanese American Redress (NCJAR) is founded. The group proposes to seek redress through Congress with a bill introduced later in the year.

August 2   Senators Daniel Inouye and Spark Matsunaga introduce a bill to establish the Commission on Wartime Relocation and Internment of Civilians Act.

November 28   Congressman Michael Lowry introduces the first redress bill (H.R. 5977), which suggests individual payments to former internment camp residents.

1980   President Jimmy Carter establishes the Commission on Wartime Relocation and Internment of Civilians (CWRIC). The NCJAR decides to focus its attention on redress through the judicial system.

1981   The CWRIC holds hearings and hears testimony from more than 750 witnesses throughout the United States.

1983   Gordon Hirabayashi, Minoru Yasui, and Fred Korematsu file a writ of error *coram nobis* to officially reopen their World War II cases.

March 16   NCJAR files a class action lawsuit, *William Hohri et al.* v. *United States* in the district court of the District of Columbia, seeking $200,000 in damages for former internees.

June   The CWRIC issues its report titled *Personal Justice Denied.* It recommends an official apology by the government and redress compensation in the amount of $20,000 per surviving internee.

November 11   Fred Korematsu's original wartime conviction is vacated by Judge Marilyn Hall Patel.

1984   California State Legislature recognizes February 19 as A Day of Remembrance, encouraging citizens to remember the rights and responsibilities of citizens as guaranteed by the U.S. Constitution.

1987   The Smithsonian Museum in Washington, D.C., commemorates the bicentennial of the U.S. Constitution with an exhibit titled "A More Perfect Union." It documents the internment of Japanese Americans during World War II and the experiences of the 100th Battalion/ 442nd Regimental Combat Team and Military Intelligence Service.

1988

August 10   H.R. 442 is signed into law by President Ronald Reagan. It provides for individual payments of $20,000 to each surviving internee and a $1.25 billion education fund.

1989

November 2   President George Bush signs Public Law 101–162. The law guarantees the funding of reparation payments to people of Japanese ancestry detained in internment camps during World War II.

1990

October 9   The first redress payments are made at a Washington, D.C., ceremony. The Reverend Mamoru Eto of Los Angeles is the first to receive a check. He is 107 years old.

1996   The Civil Liberties Public Education Fund is established. Commissioners are appointed by President Clinton and sworn in by Congressman Robert T. Matsui.

2000

July   The Japanese American Citizens League passes a
                        resolution to recognize the Nisei Resisters of Conscience
                        or Heart Mountain Draft Resisters.

October   Twenty former 442nd Nisei veterans receive medal
                        upgrades and receive the Medal of Honor.

1

The Japanese in America before World War II

For more than 100 years, people of Japanese ancestry have made their home in America. They migrated because of political and economic forces in their homeland, combined with the attraction of economic opportunity and industrial development in the United States. Before World War II, Japanese Americans formed tightly knit, self-sufficient communities within a society filled with anti-Asian sentiment, inherited from the Chinese who settled in America before them. When Japan bombed Pearl Harbor on December 7, 1941, their lives changed dramatically. The ensuing war years in which more than 120,000 Japanese Americans were interned in camps are forever embedded into the Japanese American community memory. This chapter overviews the immigration and settlement of the Japanese in America before World War II, and looks at how anti-Japanese sentiment contributed to the eventual forced exclusion and detention known as relocation.

IMMIGRATION

The Japanese presence in America began at a time of one of the greatest surges of population growth in American immigration history. During the late nineteenth century, immigrants from eastern and southern Europe were drawn to the East Coast. The West Coast received immigrants from Asia, mainly Chinese and Japanese. The distinctive physical and cultural characteristics of the Chinese and Japanese set them apart from the largely European American majority and made them targets of prejudice and discrimination.

For more than 200 years, Japanese laws prohibited emigration abroad.

In 1853, Japan's seclusion ceased when Commodore Matthew Perry sailed into Tokyo Bay. The increased contact with Western nations moved Japan rapidly into a new era. Within a year after Perry's arrival, the English and French missions arrived in Japan to establish similar diplomatic and trade relations. Internal political turmoil led to disagreements between powerful leaders, some of whom believed in restoring power to the Japanese emperor as a way of dealing with the increasing presence of Western nations. The historical period in which this occurred is referred to as the Meiji Restoration (1868–1912). The dates correspond to the reign of the Meiji emperor. In this new era, Japan began a course of modernization involving industrial and military growth accompanied by greater openness to trade relations and emigration abroad for its citizens. This growth was financially supported by increasing the taxes of landowning people. As a result, many farmers went into debt to pay the taxes or lost their land when they could not. In order to support a national army, Japan's national conscription law required men to perform military service. Japanese males could avoid military service by leaving the country and staying away until they had reached the age at which they were no longer eligible for military duty. All of these were reasons for emigration abroad.

The majority of immigrants during this time came from the prefectures of southwestern Japan where many people were experienced with agricultural work. The initial groups of immigrants were drawn to work on Hawaiian sugar plantations, and labor contractors recruited workers to fill this need. In the late nineteenth century, an estimated 80,000 Japanese men and women went to Hawaii to work as contract laborers.[1] By 1900, 39.7 percent of the population in Hawaii was of Japanese descent. Since the Japanese were such a significant percentage of Hawaii's population, they were an integral part of the local economy, and were not sent to internment centers as were the Japanese on the mainland during World War II. When plantation contract labor was outlawed in 1900, the migration of Japanese laborers to Hawaii declined. At this time there was an increase in the emigration of Japanese laborers from both Japan and Hawaii to the mainland United States (see Table 1.1).

The first Japanese settlement on the mainland was established in 1869 as the Wakamatsu Tea and Silk Colony in Gold Hill, El Dorado County, near Sacramento, California. Later this group disbanded because of crop failure and other economic hardships. By 1885, a steady stream of Japanese laborers began to migrate to the mainland United States. Among them were those who had agricultural experience and those of student and merchant classes. Regardless of their class status, they went to work in low-skilled, physically demanding jobs in the service sector and in the railroad, timber, manufacturing, and agricultural industries.

Table 1.1
Japanese Immigration to the United States, 1861–1950

Year	Numbers Immigrating
1861-1870	186
1871-1880	149
1881-1890	2,270
1891-1900	25,942
1901-1910	129,797
1911-1920	83,837
1921-1930	33,462
1931-1940	1,948
1941-1950	1,555

Source: U.S. Immigration and Naturalization Service, *Statistical Yearbook of the Immigration and Naturalization Service* (Washington: Government Printing Office, 1993), 26–8.

In 1880, the U.S. census counted 148 Japanese living in the United States. By the eve of World War II, there were 285,115. Geographically, the Japanese population was concentrated in the states of California, Oregon, and Washington, and the territory of Hawaii (see Table 1.2).

The Japanese did not experience immigration restriction until the so-called "Gentlemen's Agreement" of 1907–1908. President Theodore Roosevelt negotiated this agreement in response to anti-Japanese groups who wanted to halt emigration from Japan. The terms of the agreement were quite simple. At the request of the U.S. government, Japan stopped issuing passports to laborers. In return, Congress never passed any formal exclusion law directed toward the Japanese. The immigration agreement was a diplomatic relations side step between the two countries. The U.S. government recognized Japan's increasing military power in Asia, and saved Japan from any social and diplomatic embarrassment by not having an exclusion law passed toward its citizens.

The Gentlemen's Agreement curtailed the number of laborers emigrating to the United States, but it did not prevent the emigration of Japanese women. The common practice of this time was for arranged marriages. In Japan, matchmakers set up arrangements between eligible men and women. Issei men in America would send their picture, and they would receive a picture of a potential marriage partner. The marriage could be conducted without the groom being present. The bride would then come to America as the legal wife of the Issei laborer. The women became known as "picture brides" because they had entered into

Table 1.2
Japanese Population in the United States, 1880–1940

Year	Total U.S.	Total Japanese	California	Oregon	Washington	Hawaii
1890	62,947,714	2,039	1,147	25	360	12,610
1900	76,212,168	85,716	10,151	2,501	5,617	61,111
1910	92,228,531	152,745	41,356	3,418	12,929	79,675
1920	106,021,568	220,596	71,952	4,151	17,387	109,274
1930	123,202,660	278,743	97,456	4,598	17,838	139,631
1940	132,165,129	285,115	93,717	4,071	14,565	157,905

Source: Adapted from Kitano (1969: 162–3), O'Brien and Fugita (1991: 137), and Spickard (1996: 62).

an arranged marriage with only a picture of their husband. This type of marriage was commonplace in Japan, but frequently targeted by anti-Japanese groups as being incompatible with Western standards and norms. Pressured by these groups, picture bride emigration ceased in 1920. By 1924, worldwide immigration coupled with nativist and xeno-phobic attitudes pressured the U.S. Congress into passing the most re-strictive immigration law of the century: the Immigration Act of 1924. This act set European immigration by quota per country, but all "aliens ineligible for citizenship" were barred from immigrating, effectively ex-cluding Japanese.

Thus, the bulk of Japanese immigrants came between 1885 and 1924. This short time period of Japanese migration to the United States gave the community distinct generational groupings. Different generations of Japanese Americans are referred to as Issei, Nisei, and Sansei. Translated, these terms simply mean "first generation," "second generation," and "third generation." As sociologist Darrel Montero says, "the Japanese are the only ethnic group to emphasize geogenerational distinctions by a separate nomenclature and a belief in the unique character structure of each generational group" (Montero, 1980: 8). Thus, each generation had a certain history and a set of experiences that became part of its identity. World War II and the relocation and internment experience influenced and shaped the character of each generation.

THE FIRST GENERATION: ISSEI

The Issei are often referred to as the "pioneer" generation of Japanese Americans. These early immigrants faced the challenging and sometimes difficult adjustment to life in a new country where the language and social and cultural customs were different from their native land. Inter-estingly, the Japanese were keenly aware of the discrimination Chinese people had faced. In attempts to make themselves blend in better, Jap-anese immigrants quickly adopted Western-style clothing and encour-aged their Nisei children to be educated in American schools and participate in American-style activities. The Japanese further distinguished themselves from the Chinese by forming separate communities and neighborhoods. The non-Asian majority were often ignorant of the differences between the two groups. Although the Gentlemen's Agreement slowed the emigration of Japanese male laborers to the United States, Japanese picture brides still allowed under the agreement gave way to the formation of families and a stable Japanese community in this country.

The center of most Japanese American communities was Japantown, Little Tokyo, or "Nihonmachi," neighborhoods where people lived and worked. They housed churches, stores, doctors, boardinghouses, and a host of activities that served the Japanese ethnic community. Several organizations and groups existed to keep individuals connected. The Japanese Association of America provided visas for Japanese Americans who wanted to travel between Japan and the United States. It was quite common for families to send one or more of their children back to Japan to be educated, and the association facilitated this. There were regional associations based upon home prefecture that were called Kenjinkai, as well as both Buddhist and Christian churches, and business/employment associations for gardeners, farmers, and other merchants. Each of these groups provided a social outlet within the ethnic community for Japanese immigrants.

In terms of employment, Issei found themselves working in a variety of occupations. Many held jobs that were not in direct competition with other non-Asian immigrants. In general Japanese Americans were known to be highly successful in agriculture. They farmed land in the least desirable areas—swamplands near marshes and rivers that would flood, or barren desert strips of land that had to be irrigated. Despite the restrictions on Issei land ownership, Japanese American farmers were able to grow certain specialty, labor-intensive crops such as strawberries, deciduous fruits, and cut flowers, which allowed them to remain competitive with white farmers.

THE SECOND GENERATION: THE NISEI

The Nisei generation has often been described as growing up in two worlds, one Japanese, the other American. The issue of citizenship and nationality was complex for them. Until 1916, Japan followed the practice of *jus sanguinis*. Anyone born of a Japanese father was a Japanese citizen. The United States followed the practice of *jus solis*, which recognized citizenship by place of birth, and so anyone born in the United States was a citizen. Thus, Nisei could technically hold dual citizenship. By 1924, Japan changed its laws requiring overseas Japanese to register their children immediately in order to retain Japanese citizenship. In looking out for the interests of Japanese immigrants, the Japanese Association encouraged Issei to terminate their children's dual citizenship. By the time of World War II, fewer than 20 percent of Nisei held dual citizenship.

This difficult legal situation ameliorated but did not change the different cultural worlds Nisei had to navigate. Speaking Japanese in the home and English at school, Nisei often served as translators and interpreters for their parents. Within the Japanese American community, Japanese language schools were developed to teach Japanese language and customs to the Nisei children. This was one way of preserving and maintaining cultural ties to Japan. But Nisei participated in a variety of activities that by any standards could be defined as "American." Indeed, there was great pressure for Nisei to become Americanized and assimilated. Basketball and bowling leagues, ballroom dancing clubs, and general socializing was with other Nisei, but done with an American content.

One subgroup of Nisei called Kibei consisted of those Nisei born in the United States but reared and educated in Japan. Because the Kibei spent their formative years in Japan, but were U.S. citizens by birth, they probably experienced great conflict in loyalty between their two "mother" countries. As was the practice of the Japanese educational system, Kibei were educated in a strict militaristic tradition with emphasis on national loyalty. This often presented a dilemma for those Kibei who returned to the United States before the war, having received a good dose of Japanese nationalism, yet also having to live in American society. Oddly enough, though, many Kibei became instrumental in working for the U.S. military in intelligence gathering and translation activities during the war precisely because of their education and background.

By the 1930s, Nisei were "coming of age." Their Issei parents stressed the value of education, and many attended college and universities. They were educated in the American school system, which taught them citizenship, democracy, and equality. Yet when they tried to enter the U.S. mainstream, they still experienced discrimination in employment, housing, and in some social settings. Some Nisei professionals found themselves working within the Japanese American community; others ended up working for their parents' farms or businesses. Their social reality was not often the same as what they were taught. To combat the social prejudice and discrimination, the Nisei formed the Japanese American Citizens League (JACL) as a social and political arm of the community. As reflected in the official creed of the JACL:

Although some individuals may discriminate against me, I shall never become bitter or lose faith, for I know that such persons are not representative of the majority of the American People. True, I shall do all in my power to discourage such practices, but I shall do it in the American way—above board, in the open, through courts of law, by education, by proving myself to be worthy of equal treatment and consideration. . . . Because I believe in America, and I trust she believes in me, and because I have received innumerable benefits from her, I pledge myself to do honor to her at all times and all places; to support her constitution; to obey her laws; to respect her flag; to defend her against all enemies, foreign and domestic; to actively assume my duties and obligations as a citizen, cheerfully and without any reservations, in the hope that I may become a better American in a greater America. (Daniels, 1971: 24–5)

At the outbreak of World War II, the JACL became an important political organization representing Japanese Americans as they dealt with the issues of evacuation and internment. Although controversial at times, the organization provided leadership under tremendous pressure from the government and urged all Japanese Americans to comply with the curfew, evacuation, and relocation programs.

THE THIRD GENERATION: SANSEI

The third generation, Sansei, were the smallest number in the relocation centers. Most Sansei were not even born at the time of the internment and relocation. Because the Nisei were of the age that most people married and started families, it was quite common to see young families with infants and small children in the camps.

The majority of the Sansei, however, were born as part of the postwar "baby boom" generation. When the camps began to close in 1946, Japanese Americans were encouraged to resettle in areas throughout the United States. Although there are still large Japanese American communities throughout the West Coast, after camp, many families moved out of Japanese ethnic enclaves to integrated middle- and working-class neighborhoods, cities, and suburbs. Thus, many Sansei were raised in communities where there were few Japanese Americans. Sansei report that their parents encouraged them to be high achieving, socially and educationally. Their proof of "Americanness" was economic and social mobility. To achieve this one had to do one's best and prove oneself as a model citizen. A great deal of emphasis was placed on assimilation. That meant that Sansei were not taught to speak Japanese, thus making it difficult for them to communicate with their Issei grandparents. But more important, many Sansei were not told about their parents' and grandparents' experiences during World War II.

Although the Sansei were largely kept in the dark about Japanese American internment during World War II, the civil rights movement of the 1960s raised awareness of the racial injustices of the past. From this, Sansei began to question their parents about the war, thus shedding new light on a long, dark period of Japanese American history. Along with this relearning of forgotten history, Sansei worked with Nisei politicians and activists to seek redress for all Japanese who were affected by the internment during World War II. The redress movement, along with other significant post–World War II developments, are discussed in more detail in Chapter 6 of this book.

THE ANTI-JAPANESE MOVEMENT

The anti-Japanese movement was a part of a larger anti-Asian movement beginning with the Chinese in the late nineteenth century (Daniels, 1968). Historian Alexander Saxton calls the activities of anti-Asian violence part of a "growth sequence" of events that trigger continued outbursts of violence directed toward one Asian group, followed by another. What usually happened was a spontaneous eruption of violence toward a minority group such as the Chinese or Japanese. The perpetrators of the attack would be arrested, after which a defense committee worked to exonerate the attackers. With this support base, a more organized committee and activities emerged whose goal was to eliminate the minority group under attack, usually by advocating some type of immigration restriction measure.

Hostility toward Asian immigrants took several different forms. At one level, Japanese were stereotyped as being part of the "Yellow Peril"—an image in which hordes of Asians threatened to invade and conquer the United States. The Japanese were viewed as outsiders and strangers, their "assimilability" was questioned, and their success in agriculture was viewed as threatening the economic livelihood of the U.S. born, non-Japanese farmers.

Other types of anti-Japanese attacks were led by prominent political leaders. The *Sacramento Bee* publisher V.S. McClatchy said, "Of all races ineligible for citizenship, the Japanese are the least assimilable and the most dangerous to this country. . . . With great pride of race, they have no idea of assimilating in the sense of amalgamation. They do not come to this country with any desire or any intent to lose their race or national identity. . . . They never cease to be Japanese" (quoted in Takaki, 1989: 209).

In a speech in 1900, San Francisco mayor James D. Phelan said, "The Japanese are starting the same tide of immigration which we thought we had checked twenty years ago. The Chinese and Japanese are not bona fide citizens. They are not the stuff of which American citizens can be made. Personally we have nothing against Japanese, but as they will not assimilate with us and their social life is so different from ours, let them keep at a respectful distance." Yet another anti-Asian agitator, Dennis Kearney, an Irishman who once headed the California's Workingmen's Party, revised his slogan of the 1870s from "The Chinese Must Go!" to "The Japs Must Go!"

The Issei were largely politically powerless in the United States because they were denied the right to become naturalized citizens and thus could not vote. The Naturalization Act of 1790 guaranteed the right of citizenship to "free, white persons." Congress later extended citizenship to people of African descent in 1870, and American Indians in 1924. Only Asians were not eligible for citizenship because they were not considered in the category of "free, white" or "African descent."

One Issei who wanted to become a U.S. citizen was Takao Ozawa. He arrived in the United States as a student in 1894, and attended schools in California, including the University of California, Berkeley. Ozawa later settled in Hawaii, married, started a family, and worked for an American company. In 1914, he filed an application for U.S. citizenship. His application for citizenship was denied because the court declared that Ozawa was "in every way eminently qualified under the statutes to become an American citizen" except that he was not "white." Ozawa decided to take his case to the U.S. Supreme Court. Here, he told the Court that he was a true American, that he made sure that his wife was educated in the United States, that he spoke English at home with his children, and that he did not have any connection with the Japanese government. He also stated that he was loyal to the United States and grateful for the opportunity the country had given him. In 1922, the Court handed down their decision. Ozawa was not entitled to naturalized citizenship simply because he was not Caucasian.

Ozawa's case points out how the U.S. judicial system clearly acknowledged racial classification in determining citizenship status. No matter how loyal or "American" one professed to be, it was the racial category one belonged to that determined inclusion, or in this case, citizenship. The issue of dual citizenship was also controversial and questioned by the anti-Japanese movement. They felt that Nisei who held dual citizenship could not possibly be loyal to the United States. But for the Issei, the inability to achieve naturalized citizenship led to a lack of political power. This became evident as states begin to pass laws restricting Japanese landownership.

The Issei could do little when politicians began to pass laws affecting their livelihood that resulted in economic discrimination. In 1913, California passed the first law that prohibited any "alien ineligible for citizenship" from purchasing agricultural land or leasing it for longer than three years. Other states soon followed California: Arizona in 1917, Washington and Louisiana in 1921, New Mexico in 1922, Idaho, Montana, and Oregon in 1923, and Kansas in 1925. Only when officials felt compelled to act was the law enforced. The Japanese farmers, however, felt they had to be careful to avoid breaking the laws, or they would be punished. In order to keep farming, they found loopholes in the laws. Issei continued to farm by putting the land in the name of their American-born children, by using a non-Japanese middleman to lease the land, or by forming corporations in which American citizens formed the majority. The Alien Land Laws did not prevent Japanese farmers from continuing with their livelihood. By 1920, they were able to increase their land held under lease from 155,488 to 192,150 acres, and ownership from 26,707 to 74,769 acres (Takaki, 1989).

Other anti-Japanese activities involved attempts at segregation in housing and education. Many places restricted ownership of land or leasing property to Japanese. In 1906, the San Francisco School Board proposed to send Japanese schoolchildren to the segregated "Oriental School" where Chinese students attended. This move drew the outrage of the Japanese consulate. There were only ninety-three students who were protected by a "most favored nation" status guaranteed by an 1894 trade agreement between Japan and the United States. President Theodore Roosevelt recognized the diplomatic embarrassment and ordered the school board to rescind its decision. Roosevelt also recognized that the issue was not about education, but was a reaction by anti-Japanese groups to the growth of immigration from Japan. An agreement was reached with the school board that allowed the Japanese children to attend the public school with white children. The U.S. government negotiated an immigration agreement to have Japan stop issuing passports to its laborers, the resulting Gentlemen's Agreement of 1907.

Japanese immigrants were often targets of physical attacks. Throughout the early 1900s there were episodes of vandalism to Japanese-owned homes and businesses. As one Japanese laundry operator said, "My drivers were constantly attacked on the highway, my place of business defiled by rotten eggs and fruit; windows were smashed several times" (Takaki, 1989: 203). One night several Japanese farmworkers in Turlock, California, were loaded into trucks and told to leave town and never return. These events were a part of the longer historical series of attacks directed toward Asian immigrant groups.

Even picture bride marriages were often the target of anti-Japanese groups who felt that the practice was immoral and violated the premise of the Gentlemen's Agreement. Since the Gentlemen's Agreement was to stop the flow of Japanese laborers to the United States, these groups felt that picture brides could also be construed as potential laborers, regardless of their husband's worker status.

THE JAPANESE IN HAWAII

Japanese immigration and settlement on the Hawaiian Islands is a significant, yet often overlooked, part of Japanese American history. Beginning in 1879, the government of Hawaii looked toward Japan to hire contract laborers to work on the developing sugarcane plantations on the islands. Thousands of Japanese men and women migrated to the

Hawaiian Islands as plantation workers beginning in 1885. Between 1885 and 1894, about 29,000 emigrated to work on sugarcane plantations. Unlike the mainland United States, where female immigration was not encouraged, the Hawaiian government actively encouraged women to migrate. Japanese women were seen as workers, providing necessary "female" skills needed to support the male contract workers: cooking, sewing, and working as field laborers. There was an additional belief that having women was good because it meant men would be much happier and satisfied with their conditions and prove to be better workers. For the contract laborers, the conditions were usually a three-year working period for a plantation or farm. As contract workers, they did not have very good working or living conditions, housing and food costs were deducted from their minimal wages, and many tried to run away and break their contracts.

Government contract workers were prohibited after 1894, and, until 1908, another 125,000 migrated as independent workers not indentured into plantation contracts. Having significantly greater freedom allowed workers to organize collectively to improve their working conditions. After contract labor was disbanded, Japanese workers were able to organize several unions that called several strikes within a short period of time at the turn of the century. These labor strikes crossed ethnic barriers: Japanese organized with Chinese laborers on the Puehuehu Plantation, and later on the Kilauea Plantation, Japanese and Portuguese women workers held a strike in demand of better wages (Takaki, 1989).

Single men made up the bulk of these worker migrants on the islands. The Gentlemen's Agreement of 1907 halted the migration of male laborers to the islands as it did to the mainland United States. Thus, Japanese women constituted a small percentage of the total Japanese immigrant population. They were only 9 percent of the Japanese immigrants in 1890. Their proportions increased throughout the years as single male laborers of Hawaii entered into arranged marriages with "picture bride" Japanese women, whose immigration was not affected by the Gentlemen's Agreement. By 1900, women were 22 percent of the Japanese population; in 1910 they were 31 percent and by 1920, 41 percent (Okihiro, 1996).

The high percentage of married men and women among the Japanese immigrant population led to the growth of families and the birth of the second-generation Hawaiian Japanese. Thus, the Hawaiian Japanese population was well established within the local island society and economy. The Issei could not become U.S. citizens, but the Nisei saw themselves as Americans even though they were only living in a U.S. territory. Racial and ethnic relations in Hawaii were never quite as openly hostile as they were on the mainland United States. Thus, the Japanese of Hawaii felt integrated into island life. The consequences of such relations showed up in the fact that the Hawaiian Japanese were treated differently from the mainland Japanese once the United States entered the war with Japan.

CONCLUSION

The anti-Japanese movement was largely motivated by long-standing anti-Asian prejudices. These attitudes were fueled by the threat of economic competition, as evidenced by the passage of Alien Land Laws to slow the progress of Japanese in agriculture, as well as perceived social and cultural differences. The Japanese were simply unassimilable aliens whose culture was not compatible with the dominant European-American culture. With these factors in mind, it is not surprising that during World War II the U.S. government responded as it did. The U.S. government's policy of exclusion, removal, and detention of more than 120,000 Japanese citizens and noncitizens during World War II was the result of historical circumstances "shaped by racial prejudice, war hysteria, and a failure of political leadership" (Commission on Wartime Relocation and Internment of Civilians, 1982: 18).

NOTE

1. Yamato Ichihashi, *Japanese in the United States* (Stanford, Calif.: Stanford University Press, 1932), p. 27.

2

Evacuation

The Japanese bombing of Pearl Harbor on December 7, 1941, came as a surprise to the Japanese American population of the Hawaiian Islands and the mainland. Although the government was aware of the potential for a Pacific attack by Japanese forces, they were unprepared. Once President Roosevelt declared war with Japan, the Japanese American population, both citizen and alien, became suspect. Issei community leaders were arrested, curfew orders were implemented, and officials within the government set into motion a plan to evacuate and remove both Japanese aliens and Japanese Americans from their homes on the West Coast.

FACTORS LEADING UP TO THE EVACUATION ORDER

The decision to evacuate and remove Japanese living on the West Coast was not based only on the Pearl Harbor disaster. The removal of Japanese was a consequence of anti-Japanese sentiment from the early part of the twentieth century. The government maintained that "military necessity" was the main reason behind the evacuation and internment program. In other words, enemy aliens presented a potential threat to national security during wartime. General John L. DeWitt's *Final Report* (1943) cites a number of factors supporting the government's claims: arms found in Japanese homes and businesses when they were searched by the FBI shortly after Pearl Harbor; concentrations of Japanese in close proximity to highly sensitive military areas; the presence of Japanese ethnic organizations that would support the Japanese emperor and the country; and the presence of Kibei, second-generation Japanese Americans, educated in Japan, who were likely to be pro-Japanese. A second reason given by the government was that the ethnic Japanese needed "protection" from vigilantes and other anti-Japanese forces during wartime.

Although military justification was the main reason given for the evacuation and internment, government intelligence had already determined that the Japanese were not likely to be a national security threat. In the fall of 1941, Chicago businessman Curtis B. Munson was appointed to work as a special representative of the State Department. His assignment was to gather intelligence material on Japanese living in the United States, and to investigate whether there was any possibility of the Japanese presenting an internal military threat to the United States government. Though Munson was not a professional intelligence officer, he was able to gather information from a number of reputable sources. He spoke with Naval Intelligence, British Intelligence, and FBI agents in Hawaii. Based upon his investigation, more commonly referred to as the Munson Report, he wrote, "There will be no armed uprising of Japanese. . . . For the most part the local Japanese are loyal to the United States or, at worst, hope that by remaining quiet they can avoid concentration camps or irresponsible mobs. We do not believe that they would be at least any more disloyal than any other racial group in the United States with whom we went to war" (CWRIC, 1982: 52). Munson concluded that the Japanese living in the United States would not threaten national security.

The government's first reaction after Pearl Harbor was to ready the country for war by examining the "enemy alien problem." Entering World War II heightened a sense of American patriotism. People of any enemy nationality immediately became suspect and could be arrested and detained for reasons of national security. People of Japanese descent were easily identifiable and became targets of suspicion. Immediately after December 7, the FBI arrested people who were in their "at-risk for security" categories. They had already devised a list of those to be arrested depending upon their potential "risk" for intelligence activity. There were three categories: "A" category were aliens who led cultural organizations; "B" were slightly less suspicious aliens; and "C" categories were those people who were members of a particular "enemy" ethnic group, or who had ever donated to an enemy alien group or organization. The "C" group consisted of Japanese language teachers and Buddhist priests. Of these there were 1,291 Japanese (367 in Hawaii, 924 in the mainland United States), 857 Germans, and 147 Italians.

In addition to the arrest of Issei leaders, the financial assets of many Japanese were frozen and taken over by the U.S. government. Those who had money in Japanese-owned banks no longer had access to their funds. Because the United States was at war with Japan, business transactions between the two countries ceased. These constraints affected many Issei, especially those who had business relations with Japan. Radio transmitters, weapons, cameras, and other possible instruments of espionage were also confiscated.

The issue of enemy aliens concerned those in U.S. government intelligence. Besides the Japanese, German and Italian aliens were also considered suspect. But the Japanese, both aliens and U.S. citizens, appeared to be singled out for different treatment. Thus, Japanese Americans did their best to promote a more positive image of their loyalty in the Pearl Harbor aftermath. Japanese American communities offered their pledge of loyalty to the United States, enlisted as air raid wardens, and helped guard the water supply in the California central valley town of Parlier. There was even a comic strip called "Joe Palooka" that had Nisei GIs as loyal citizens.

Positive images of Japanese were largely overshadowed by negative reaction from nativist organizations. Nativist groups can best be described as pro-American, patriotic groups that believed that the United States should be a country comprising native-born individuals of European descent, preferably western European. These groups were anti-immigrant, anti-foreigner, and at different periods of time, even anti-Catholic. Relative to the situation of the Japanese in America at the time of World War II, nativist groups held the perception of Japanese as immigrant foreigners who did not belong in America and could not be trusted once the country was at war with Japan. The American Legion was one of the first organizations that called for the removal of Japanese from the West Coast. The California Joint Immigration Committee, an organization that formerly was known as the Japanese Exclusion League, reasserted its earlier claims that Japanese could not assimilate into American society. In a press release to California newspapers, they declared that "those born in this country are American citizens by right of birth, but they are also Japanese citizens, liable . . . to be called to bear arms for their Emperor, either in front of, or behind, enemy lines" (tenBroek et al., 1968: 78). Because the American-born Japanese, or Nisei, could hold dual citizenship, they questioned the loyalty of such individuals. Several local chapters of the Native Sons and Daughters of the Golden West passed resolutions to remove all ethnic Japanese from the West Coast. Agricultural organizations such as the Western Growers Protective Association and the California Farm Bureau Federation also called for their removal. A spokesman for the Grower-Shipper Vegetable Association stated,

We're charged with wanting to get rid of the Japs for selfish reasons. We might as well be honest. We do. It's a question of whether the white man lives on the Pacific Coast or the brown man. They came into this valley to work, and they stayed to take over. . . . If all the Japs were removed tomorrow, we'd never miss them in two weeks, because the white farmers can take over and produce everything the Japs grows. And we don't want them back when the war ends, either. (quoted in tenBroek et al., 1968: 80)

Shortly after Pearl Harbor, Congress established a commission to investigate the bombing. The commission was headed by Supreme Court Justice Owen J. Roberts and included Major General Frank McCoy, Brigadier General Joseph McNarney, Admiral William Standley, and Rear Admiral Joseph Reeves. Most notably, the commission was composed of military officers. Their report suggested that the Japanese consulate in Hawaii was the center of intelligence activity for Japan and that counterespionage efforts could have been employed to prevent the disaster from occurring. Although there seemed to be no direct implication of Japanese American spying, the Roberts Report helped to support rumors of disloyalty among the Japanese in Hawaii and by extension, further doubts about the loyalty of mainland Japanese. Thus, it was likely to have influenced War Department officials in their quest to evacuate and exclude the Japanese population from the West Coast of the United States.

Several key individuals, civilian and military, were instrumental in the decision to evacuate the Japanese. They were in high-level positions within the presidential cabinet (see Table 2.1). Some strongly insisted that the evacuation program was a military necessity. Others, were less inclined to see the military justification of the evacuation, but did little to inform the president or stop the mass evacuation from taking place.

The Western Defense Command (WDC) was headed by Lieutenant General John L. DeWitt. This area included much of the Western states of Washington, Oregon, California, and Arizona. Dewitt's main charge was "the defense of the Pacific Coast . . . against attacks by land, sea, and air; and the local protection of establishments and communications vital to the National Defense for which adequate defense cannot be provided by local civilian authorities" (tenBroek et al., 1968: 100).

DeWitt played an influential and strategic role as commanding officer of the WDC and the decision to evacuate and remove Japanese from the West Coast. He was strident in his statements about the military necessity of Japanese incarceration. He stated, "We are at war and this area— eight states—has been designated as a theater of operations. . . . [There are] approximately 288,000 enemy aliens which we have to watch and I have little confidence that the enemy aliens are law-abiding or loyal in any sense of the word. . . . Particularly the Japanese. I have no confidence in their loyalty whatsoever" (quoted in Takaki, 1989: 387).

Japanese Americans had to live under suspicion from their neighbors and surrounding communities. It was a difficult period for them because of the war with Japan and simply not knowing what was going to happen. Their community leaders had been rounded up and arrested by the

Table 2.1
Key Individuals in the Decision to Evacuate and Relocate the Japanese Population in the United States

Individual	Position	Role/Involvement
Franklin D. Roosevelt	President of the United States	Signed Executive Order 9066
Francis Biddle	Attorney General	Believed exclusion and evacuation was unnecessary, but did not advise the President of this option.
Henry L. Stimson	Secretary of War	Cabinet member who advocated evacuation and internment plan.
John J. McCloy	Assistant Secretary of War	Supported evacuation and internment plan.
Frank Knox	Secretary of Navy	Supported evacuation of Terminal Island and Bainbridge Island Japanese from Navy installations.
J. Edgar Hoover	Director of FBI	Supported limited involvement with Japanese enemy aliens. Did not actively support full evacuation of entire Japanese population.
Edward Ennis	Attorney, Justice Department Head, Alien Enemy Control Unit	Opposed the internment program on constitutional grounds, but directed the Justice Department's detention centers for enemy aliens.
Curtis B. Munson	Intelligence, Special Investigator	Produced the Munson Report, investigation of the loyalty of Japanese in the United States.
Owen J. Roberts	Supreme Court Justice	Chaired the Roberts Commission investigation of Pearl Harbor
John L. DeWitt	Lieutenant General, Army	General in charge of evacuation program and assembly center program.
Karl Bendetson	Colonel, Army	Supervised evacuation.

FBI. Some were financially strapped. Even the immigrant Issei who were not arrested were still considered "enemy aliens." The Nisei were also in a difficult situation. They were American citizens, but their racial-ethnic background made them easily identifiable and targets of discrimination. They would remain suspect as long as war with Japan prevailed. The U.S. government's next step of evacuation and exclusion would remedy the problem of living in this hostile society, but would also deprive them of their freedom and liberty as residents of the United States.

EXECUTIVE ORDER 9066

By early 1942, despite intelligence reports stating that the Japanese were not a military threat, top military officials began to investigate the possibilities of removing the Japanese population from the West Coast. Within the executive branch of government, the president relied on the advice and counted on the competency of his advisers and cabinet. Among the individuals who advised the president were Secretary of the Navy Frank Knox, Secretary of War Henry L. Stimson, Assistant Secretary of War John J. McCloy, and Attorney General Francis Biddle. There was political pressure upon the War Department to carry out a mass evacuation of the Japanese population on the West Coast. By the middle of February 1942, the War Department drafted an executive order that was forwarded to the president.

On February 19, 1942, President Roosevelt signed Executive Order 9066. The order did not directly mention Japanese Americans or aliens, but designated certain areas of the West Coast that would fall under military jurisdiction "from which any and all persons may be excluded as deemed necessary or desirable" (Chan, 1991: 125). The effect of the order gave power to the military to remove Japanese aliens and citizens according to their needs.

Roosevelt's direct role in the evacuation and internment of Japanese Americans is questionable. Throughout his presidency he was known as a liberal in terms of race relations and the government's social policies. He had supported and instituted a number of different pieces of legislation that affected racial minority groups, such as the 1934 Indian Reorganization Act and Fair Employment Practices of 1940. His support of the executive order to exclude a population based on national origin, and racial and ethnic ancestry stands in contradiction to his previous decisions about civil rights. As chief executive officer of the U.S. government, he bore responsibility for the decision to evacuate and incarcerate citizens and aliens of Japanese descent.

During late February to early March 1942, Congressman John H. Tolan (D-Oakland, California) was chairman of the House Select Committee Investigating National Defense Migration, which held hearings examining the necessity for evacuation. Most of the testimony presented at the hearings were negative toward the Japanese, particularly the remarks by Earl Warren, attorney general of California, and the anti-Japanese group called the California Joint Immigration Committee. Warren said,

In some instances the children of those people [i.e., the Kibei] have been sent to Japan for their education, either in whole or in part, and while they are over there they are indoctrinated with the idea of Japanese imperialism. They receive their religious instruction which ties up their religion with their Emperor, and they come back here imbued with the ideas and the policies of Imperial Japan. While I do not cast a reflection on every Japanese who is born in this country—of course we will have loyal ones—I do say that the consensus of opinion is that taking the group by and large there is more potential danger to this State from the group that is born here than from the group born in Japan. (U.S. Congress Select Committee, 1942: 11014–15)

Some positive testimony was presented by scholars and religious and labor leaders who were sympathetic to the Japanese. Within the Japanese American community, the Japanese American Citizens League leaders spoke on behalf of the Japanese population on the West Coast. While hoping that mass removal would not be an option, they assured the committee members that there would be full cooperation among all people of Japanese descent should there need to be any type of evacuation from the West Coast. JACL leader Mike Masaoka even boldly proposed that a volunteer "suicide" battalion of Nisei soldiers be formed to prove their loyalty to the United States.

Only one Japanese American spoke out at the Tolan Committee hearings who was not affiliated with the JACL. James Omura, a Nisei journalist and founder of a Japanese American literary/public affairs magazine *Current Life*, spoke out against any type of mass evacuation or relocation plan. He felt that the JACL was not representative of the Japanese American community, and was not willing to accept the JACL's plan for cooperation with the U.S. government. In his testimony he asked, "Has the Gestapo come to America? Have we not risen in righteous anger at Hitler's mistreatment of the Jews? Then, is it not incongruous that citizen Americans of Japanese descent should be similarly mistreated and persecuted?" (quoted in Weglyn, 1976: 67). Eventually, he and his wife relocated to Denver, Colorado, during the war and were not detained in any relocation center.

The Tolan Committee did little to change public opinion toward the Japanese on the West Coast, and in conclusion supported the Executive Order 9066 already enacted by the president. The committee did not directly recommend mass evacuation and removal for people of Japanese ancestry; it suggested a program in which assembly centers would serve as sites for hearings on the "loyalty" of citizens and aliens of Japanese ancestry. Those who passed loyalty screenings would be eligible for re-settlement outside of the restricted military zone on the West Coast. The committee did not recommend any program of mass removal for Germans and Italians.

Several different U.S. government agencies were involved with the evacuation, relocation, and eventual internment of the Japanese American population. Initially, the FBI and the Department of Justice were involved with intelligence activities, search and seizure of contraband, and the arrest of Issei leaders within the Japanese American community. The War Department supervised the mass evacuation and management of the temporary assembly center facilities.

Within the government, there was not uniform support for a mass evacuation program. Attorney General Francis Biddle and Alien Enemy Control Unit members James Rowe and Edward Ennis opposed the mass evacuation, believing that the United States was not in danger of attack or internal sabotage by the Japanese. A mass evacuation would disrupt agricultural production in California. There was the additional problem of supervising the removal of the Japanese population, along with trans-portation and resettlement issues. Biddle raised questions about the mo-rale of the 60,000 Japanese who were American citizens and how such a mass evacuation would affect them.

The idea of Japan using Japanese nationals or Japanese Americans as spies was also questionable. Intelligence reports from the FBI indicated that Japan would not use its overseas citizens for intelligence. In the past they had used Westerners for spying. FBI Director J. Edgar Hoover also felt that a mass evacuation program was unnecessary. He stated,

The necessity for mass evacuation is based primarily upon public and political pressure rather than on factual data. Public hysteria and in some instances, the comments of the press and radio announcers, have resulted in a tremendous amount of pressure being brought to bear on Governor Olson and Earl Warren, Attorney General of the State, and on the military authorities. . . . Local officials, press and citizens have started widespread movement demanding complete evacuation of all Japanese, citizen and alien alike. (CWRIC, 1982: 73)

There were other sympathetic organizations such as the American Friends Service Committee and the American Civil Liberties Union (ACLU) who opposed the evacuation and relocation program and felt it was simply wrong. For the most part, these opinions ran counter to the prevailing sentiment that favored an evacuation program. Indeed, a number of social liberals supported evacuation and internment. Walter Lippmann, a liberal writer, was concerned with the potential for sabo-tage on the West Coast by the American-born Nisei. His writing incited others to take the stand for excluding Japanese from the West Coast. Manchester Boddy, another liberal editor and the publisher of the *Los Angeles Daily News*, felt that the general public did not easily distinguish between the American citizen Japanese population and the alien (non-citizen) and that both should be moved from the West Coast.

In the end, even the attorney general's office supported the executive order. In a memo to the president, Biddle wrote,

This authority gives very broad powers to the Secretary of War and the Military Commanders. These powers are broad enough to permit them to exclude any particular individual from military areas. They could also evacuate groups of persons based on a reasonable classification. The order is not limited to aliens but includes citizens so that it can be exercised with respect to Japanese, irrespective of their citizenship. The decision of safety of the nation in time of war is necessarily for the Military authorities. (CWRIC, 1982: 86)

THE EVACUATION

The War Department oversaw the removal of people of Japanese ancestry from the West Coast based upon wartime military necessity. Shortly after the passage of Executive Order 9066, General DeWitt issued Public Proclamation 1, which created Military Areas 1 and 2. Military Area 1 covered the western portion of Washington, Oregon, California, and the southern half of Arizona. Military Area 2 consisted of portions of all those states that were not in Area 1. In these areas, all enemy aliens included Japanese, German, and Italian aliens (noncitizens) as well as American citizens of Japanese descent. Enemy aliens had to register with the government and let government officials know if they were to move. Later, a curfew regulation was added that required all enemy aliens and people of Japanese ancestry to be in their homes between 8 P.M. and 6 A.M.

Initially, General DeWitt tried a "voluntary" resettlement program. Issei and Nisei could move inland out of the restricted military zones on their own. Approximately 5,000 Japanese left Washington, Oregon, and California to states outside the Western Defense Command zone. Nevada, Utah, and Colorado were the first states to see voluntary evacuees. In theory, this program contradicted the government's claims that the Japanese were a potential military threat. Why would the Japanese be allowed to move to areas inland where they could potentially sabotage transportation or utility lines, or spy on war industries? Japanese American voluntary evacuees experienced mixed reactions from those states that allowed resettlement during this interim period. Governor Carvill of Nevada thought that allowing enemy aliens would create the potential for espionage:

I have made the statement that enemy aliens would be accepted in the State of Nevada under proper supervision. This would apply to concentration camps as well as to those who might be allowed to farm or do such other things as they could do in helping out. This is the attitude that I am going to maintain in this State and I do not desire that Nevada be made a dumping ground for enemy aliens to be going anywhere they might see fit to travel. (CWRIC, 1982: 102)

On the other hand, Governor Ralph L. Carr of Colorado was cautiously supportive of the voluntary relocation program. But his remarks still hint at suspicion of Japanese. He said,

If the enemy aliens must be transferred as a war measure, then we of Colorado are big enough and patriotic enough to do our duty.... We announce to the world that 1,118,000 red-blooded citizens of this State are able to take care of 3,500 or any number of enemies. ... The people of Colorado are giving their sons, are offering their possessions, are surrendering their rights and privileges to the end that this war may be fought to victory and permanent peace. If it is our duty to receive disloyal persons, we shall welcome the performance of the task.... This must not be construed as an invitation, however. ... In making the transfers, we can feel assured that governmental agencies will take every precaution to protect our people, our defense projects, and our property from the same menace which demands their removal from those sections. (CWRIC, 1982: 103)

Under pressure from the inland states to which some Japanese were moving, DeWitt terminated the voluntary program. The government moved to take full control of an evacuation and relocation program. The Wartime Civil Control Authority (WCCA) was created as a part of the Western Defense Command to oversee the evacuation and relocation program. From the very beginning, the evacuation and relocation program was orchestrated by the military to justify their need for national security. Although all enemy aliens were said to be suspect, it was the Japanese, both alien and citizen, who were singled out for removal.

Even before the formation of the Western Defense Command, the communities of Terminal Island (near Los Angeles, California) and Bainbridge Island (near Seattle, Washington) were evacuated. The process of evacuation in these communities foreshadowed what was to take place before the mass evacuation of West Coast Japanese. Terminal Island was an isolated island bordered by the Los Angeles harbor across from San Pedro and could be reached only by ferry or small drawbridge. The Japanese community there numbered about 3,500, about half of whom were American born Nisei. In early February 1942, all Japanese aliens were told to leave the island. Later that month, February 25, all Terminal Islanders were told they had forty-eight hours to leave the island. By that time, the FBI had already removed many of the men whom they had considered dangerous aliens and left a community filled with older women and small children. They had to dispose of all their personal property in a very short time, leaving the island a virtual ghost town littered with abandoned household goods and equipment. Dr. Yoshihiko Fujikawa, a former resident of Terminal Island, described the chaotic conditions of evacuation:

It was during these 48 hours that I witnessed unscrupulous vultures in the form of human beings taking advantage of bewildered housewives whose husbands had been rounded up by the FBI within 48 hours after Pearl Harbor. They were offered pittances for practically new furniture and appliances: refrigerators, radio consoles, etc., as well as cars, and many were falling prey to these people. (CWRIC, 1982: 108–9)

Bainbridge Island was the next community to be evacuated because it was in an area considered highly sensitive to navy operations. On March 24, 1942, residents received orders from the army for an evacuation one week later. For the forty-five Japanese families of this small community, there was much confusion during the evacuation process. There was little plan for disposal of their personal property, and they were not prepared for what they could or could not bring during their evacuation. Shortly after the Bainbridge Island evacuation, exclusion orders were issued for other areas in the West Coast Civil Defense Command. The Japanese were now part of one of the largest forced removal programs of civilians in U.S. history.

THE JAPANESE IN HAWAII

At the time of Pearl Harbor, the Hawaiian Japanese accounted for 37.3 percent (157,000 in 1940) of the islands' population. Almost 75 percent of the ethnic Japanese population was born in Hawaii. Most were descendants of the early plantation laborers who arrived between 1885 and 1894. Many in the second generation had moved out of the plantation fields and into Hawaii's territorial government, into the professions (teaching, medicine, administration), and into business. By World War II, Hawaii's society was a multi-ethnic mix of Chinese, Japanese, Korean, Filipino, Portuguese, Native Hawaiian and *haoles*, as the Anglo/European Americans were called. A racial-ethnic hierarchy placed the *haole* at the top in terms of social and economic power, but in general, race relations in Hawaii were better than on the mainland, both between the *haole* and the Japanese, and between and among the other ethnic groups on the islands.

Many Japanese American families lived near the Pearl Harbor area. The morning it was bombed remains etched in their memories. One person recalled,

I got up at 9:00 that morning. Everyone in the household was out in the yard shouting and pointing towards the sky. I hurried downstairs to see what was the matter and my mother was the first to tell me that the "Japs" had come. My reaction was one of complete disbelief. Even after I had looked towards the sky and had seen planes flying overhead and had heard the sound of cannon fire, I was still convinced that the army and navy were on maneuvers. I was so firm in my arguments that half of the family were ready to believe me until the radio announcer uttered the fatal words that we were being attacked by the "Japs." My mother kept running up and down the house, muttering a prayer as she did. (quoted in Okihiro, 1996: 157)

Immediately following the Pearl Harbor attack, Hawaii was placed under military control. As a U.S. territory, the islands were governed by the laws of the United States. The territorial governor used the Hawaii Defense Act and placed the islands under martial law "during the emergency and until the danger of invasion is removed" (CWRIC, 1982: 263). By doing this, anyone could be arrested if they were believed to present potential risks to the security of the territory or to any of the wartime operations. In essence, this allowed the military to arrest anyone without any formal charges, and suspended the writ of habeas corpus.

There was great debate among the military commanders and government about whether all Japanese in the islands, both alien and citizen, should be transported to the mainland and placed in internment camps. Secretary of the Navy Frank Knox proposed that all Japanese in Hawaii, citizen and alien, be interned on the island of Molokai (Okihiro, 1996: 175). Indeed, there was great concern by several members of President Roosevelt's cabinet that Hawaii's Japanese were partially responsible for the attack and should be removed, or at the very least, closely watched.

Thus, under martial law, a number of people were immediately arrested on the island of Oahu. They were detained at the Sand Island Detention Center near Honolulu's harbor. Originally Sand Island was an Immigration and Naturalization Service center, but it was activated as an army detention center/jail on December 8, 1941, right after Pearl Harbor. The first group of Sand Island detainees arrived on December 9, 1941. Sand Island detained aliens of Japanese ancestry, Japanese Americans, Germans, and Italians. Eventually, the detention facility closed in March 1943 and detainees were evacuated to War Relocation Authority camps on the mainland. Others were arrested and detained in the local county jails, immigration stations, and an internment camp on the island of Maui.

Because the territory of Hawaii was under martial law, the military argued that a mass removal program of so many people would be difficult if not impossible. Further, Japanese labor was needed to rebuild the damaged facilities. If the Japanese were removed, they would have to be replaced by an equivalent skilled labor force from the mainland. Because the Japanese in Hawaii accounted for such a large population, their absence might also cause the collapse of the community's economic infrastructure. Eventually, about 1,500 people, one-third of whom were American citizens, were arrested, evacuated, and detained. One of the first groups moved were Japanese farmers who had to leave their farms, being allowed back only during daylight hours to tend to their livestock and harvest their crops. Later, Japanese living in the area of Honolulu's harbor and the railroad terminal had to move out. They quickly had to sell their belongings and arrange for other places to live.

One of the critical factors influencing the treatment of the Hawaiian Japanese during wartime were the attitudes held by the top commanding military officials. On the West Coast, Lieutenant General John DeWitt held negative attitudes toward the Japanese population. In Hawaii, General Delos Emmons, who became commanding general shortly after Pearl Harbor, held a more rational, less negative view of the situation of Japanese on the islands. Emmons concurred with the Munson Report that laborers were needed to continue with the daily operations and local economy, and did not advocate for immediate evacuation or detention of Japanese individuals. As military governor of Hawaii, he stated,

There is no intention or desire on the part of the federal authorities to operate mass concentration camps. No person, be he citizen or alien, need worry, provided he is not connected with subversive elements.... While we have been subjected to a serious attack by a ruthless and treacherous enemy, we must remember that this is America and we must do things the American Way. We must distinguish between loyalty and disloyalty among our people. (quoted in Takaki, 1989: 380)

More than forty years after the war, Emmons is noted for his fair treatment of the Japanese in Hawaii. The Commission on Wartime Relocation and Internment of Civilians reports that "Emmons does not appear to have been a man of dogmatic racial views, in rather practical terms, he appears to have argued quietly but consistently for treating the Issei and Nisei as loyal to the United States, unless evidence to the contrary appeared" (CWRIC, 1982: 262). For the Japanese in Hawaii, this attitude of civility was important. The quality of life under martial law could have been repressive and restrictive, yet Emmons's views tempered the potentially volatile situation.

Beyond the military, the local kamaaina elite (haoles who had lived in Hawaii for such a long time they were considered "native") did not

support mass incarceration. Businessmen felt it would destroy the islands if the Japanese were removed. What is evident in the social-cultural
interactions in Hawaii was a type of benevolent "genteel" paternalism
(Takaki, 1989). This attitude permeated much of the social interaction
between upper-class *haoles* and other ethnic groups in lower-status positions. Social relations were such that *haoles* benefited from the Japanese
who worked for them and the entire structure of Hawaiian business
economy; there was an implicit understanding from both *haoles* and Japanese in which each understood their "place" as a social class and their
status within the Hawaiian society.

Even though the majority of Japanese in Hawaii were not interned,
they were still under strict scrutiny by the rest of the population. They
had to be carefully guarded about their actions, lest anything be misin-
terpreted as potentially disloyal. One indicator of how the Hawaiian Japanese responded to the wartime situation was their reaction to the call
for volunteers to the all-Japanese 442nd Regimental Combat Team. Initially, on the mainland, only 1,181 volunteers came forward from the ten
relocation centers; in Hawaii, 9,507 volunteered. Since the entire Japanese
population in the islands was not evacuated and interned, there was a
higher rate of volunteering for the military. Many of the Hawaiian volunteers were already in the Hawaiian National Guard, which eventually
became the foundation for the 100th Battalion.

Thus, the situation in Hawaii was both different from and similar to
the mainland Japanese. On the one hand, the Japanese were an integral
part of the island economy and social structure. There was an established
ethnic community with Japanese-centered schools, churches, and other
social organizations. To some degree, Hawaii did not have the same
virulent anti-Asian sentiment as was the case on the West Coast, there
was greater tolerance because of the ethnically diverse Hawaiian society.
This did not mean, however, that the Japanese population held any
meaningful social and political power, which was still largely a part of
the white/*haole* elite, plantation owners, businessmen, and military officials of the islands.

According to Curtis B. Munson's "Report on Hawaiian Islands," Hawaiian Japanese were likely to be loyal to the United States. He also
believed that the "disloyal" would be easily controlled because of the
large military presence on the islands, and that the possibility of mass
incarceration or detention of Japanese in Hawaii would be difficult.

The consensus of opinion is that there will be no racial uprising of the Japanese
in Honolulu. The first generation, as on the Coast, are ideologically and culturally
closest to Japan. Though many of them speak no English [*sic*], or at best only
pigeon-English, it is considered that the big bulk of them will be loyal. This is
especially so, for in Hawaii the first generation is largely on the land and devoted

to it. . . . The second generation is estimated as approximately ninety-eight percent loyal. . . .

The general background and characteristics of the Japanese are the same in the Islands as they are on the mainland. . . . This reporter believes there is this fundamental difference between the Japanese "Problem" on the Coast [West Coast/mainland United States] and the Japanese "Problem" in the Hawaiian Islands. On the Coast, the Japanese are discriminated against on a racial basis. In Hawaii it is really only on a social and economic basis. This is peculiarly American. . . .

The report also discussed,

One important difference between the situation in Hawaii and the mainland is that if all the Japanese on the mainland were actively disloyal they could be corralled or destroyed within a very short time. In the Hawaiian islands, though there are sufficient American troops and Navy present to overwhelm the Japanese population, it would simply mean that the Islands would lose their vital labor supply by so doing, and in addition to that we would have to feed them, as well as import many thousands of laborers to take their place. Since a large part of the vital essential work of the Islands is ably carried on by the Japanese population, it is essential that they should be kept loyal—at least to the extent of staying at their tasks. (quoted in Ogawa, 1978: 299–301)

Thus, although there was some concern over the possibility of spies and fifth column activity among the Japanese in Hawaii, the population was an integral part of the Hawaiian social and economic structure. Even within the military, there were many Hawaiian Japanese. On the mainland, military necessity was given as the main justification for the mass evacuation and internment program, yet in Hawaii, no mass evacuation program ever took place.

CONCLUSION

The decision to evacuate and intern people of Japanese ancestry on the West Coast was influenced by the anti-Japanese attitudes held by individuals in strategic decision-making positions in the U.S. government. Scholarly sources suggest that there was not one person directly responsible, but a number of individuals were in a position and had the authority to draft and put forward the executive order signed by President Roosevelt.

According to historian Roger Daniels, President Roosevelt, as leader of the nation, should bear the responsibility for the evacuation and internment of Japanese Americans. Daniels writes,

The leader of the nation, was, in the final analysis, responsible. It was Franklin Roosevelt, who in one short telephone call, passed the decision-making power to two men who had never been elected to any office, saying only, with the politician's charm and equivocation: "Be as reasonable as you can." Why did he agree? Probably for two reasons: in the first place, it was expedient; in the second place, Roosevelt himself harbored deeply felt anti-Japanese prejudices. (Daniels, 1971: 72)

The issue of expediency had more to do with the United States entering the war. Japan's army was rapidly moving into Singapore and Burma. Handling the internal crisis by simply removing the Japanese allowed Roosevelt to move on to deal with international issues and toward winning the war. As for harboring anti-Japanese prejudices, Daniels asserts that Roosevelt along with his top-level cabinet members felt that Japanese, both alien and citizen, were threats to national security. They wanted to intern the Japanese in Hawaii, but never succeeded in doing this because they heeded the advice of the commanding general of the Hawaiian territory, Delos Emmons. He felt that the Japanese were indispensable to the Hawaiian economy. If the Japanese were to be removed, Hawaii would experience an extreme labor shortage that could paralyze the island's activities, particularly support for the military now that the United States had entered the war. There was also the logistical problem of transporting the population to a secure mainland facility.

The report of the Commission on Wartime Relocation and Internment of Civilians suggests several conditions that permitted the decision to evacuate to be made. These conditions rely heavily on the attitudes held by key military and cabinet officials. In the military, General DeWitt fully believed that ethnic Japanese could not be trusted. He relied on the reports of civilian politicians, rather than using military judgment, who held anti-Japanese attitudes, and he tended to exaggerate conditions, placing security ahead of civil liberties for citizens. Intelligence reports (FBI and Naval Intelligence) suggesting that the Japanese could likely be trusted were ignored.

Within the presidential cabinet, Secretary of War Stimson and Assistant Secretary of War McCloy blindly agreed with what DeWitt wanted to do with regard to evacuating and interning a civilian population, and they failed to require a strict military justification for the event. Also in the cabinet, Attorney General Francis Biddle was a reluctant participant in the exclusion decision. He did not feel it was necessary, but did not present strong counsel to the president on this.

At the national and congressional level, there were not very many public forums nor was there much opposition to the evacuation and internment plans. There were probably many people who were strong advocates of civil liberties but who remained silent about the proceedings. Thus, in some respects, the public can be held responsible for their complacency, but also for electing those into office who had the power to enact the laws.

Finally, the commission concluded that President Roosevelt bore ultimate responsibility for signing the order without having it reviewed thoroughly by his cabinet and for not publicly refuting any rumors of sabotage on the West Coast. In other words, as president, Roosevelt's responsibility was to bring a sense of nationhood and calm as the nation entered the international arena of war, and in dealing with the domestic crisis brought about by the distrust of people of Japanese ancestry. At this time, unfortunate as this seems, he did little as a national leader to protect the rights and civil liberties of U.S. citizens and residents.

3

Life within Barbed Wire

The removal of Japanese residents from Terminal Island in California and Bainbridge Island in Washington occurred quickly with little planning and foresight. These communities had very little warning of their impending evacuation and removal, giving residents little time to plan their lives. As the possibility of a full-scale West Coast evacuation began to become a reality, the Wartime Civil Control Administration (WCCA) began to plan for the process of evacuation of Japanese living in the Western Defense Command. This area included the western portions of the states of Washington, Oregon, and California.

TEMPORARY REMOVAL: THE ASSEMBLY CENTERS

By early 1942, the army had begun to consider suitable areas for temporary and permanent sites for housing the Japanese American population. The assembly centers[1] had to be large enough to house several thousand evacuees, with necessary facilities such as water, electricity, and close to transportation lines. They had to be far enough away from strategic military areas, and close enough for evacuees to get there within a short period of time.

In March 1942, a site was selected in eastern California in the Owens Valley, later to become known as Manzanar. A second assembly center area in northern Arizona was part of the Northern Colorado Indian Reservation and was administered by the Office of Indian Affairs. All total there were sixteen assembly centers in Washington, Oregon, California, and Arizona (see Table 3.1 and Figure 3.1). They included large

Table 3.1
List of Assembly Centers, 1942

9\223

Assembly Center	Population	Dates Open, 1942
Puyallup, Washington	7,390	April 28 to September 12
Portland, Oregon	3,676	May 2 to September 10
Marysville, California	2,451	May 8 to June 29
Sacramento, California	4,739	May 6 to June 26
Tanforan, California	7,816	April 28 to October 13
Stockton, California	4,271	May 10 to October 17
Turlock, California	3,661	April 30 to August 12
Salinas, California	3,586	April 27 to July 4
Merced, California	4,508	May 6 to September 15
Pinedale, California	4,792	May 7 to July 23
Fresno, California	5,120	May 6 to October 30
Tulare, California	4,978	April 20 to September 4
Santa Anita, California	18,719	March 27 to October 27
Pomona, California	5,434	May 7 to August 24
Mayer, Arizona	245	May 7 to June 2
Manzanar, California *	9,837	March 21 to June 2

*Manzanar was transferred to the War Relocation Authority for use as a relocation camp.

Source: Commission on Wartime Relocation and Internment of Civilians, 1982: 138.

fairgrounds, stockyards, and exposition centers, and a former Civilian Conservation Corps facility.

The evacuation to assembly centers began at the end of March 1942. More than 90,000 people went to assembly centers and stayed an average of 100 days. About 70 percent were U.S. citizens. With such a large population, how did the government accomplish the task of removing the Japanese population from the West Coast? Evacuation notices were posted in prominent public areas in Japanese American communities. The instructions required that one member of the family report to a control center and register the family. Each family was then issued a number and told when they would have to leave and what they could take. The evacuation notices were issued so quickly that most people had little time to make the necessary arrangements for their personal property.

Figure 3.1
Map of Assembly Centers and Internment Camps

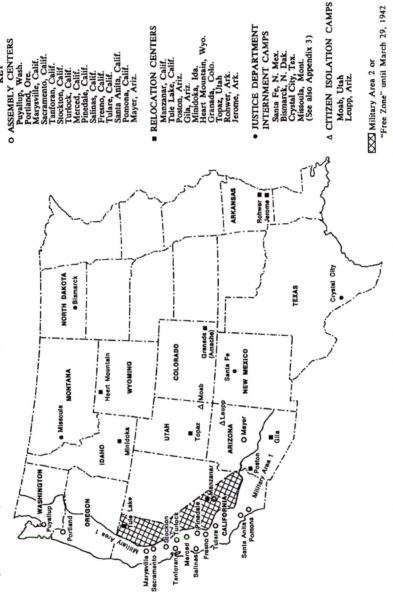

KEY

○ ASSEMBLY CENTERS
Puyallup, Wash.
Portland, Ore.
Marysville, Calif.
Sacramento, Calif.
Tanforan, Calif.
Stockton, Calif.
Turlock, Calif.
Merced, Calif.
Pinedale, Calif.
Salinas, Calif.
Fresno, Calif.
Tulare, Calif.
Santa Anita, Calif.
Pomona, Calif.
Mayer, Ariz.

■ RELOCATION CENTERS
Manzanar, Calif.
Tule Lake, Calif.
Poston, Ariz.
Gila, Ariz.
Minidoka, Ida.
Heart Mountain, Wyo.
Granada, Colo.
Topaz, Utah
Rohwer, Ark.
Jerome, Ark.

● JUSTICE DEPARTMENT
INTERNMENT CAMPS
Santa Fe, N. Mex.
Bismarck, N. Dak.
Crystal City, Tex.
Missoula, Mont.
(See also Appendix 3)

△ CITIZEN ISOLATION CAMPS
Moab, Utah
Leupp, Ariz.

▨ Military Area 2 or
"Free Zone" until March 29, 1942

Source: Michi Nishiura Weglyn. *Years of Infamy: The Untold Story of America's Concentration Camps* (New York: William Morrow, 1976), p. 6.

Many were forced to store or sell their personal property and make sure that their finances and other aspects of their personal lives were in order within a few weeks' time. An even larger question loomed in many minds: What was going to happen to them?

The day that evacuees left their homes and reported to the evacuation center was chaotic. Although they were told they could bring two suitcases per person, a lot of luggage and other personal items had to be transported to the evacuation centers. Among the many families who had to evacuate, there were many single female–headed households, many with young children. Many male leaders had already been arrested and taken away by the FBI immediately after the bombing of Pearl Harbor, which left some families without a male head of household.

The first stop for most evacuees was the local registration station. These were community centers, schools, and churches in their neighborhoods. The scenes of this day were chaotic. Luggage was piled high, and children and older people were sitting on the piled luggage. As if humans were a piece of baggage, paperboard tags hung from their neck identifying their family number. From there, they would be transported by train or bus to the nearest assembly center. For most evacuees, the living conditions of the assembly centers were unpleasant and uncomfortable. The Wartime Civil Control Administration policy was to allot 200 square feet per couple, and to house family groups together. Everyone was to be furnished with a cot, mattresses, blankets, and pillows. Each living area was to have electricity. But this was wartime, so there were shortages of supplies that would meet the needs of the evacuee population. The reality of assembly center life was that these places were not meant to be inhabited by humans. Former residents describe the conditions in the following way:

Pinedale. The hastily built camp consisted of tar paper roofed barracks with gaping cracks that let in insects, dirt from the dust storms . . . [there were] no toilet facilities except smelly outhouses, and community bathrooms with overhead pipes with holes punched in to serve as showers. The furniture was camp cots with dirty straw mattresses.

Manzanar. [The barracks were] nothing but a 20 by 25 foot of barrack with roof, sides of pine wood and covered with tar paper . . . no attack, no insulation. But the July heat separated the pine floor and exposed cracks to a quarter of an inch. Through this a cold wind would blow in or during the heat of the day dusty sand would come in through the cracks. To heat, one pot bellied wood stove in the center of the barracks.

Portland. The assembly center was the Portland stockyard. It was filthy, smelly, and dirty. There was roughly two thousand people packed in on large building. No beds were provided, so they gave us gunny sacks to fill the straw, that was our bed.

Santa Anita. We were confined to horse stables. The horse stables were whitewashed. In the hot summers, the legs of the cots were sinking through the asphalt. We were given mattress covers and told to stuff straw in them. There were no partitions. Toilet paper was rationed by family members. We had to, to bathe, go to the horse showers. The horses all took showers in there, regardless of sex, but with human beings, they built a partition. . . . The women complained that the men were climbing over the top to view the women taking showers. [When the women complained] one of the officials said, "Are you sure you women are not climbing the walls to look at the men. . . ." It had extra guard towers with a searchlight panoraming the camp, and it was very difficult to sleep because the light kept coming into our window. (CWRIC, 1982: 138–9)

One of the greatest complaints was the lack of privacy. It was not uncommon for large families to share a 20-by-20-foot room, or even smaller families of four to live in an 8-by-20-foot room. Some newly married couples shared rooms with only sheets strung on wires to give them privacy. Initially, in the latrines, there were no partitions between the toilets or shower curtains.

Finally, the weather created uncomfortable living conditions. On hot days in California's Central Valley, temperatures could reach more than 110 degrees. At Puyallup in Washington State, they had to battle with the "carnivorous Puyallup mud. The ground was a vast ocean of mud, and whenever it threatened to dry and cake up, the rains came and softened it into slippery ooze" (CWRIC, 1982: 140).

Even after the initial shock of the living conditions, evacuees were continually being challenged with day to day living. Family and community life was severely disrupted from the routines of pre-evacuation life. Since families were housed in one room facilities, all other facilities were based upon the army model of living: communal latrines and shower facilities, large recreation halls, and mess halls with institutional food. Meals in the communal mess hall meant that families no longer had to eat together at the same time. The WCCA food allowance was the same as the army's—50 cents per day. It was actually less than that, about 39 cents per day. Former evacuees remember getting food that was less than appetizing. They reported that food consisted of "discolored cold cuts, overcooked Swiss chard, and a slice of moldy bread . . . brined liver—salted liver. Huge liver. Brown and bluish in color, rice and for dessert, maybe half a can of peach or a pear" (CWRIC, 1982: 142). Thus, food was a common source of complaint for the evacuees.

Obtaining items from "outside" the center was difficult. Evacuees could bring only a limited amount of personal property with them. A few individuals had very little or inappropriate clothing for the climate of the assembly centers. The army allocated between $24 and $42 for clothing allowances, depending on the age and sex of the individual. But since evacuees were not allowed to go outside the assembly center to shop for clothing, everything had to be mail ordered. The assembly centers had small canteens (stores), but there was not much available to be purchased.

Health and medical care were also problematic in the assembly centers. The Public Health Service provided the medical care, but there was a shortage of medical personnel who were recruited from the evacuee population. Medical equipment and supplies were also needed. Those with serious medical emergencies were taken to medical facilities outside of the assembly center.

Because the assembly centers were only temporary holding facilities for the evacuees, there was little constructive activity in the beginning. Eventually, different programs were developed to fill the time. School-age children attended educational programs that were staffed by evacuee teachers who were paid $16 a month. Although there were few textbooks and supplies, traditional subjects such as math, history, music, and art were taught. Recreational activities began to fill some of the time. Some assembly centers had Scout troops, and most had some form of limited recreational activities that were initiated by the evacuees, such as movie theater night. At Tanforan Assembly Center, artist Chiura Obata started the Tanforan Art School as an affiliated program of the Tanforan Adult Education program. According to him, the philosophy of the art school was its "determination to maintain one spot of normalcy" for the evacuees during their confinement (Hill, 2000: 37). His faculty included many college graduates. Two had master's of architecture degrees, and three had master's of arts degrees from the University of California, Berkeley. More than 600 students from grade school through adult could take more than twenty-three different courses in fine art, commercial art, and art technique for as little as a dollar per class for adults and 50 cents for children.

Church and religious services also were held in the assembly centers, as most evacuees were either Buddhist or Protestant. Although the Protestant services could be conducted in English, it was difficult to conduct Buddhist services because speaking Japanese in public was forbidden. The camp officials feared that there would be propaganda and subversive activity going on if services were conducted in Japanese.

Although every attempt was made to keep families together, there was always the potential for members to be separated during the evacuation process. Some evacuees had family members who were hospitalized and ill whom they were not allowed to see. If members of a family lived in different communities, they could be sent to different assembly centers. There were also Caucasian individuals who were married to Japanese who were free to leave the assembly centers, but their mixed-parentage children were not allowed to leave. In many cases, Caucasian spouses chose to stay with their Japanese husbands and wives. Estelle Ishigo was of English, Dutch, and French ancestry, married to Nisei Arthur Ishigo.

As an artist she documented the life of Heart Mountain Relocation Center in her drawings and paintings. Before camp, she and her husband were shunned by the white community, but in the lonely isolation of the camps, she felt accepted and welcomed into the Japanese American community.

Another woman, Elaine Black Yoneda, was married to Kibei activist Karl Yoneda and interned at Manzanar Relocation Center. Initially, she was told that she would not have to go to camp, but that her son who was half Japanese would have to go and live in the children's village at Manzanar, cared for by the Maryknoll Sisters. According to Colonel Karl Bendetsen's orders, anyone with at least one-sixteenth "Japanese blood" was to be evacuated. Elaine refused, and joined her husband where he had gone earlier to help set up the site for inhabitants. After her arrival, Elaine's many years as a social activist made her aware of the living situation. It was clearly a prison, with barbed wire and watchtowers manned by armed guards with searchlights on the roof.

For many evacuees, their stay in the assembly center was overshadowed by the fear of not knowing what might happen next. For the most part, they had gone to the assembly centers cooperatively, with little fanfare or complaint. But they had also been uprooted from their homes and communities with very short notice, and forced to live under makeshift, temporary housing conditions. Surrounded by barbed wire and armed military guards, they relinquished both their freedom and privacy when they entered the assembly center. Many were hopeful that the more permanent relocation centers would have much better conditions than what they had just experienced. Still not knowing what to expect, they left the assembly centers by train and by bus, to begin a new journey and a new phase in their lives.

RELOCATION CENTERS

Most residents lived at the assembly centers from one to four months. Soon, more permanent residential facilities were built by the War Department. The relocation centers were to be managed by a new division of the Department of the Interior. It was called the War Relocation Authority (WRA) and was created by Executive Order 9201 in March 1942. By October 1942, all of the assembly centers were closed and residents were transferred to the War Relocation Authority centers.

The relocation camps, as they came to be known, were in isolated areas throughout the West, Rocky Mountains, and Southeast. The ten "camps" were in areas that were "at a safe distance" from military outposts and on federal as well as private property. Part of the WRA plan for developing relocation centers was to have sites that would be suitable for large-scale agricultural development. The land that was available was

Table 3.2
Location and Population of Relocation Centers

Center	Location	Population	Date Opened	Date Closed
Topaz	Utah	8,130	September 11, 1942	October 31, 1945
Poston	Arizona	17,814	May 5, 1942	November 28, 1945
Gila River	Arizona	13,348	July 20, 1942	November 10, 1945
Granada	Colorado	7,318	August 27, 1942	October 15, 1945
Heart Mountain	Wyoming	10,767	August 12, 1942	November 10, 1945
Jerome	Arkansas	8,497	October 6, 1942	June 30, 1944
Manzanar	California	10,056	June 1, 1942	November 21, 1945
Minidoka	Idaho	9,397	August 10, 1942	October 2, 1945
Rohwer	Arkansas	8,475	September 18, 1942	November 30, 1945
Tule Lake	California	18,789	May 27, 1942	March 20, 1946

Source: War Relocation Authority, 1946: 197.

not very desireable in terms of the climate and resources needed to farm. Each of the ten sites selected posed different climactic problems and challenges for the residents. Manzanar in California, and Poston[2] and Gila River in Arizona were in dry desert areas; Minidoka and Heart Mountain in Idaho and Wyoming had problems with harsh cold winters and summer dust storms, as did Granada in Colorado; Rohwer and Jerome in Arkansas were located in swampland with drainage problems. Topaz in Utah also had cold winters, and the land was covered by greasewood brush making it difficult to cultivate crops. Tule Lake in California, located on the site of a dry lake bed, had the most potential for development.

The largest camp was Tule Lake in California with 18,789 residents. The smallest camp was Granada in Colorado with 7,318 residents (see Table 3.2). In all, more than 120,000 people were held in WRA custody during the war (see Figure 3.2).

Milton S. Eisenhower (brother of General Dwight D. Eisenhower) was the first director of the WRA. He had previously served in the Department of Agriculture and had very little experience with or exposure to Japanese Americans. His tenure with the WRA was a scant three months. He resigned in May 1942, just as the evacuation was under way and the permanent relocation centers were being built. His successor was Dillon S. Myer, also a former bureaucrat from the Department of Agriculture.

Evacuees were told that the conditions of the War Relocation Author-

Figure 3.2
The Evacuated People

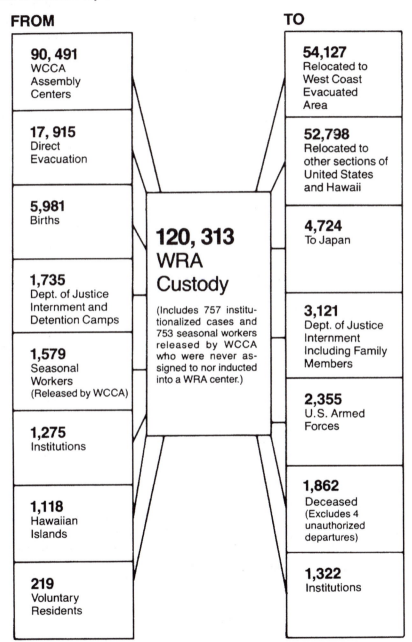

FROM

90,491
WCCA
Assembly
Centers

17,915
Direct
Evacuation

5,981
Births

1,735
Dept. of Justice
Internment and
Detention Camps

1,579
Seasonal
Workers
(Released by WCCA)

1,275
Institutions

1,118
Hawaiian
Islands

219
Voluntary
Residents

120,313
WRA
Custody

(Includes 757 institutionalized cases and 753 seasonal workers released by WCCA who were never assigned to nor inducted into a WRA center.)

TO

54,127
Relocated to
West Coast
Evacuated
Area

52,798
Relocated to
other sections of
United States
and Hawaii

4,724
To Japan

3,121
Dept. of Justice
Internment
Including Family
Members

2,355
U.S. Armed
Forces

1,862
Deceased
(Excludes 4
unauthorized
departures)

1,322
Institutions

Source: U.S. Department of the Interior, WRA, *The Evacuated People: A Quantitative Description* (1946), p. 8.

ity camps would be more hospitable than the assembly centers. Most were probably eager to leave the temporary living arrangements of the assembly centers and move to more permanent living structures. The trips to the relocation centers were usually by train, some taking several days to the centers far inland. Some trains had sleeping areas for invalids and mothers with small children, which meant they had to be separated from their husbands. Most evacuees sat upright during the entire trip. The military ordered that all window shades on the train be drawn during the trip, so ventilation and lighting were poor.

The train trip was uncomfortable, but even more denigrating was the treatment by military guards and other personnel. Interviews with former evacuees report:

When we finally reached our destination, four of us men were ordered by the military personnel carrying guns to follow them. We were directed to unload the pile of evacuees' belongings from the boxcars to the semi-trailer truck to be transported to the concentration camp. During the interim, after filling one trailer-truck and waiting for the next to arrive, we were hot and sweaty and sitting, trying to conserve our energy, when one of the military guards standing with his gun, suggested that one of us should get a drink of water at the nearby water faucet and try and make a run for it so he could get some target practice.

Another evacuee reported:

At Parker, Arizona, we were transferred to buses. With baggage and carryalls hanging from my arm, I was contemplating what I could leave behind, since my husband was not allowed to come to my aid. A soldier said, "Let me help you, put your arm out." He proceeded to pile everything on my arm. And to my horror, he placed my two-month old baby on top of the stack. He then pushed me with the butt of the gun and told me to get off the train, knowing when I stepped off the train my baby would fall to the ground. I refused. But he kept prodding and ordering me to move. I will always be thankful [that] a lieutenant checking the cars came upon us. He took the baby down, gave her to me, and then ordered the soldier to carry all our belongings to the bus and see that I was seated and then report back to him. (CWRIC, 1982: 151)

All of the camps were built based upon the army model and resembled military housing of that period. The only difference was that the entire site was surrounded by barbed-wire fences with watchtowers staffed by armed guards. The evacuees lived in barrack-style housing. Each barrack measured 20 by 100 to 120 feet, divided into four to six rooms, each from 20 by 16 to 20 by 25 feet. Each room housed one family, no matter how large the family. In a few cases, two families might share a room. The barracks were arranged in what was called a "block" consisting of twelve to fourteen barracks, a communal mess hall, bath and shower facility, toilets, laundry, and recreation hall. The barracks were constructed of planks nailed to studs, covered with tar paper, with no interior wall. Since they were newly constructed, many had cracks in the floors and walls, which let dust settle into the living area. The Caucasian military and administrative personnel had their own housing, which was generally larger and better equipped than the internee living quarters.

When they first arrived, evacuees found two canvas cots, sometimes a cotton mattress, minimal bedding (sheets, pillow, and blanket), a pot-bellied stove for coal heating, and a naked ceiling lightbulb. The several apartment rooms in one barrack gave little privacy to each family. For example, the coal heating stoves were ventilated to the outside with chimneys that cut through each room. The holes cut between the walls had to be large enough so that the wall would not burn, but it meant that conversations could be heard from one room to another. There were no cooking utensils, housekeeping items, or things that one would want in creating a home. Rooms had no running water.

Perhaps the most sensitive situation was the bathroom and toilet facilities. The facilities at Manzanar were less than private. There were no partitions or doors, just toilets back to back. According to Elaine Yoneda Black, "Because I had been in jails before, in solitary as well as the main prison tank, I wasn't appalled by it. I began encountering frustrated, horrified faces, primarily among teen-aged girls, as they came into the latrine. Some would run away crying."[3] Elaine complained to the camp administration, and eventually, partitions and doors were erected.

The eating area or mess hall was designed to feed the 300 people living in that block. In actuality, they often had to accommodate 600 to 900. The meals were of basic institutional standard, but their quality and quantity varied from camp to camp. Because it was wartime, food shortages were evident. WRA officials did not want to make it appear as if the evacuees were getting any special privileges because of their confined status. Thus, the food that was made available for their use for the most part reflected their caution. The foods evacuees report eating were wieners (hot dogs), dry fish, rice, macaroni, and pickled vegetables. Once evacuees began to produce food and to cook and run the mess hall operations in the camps, food quality improved. In Jeanne Wakatsuki Houston's book *Farewell to Manzanar*, she described her shock at being served food unfamiliar to her as a Japanese:

We had pulled up just in time for dinner. The mess halls weren't completed yet. An outdoor chow line snaked around a half-finished building that broke a good part of the wind. They issued us army mess kits, the round metal kind that folded over, and plopped in scoops of Vienna sausage, canned string beans, steamed rice that had been cooked too long, and on top of the rice a serving of canned apricots. The Caucasian servers were thinking that fruit poured over rice would make a good dessert. Among the Japanese, of course, rice is never eaten with sweet food, only with salty or savory foods. Few of us could eat such a mixture. But at this point no one dared protest. It would have been impolite. I was horrified when I saw the apricot syrup seeping through my little mound of rice. (Houston, 1973: 17–18)

Camp living also ran on a fairly predictable military model of activity. A siren alarm blast rang every morning at 7 A.M., breakfast was served at the cafeteria, adults went to work, and children went to school. As one internee reported,

Camp life was highly regimented and it was rushing to the wash basin to beat the other groups, rushing to the mess hall for breakfast, lunch, and dinner. When a human being is placed in captivity, survival is the key. We developed a very negative attitude toward authority. We spent countless hours to defy or beat the system. Our minds started to function like any POW or convicted criminal. (CWRIC, 1982: 169)

A large number of the evacuee population were of school age. The camps were not designed with their education in mind. School programs took place in large, open barracks that were often also used for recreation halls. There was little in the way of furniture, desks, and chairs, as well as schoolbooks. Students had to sit on the floor or stand during classes. Eventually, in some camps, schools were built to accommodate the population, but that was only for elementary through high school. There were no provisions for higher education, but outside the camps, the National Japanese Student Relocation Council was formed to assist in the relocation of Nisei to colleges and universities in the East and Midwest.

Qualified teachers were also in short supply. It was difficult to recruit teachers from outside the Japanese population because of the harsh living conditions in camp, although there were Caucasian teachers who were employed by the WRA at many of the camp schools. Other teaching positions were filled by internees who had a few years of college and became assistant teachers, but often had full responsibility for teaching classes. The school curriculum followed the standards and guidelines of the state in which the camp was located. Overall, the curriculum covered standard subjects, but underlying this education was an emphasis on Americanization, citizenship, and loyalty to America. In some ways this was an irony of the camp educational system. As students pledged their allegiance and saluted a flag, they were captives, incarcerated people living behind guarded, barbed wire fences in isolated portions of the United States.

The camps replicated much of the social and recreational activities that were popular at that time period. There were local chapters of national organizations such as the Boy Scouts and Girl Scouts, YMCA, and

YWCA. Athletics was also popular with baseball, basketball, and football teams. But there were also activities that were unique to Japanese Americans, such as sumo wrestling, flower arranging and sumi (ink) painting, and go (Japanese board game) tournaments. The forms of recreation accommodated both Japanese and so-called American activities.

Perhaps one of the most difficult adjustments many of the evacuees had to make was deciding what to do with their time. Before camp, adult family members were active in productive paid employment. Many were in family-run businesses or farms. Now that they were temporarily taken away from their income-producing jobs, what would they do? Were they obligated to work under their conditions of confinement, or were they prisoners of the government that was to provide for their welfare during their incarceration? The WRA administration felt that establishing a work/employment program in the camps should be a high priority. Director Milton Eisenhower felt that internees should be as independent as possible and tried to find employment opportunities for those in the camps. This was difficult to do because evacuees were not allowed to leave the camps without permission of the WRA authorities and because of the geographic and physical isolation of the camps. On the other hand, evacuees were not always eager to jump into the WRA plans for work, especially when there were very few incentives to perform, and they were still denied the freedom to leave the confines of the camp.

One plan was to have an internee work corps in which volunteers could enlist to be eligible for work. The corps would develop land, build camp structures, provide irrigation, produce food, and manufacture war-related items. Manzanar manufactured camouflage net as a war goods production facility, but only U.S. citizens could work in the factory. In general, the idea of "partnership enterprises" never received widespread acceptance among the evacuees. Few signed up for the work corps, and eventually this idea floundered.

Although it was agreed that all internees would receive food, shelter, medical care, and education without charge, they needed money to buy things that were not provided by the government. Opportunities for employment were limited, and were in the clerical, construction, medical, and service-related areas. Wages ranged from $12 to $19 a month, depending upon the skill level of the job. Still, salaries were a source of constant conflict. Non-Japanese WRA staff were paid more than the internees. Financial hardships were a reality for many internees. Those who owned land still had to make mortgage payments. They could not do this on the salaries that were offered. Money was needed to buy certain goods that the WRA did not provide: personal items, clothing, and shoes. These items were usually bought from a mail order catalog and sent to the camps.

Many former internees have selective memories of camp in the way that young children remember things. They may not have been aware of their parents' and other adults' fears and anxiety, but grew to see the camp experience as a part of their everyday life routine:

In some ways, I suppose, my life was not too much different from a lot of kids in America between the years 1942 and 1945. I spent a good part of my time playing with my brothers and friends, learned to shoot marbles, watched sandlot baseball and envied the older kids who wore Boy Scout uniforms. We shared with the rest of America the same movies, screen heroes and listened to the same heartrending songs of the forties. We imported much of America into the camps because, after all, we were Americans. Through imitation of my brothers, who attended grade school within the camp, I learned the salute to the flag by the time I was five years old. I was learning, as best as one could learn in Manzanar, what it meant to live in America. But I was also learning the sometimes bitter price one has to pay for it. (CWRIC, 1982: 172)

RELOCATION CENTERS: DIVERSITY AND UNITY

Each of the camps functioned in ways similar to a small city or town. They developed a form of governance, and dealt with unique issues having to do with the challenges of the physical setting, geography, and landscape of the region they were in. Layered upon the physical surroundings were the differences in the people who settled together in the camp. Although they shared a common Japanese ancestry, they came from different places, rural and urban, were of different religious backgrounds, Buddhist and Christian, and had economic and social class differences, based upon occupation and different status in their respective communities. Now, they were confined in one all-Japanese community, living under the rules and mandates of the War Relocation Authority, and had to deal with issues of civic responsibility, decision making, and camp governance in the small city-towns of the relocation centers.

Camp governance took the form of resident councils. Each unit of twelve to fourteen barracks was called a "block" and had an elected leader called a "blockhead." Their job was to handle grievances and problems associated with their block. The idea was to form a system of community councils that could handle issues within the community. For obvious reasons, though, the WRA had the final word on all recommendations of the community councils, and designed the policies structuring the councils themselves. The WRA was criticized for handling community governance in this way, since the councils had very little power and it amounted to little more than lip service to the residents. One of the restrictions was that Issei could not serve on the elected community councils.

Block managers could be appointed or elected, depending on the camp. In many instances, a respected Issei would be appointed. Their three main responsibilities were to maintain a line of communication between the WRA and the internees, to supervise the maintenance of the block grounds, and to make sure that evacuees had what they needed. Although their power and authority was limited by the cooperation with the camp administrator, block managers did have a degree of respect, much as a community elder would.

At the relocation centers, internees were subjected to restricted living conditions. The centers were surrounded by barbed-wire fences and towers manned by guards armed with machine guns. Security was controlled by the army, although the WRA itself was a civilian agency. The army controlled the traffic in and out of the center, as well as inspection of items sent in and out of camp. The military police were called into the camp only when requested by the camp director. Ironically, internees at Topaz (Utah) had to build the fences and towers after they arrived.

The presence of armed military police guards presented potentially dangerous situations and confrontations between the internee population and the guards. At Manzanar, Hikoji Takeuchi was shot at for being outside the center of the camp. The guard said that he ordered him to stop, but that Takeuchi ignored his warnings. The guard shot and wounded Takeuchi, who later recovered. He said he was collecting wood to make shelves in his home, and did not hear the guard yell at him. Army reports of the incident note that Takeuchi's bullet wounds were in the front, not in the back, as would have occurred if he was actually trying to escape.

In April 1943, another shooting occurred at Topaz that was fatal. James Hatsuki Wakasa was shot when he failed to respond to a command of "Halt!" in broad daylight as he approached one of the outer fences of the camp compound. The guard believed he was trying to escape. The "Wakasa incident" is described this way:

An elderly resident was shot and killed within the center area inside the fence, by a guard in one of the watchtowers. Particulars and facts of the matter were never satisfactorily disclosed to the residents. The anti-administration leaders again started to howl and the rest of the residents shouted for protection against soldiers with guns. As a result, the guards were later removed to the rim of the outer project area and firearms were banned. An impressive memorial service was held for the unfortunate victim. The women of each block made enormous floral wreaths with paper flowers. (Okubo, 1946: 180–1)

There were incidents at other camps that involved shootings. A guard shot and wounded a mentally ill internee at Gila River. At Tule Lake, an internee was killed in an altercation with a guard.

Camp living was not without its discontentment. Tensions erupted from time to time over the living conditions, the amount and quality of food, shortages of supplies for households, education, and recreation. Within the internee population, there was suspicion and mistrust among different groups. There were conflicts between Issei and Nisei over the WRA-mandated self-governing procedures. Only citizens (Nisei) could hold positions within the community councils. There were also conflicts between early arrivals and later arrivals. Those who had been displaced from other camps (e.g., moved from Tule Lake once it became a segregation center) or were just arriving from the assembly centers found it difficult to adjust to the new surroundings, neighbors, and communities that had formed before they got there. There was even said to be favoritism toward those leaders who were affiliated with the JACL. Camp officials looked to JACL members as spokesmen for the entire population, but they did not always represent the sentiment of all Japanese in the camp. As a result, there was increasing distrust of those Japanese Americans who were perceived "close" to the WRA camp officials. Individuals who held positions within the camp administration were seen as privileged. Some outside of the camp administration grew suspicious and distrustful of those insiders. Those close to the administrators and Japanese American leaders were nicknamed *inu*, or dog.

As with any incarcerated population, there were bound to be disturbances. This was no less true for the Japanese American population during internment. Two major riots occurred: one at Poston, the other at Manzanar. In November 1942 at Poston, an internee who was believed to have cooperated with the WRA was beaten by a group of unidentified men. Two men were arrested on suspicion of being the assailants and were held while the beating was investigated.

One of the most serious outbreaks of violence occurred at Manzanar in December 1942. One evening, Fred Tayama, a leading JACL official was attacked and beaten by an unknown group of assailants. His condition was serious enough to cause him to be hospitalized, but since he could not positively identify his attackers, the WRA officials arrested several Kibei activists. One of the key figures in this incident was Harry Ueno, a Kibei who had tried to organize a Kitchen Workers' Union. Ueno accused the WRA officials of taking sugar and meat rations from the internees, and had also tried to organize for better working conditions. His arrest sparked a larger demonstration led by Joe Kurihara, a Hawaiian-born Nisei, another WRA agitator and anti-JACL leader. Kurihara was a World War I veteran and was obviously bitter about his detainment in camp. The demonstrators demanded two things: the release of all those who were arrested and investigation of the conditions of Manzanar by the Spanish consul (the Spanish government represented Japanese nationals during the war).

Eventually the military police were called in to quell the disturbance.

The demonstrators were teargassed, and the crowd temporarily dispersed. They later regrouped and this time, shots were fired, apparently without orders. Machine guns, shotguns, and rifles were fired into the crowd. Two men were killed and ten others were treated for gunshot wounds. The WRA insisted that the disturbances were over. In fact, what they had done was to remove the so-called troublemakers from the general camp population and sent them to citizen isolation centers in Moab, Utah, and Leupp, Arizona. JACL leaders were moved out of camp for their "protection" to a Civilian Conservation Corps camp in the Mohave Desert in California.[4]

Although living in the relocation camps had its conflicts and problems, internees tried to bring about some type of normalcy to the conditions of incarceration. With limited resources, they tried to recreate, the best they could, life as they might have lived it outside of their confinement. In addition to the schools, there were festivals, dances, movies, and other activities to fill the time. Berkeley artist Chiura Obata, who had founded the Tanforan Art School, also founded the Topaz Art School and employed many notable art teachers who had worked with him at Tanforan. His faculty included Matsusaburo and Hisako Hibi, along with Mine Okubo (author of *Citizen 13660*), Frank Taira, Teruo Iyama, and Byron Takashi Tsuzuki.

All camps had a camp newspaper. They were written in English with a Japanese section. Their primary purpose was to disseminate information to the camp population, including announcements from the camp administration and other camp news, especially information about "resettlers"—people who had left the camps—and what they were doing. The newspapers were funded by the WRA, published two or three times a week, or in the case of the Gila River Center, every day.

LEAVE: THE NISEI COLLEGE RELOCATION PROGRAM

The relocation centers provided basic elementary through high school education for children, but did not offer college or university education. In March 1942, the Student Relocation Council formed and held their first meeting at the University of California, Berkeley. A group of educators met to address the problems and issues facing the Nisei students who were attending West Coast colleges and universities, and how the impending evacuation orders might affect them. Eventually, this group coalesced into a national organization with regional offices in the Pacific Northwest, Northern California, and Southern California that coordinated the activities of Nisei college students. One educator's suggestion was to exempt from evacuation all Nisei who were attending college and living with a Caucasian family. President Robert Sproul of the University of California at Berkeley felt that the Nisei college students represented the leadership of the future Japanese American community and that the federal government should provide scholarships to those who wanted to continue their education at colleges and universities outside the restricted area. None of these ideas prevented the eventual evacuation of all Nisei college students from the West Coast restricted area. By May 1942, continued meetings with the State Department, American Friends Service Committee, the National YMCA and YWCA, along with the Japanese American Citizens League and church programs brought about the formation of the National Student Relocation Council. This group was to coordinate efforts to allow Nisei college students to leave the camps and attend colleges in the Midwest and East. By 1943, the name had changed to the National Japanese American Student Relocation Council with one main office in Philadelphia.

By the time the council had organized into a central office, evacuation was completed, assembly centers were closed, and the lives of Nisei college students were under the jurisdiction of the WRA. The council worked with the WRA to facilitate Nisei students leaving the camps for educational purposes. Under the educational leave program, college-age Nisei had to have their leaves approved by the WRA. The council helped to facilitate the leave process by making sure the students' paperwork was in order (application, letters of recommendation, and the Application for Leave Clearance/loyalty questionnaire) so that they could leave the camp and attend college elsewhere. Students were granted educational leaves once they had been accepted at an institution of higher education and showed that they had the finances to support themselves through at least one semester. The students had to receive clearance from the Federal Bureau of Investigation. Ultimately, WRA officials made the final decision of whether they were "cleared" to leave the camp.

Another job of the council was to provide financial assistance for those who wanted to attend college but did not have the means. This was a particular problem because of the serious financial losses many families faced after their forced evacuation, and because the Nisei would be considered out of state students paying higher tuition at many colleges. A substantial scholarship fund was established totaling more than $90,000, no small sum in those days. Scholarship funds were also set up within the camps to raise money for those Nisei accepted at colleges and universities.

In 1941, shortly before evacuation, there were 3,530 Nisei students in colleges and universities throughout the United States, most concentrated on the West Coast. By 1943, after evacuation, and within a year after the National Japanese American College Relocation Council formed, there were 1,493 Nisei students at colleges concentrated in the Midwest and East, with a few at colleges in eastern Arizona, Oregon, and Washington in the areas that were not evacuated (O'Brien, 1949).

The decline in the number of students most likely was caused by the reluctance of many students to leave the camps. The colleges they attended were diverse: Oberlin, St. Olaf, Harvard, Boston University, New York University, Michigan State University, and Iowa State. They were spread out among the public and private schools throughout the nation. Many were the only Nisei in their college. After restrictions and the ban on Japanese living on the West Coast were lifted, Nisei returned to colleges in the West.

The relocated Nisei college students entered an entirely different world from the one they left, both from their West Coast homes before internment, and the relocation centers. People at schools in the Midwest and East had very little exposure to Japanese American students, and the Nisei students saw themselves as "ambassadors" for their ethnic group. Robert W. O'Brien's (1949) study of the college Nisei found that the group had greater chances for exploring different occupational fields, intermixing with non-Japanese and other minority groups, relative to their experiences in West Coast colleges and universities. In other words, the college Nisei had to accommodate to living under isolated conditions, forcing them to interact with non-Japanese. Sociologist O'Brien suggests that this forced them to assimilate, providing greater opportunities for acceptance and a new pattern of race relations that held less conflict for Nisei than before.

OTHER CAMPS AND DETENTION FACILITIES

The vast majority of people of Japanese ancestry were interned in the ten WRA centers. There were others who were detained at Department of Justice camps. Shortly after Pearl Harbor, the FBI rounded up enemy aliens, Japanese, German, and Italian. Among those who were arrested and taken away were leaders of Japanese community organizations, Japanese language school teachers, Buddhist and Shinto priests, Japanese newspaper editors, and other identifiable leaders within the Japanese American community. They were often arrested and taken away without their families' knowing where they were going. These men, along with about fifty women, were detained at Department of Justice camps administered by the (INS). There were eight camps located in Idaho, Montana, New Mexico, North Dakota, and Texas that served as prison camps for a number of different groups (see Table 3.3). Two other camps administered by the Department of Justice were called Citizen Isolation Centers and housed Americans of Japanese descent who, for various reasons, were removed and isolated from the general relocation center population. These were located at Moab, Utah, and Leupp, Arizona.

In addition to the noncitizen, mostly male, Japanese population, the camps also held German and Italian nationals; German and Japanese

Table 3.3
Other Camps and Detention Facilities

Location	Authority/Type	Population Detained
Fort Lincoln (Bismarck), North Dakota	Department of Justice/INS	Males, non-citizen Japanese, German and Italian nationals, renunciants
Crystal City, Texas	Department of Justice/INS	Males, families, non-citizen Japanese families, Germans, Italians, Japanese Latin Americans
Fort Stanton, New Mexico	Department of Justice/INS	Males, non-citizen Japanese, German nationals
Kenedy, Texas	Department of Justice/INS	Males, Japanese Latin Americans, German/Italian Latin Americans, German and Japanese POWs
Kooksia, Idaho	Department of Justice/INS	Males, non-citizen Japanese, Japanese Latin Americans
Fort Missoula, Montana	Department of Justice/INS	Males, non-citizen Japanese, Italian nationals, Japanese Latin Americans
Santa Fe, New Mexico	Department of Justice/INS	Males, non-citizen Japanese Americans, German and Italian nationals, Japanese Latin Americans, renunciants
Seagoville, Texas	Department of Justice/INS	Females, Japanese non-citizens, Japanese Latin American families
Moab, Utah	War Relocation Authority Citizen Isolation Center	Males, U.S. Citizens
Leupp, Arizona	War Relocation Authority Citizen Isolation Center	Males, U.S. Citizens

Sources: CWRIC, *Personal Justice Denied* (Washington, D.C.: U.S. Government Printing Office, 1982); <http://www.cr.nps.gov/history/online_books/anthropology74/index.htm>.

POWs; Japanese, Germans, and Italians who were from Latin America; and later, Japanese American citizens who had decided to renounce their U.S. citizenship and were to return to Japan.

One of the largest and most diverse of all the Department of Justice detention centers was Crystal City, Texas. Located in southwestern Texas, not far from the Mexico border, Crystal City was in a region of extreme climate conditions; weather was hot in the summer and known to be quite cold in the winter. The housing was similar to the WRA camps—standard government military-style barrack housing—and afforded little privacy. The main difference in the camp atmosphere though, was the presence of women and children. Crystal City was a "family camp." In addition to noncitizen Japanese and their families, it detailed Japanese from Latin America, who were considered "voluntary detainees." Similar to the ten relocation centers run by the WRA, Crystal City had schools and activities appropriate for the school-age population and families who lived there. For men who had once been detained in virtually all-male Department of Justice camps, living at Crystal City gave them an opportunity to reunite with their families and to have some semblance of a normal life.

The diversity in the population stemmed from the German nationals and Japanese from Latin America and their families. Each of the groups were segregated into separate living compounds, and even the schools had to cater to the needs of the different populations of children. The education director of the camp was R. C. Tate, former principal of Crystal City High School. His job was to operate three schools at the camp: one to educate the American-born English-speaking population of Japanese, a second for the children of German detainees, and a third—Japanese—for those children who were from Peru. The school for the English-speaking Japanese American population followed Texas state curriculum guidelines and was staffed by local teachers. The other two schools had teachers from within the detained population and established their own curriculums.

THE JAPANESE LATIN AMERICANS

In the interest of national security throughout the Western Hemisphere, the U.S. internment program also covered people of Japanese, German, and Italian ancestry who were living in Latin America. One of the least known situations during World War II was the experience of Japanese Latin Americans who were brought to the United States and detained at Department of Justice camps. More than two-thirds of the people who were deported from Latin American countries were of Japanese ancestry.

The Latin American deportation program was based on a program instituted in Panama. Concerned about the security of the Panama Canal, the U.S. government brokered an agreement that would have all Japanese residents in Panama arrested, turned over to U.S. authorities, and brought to the United States for detainment. Shortly after the arrest of Panamanian Japanese, Japanese in other Latin American countries were also arrested and interned, most from Peru.

The history of the Japanese in Peru has parallels to the experience of Japanese in the United States. They first immigrated at the turn of the nineteenth century, attracted to the rich agricultural land of Latin America. When the United States enacted restrictive laws barring immigration, Peru had a surge in Japanese immigrants. But, similar to the experiences of Japanese in the United States, the Japanese in Peru inherited the anti-Chinese sentiment that had grown since the immigration of Chinese during the mid-nineteenth century.

Although initially attracted to agriculture, the Japanese formed a sizable community in urban areas of Peru. Here they formed small businesses and catered to Peruvian and Japanese clientele. Some men intermarried with native Peruvian women and joined the Roman Catholic Church. Others married Japanese picture brides. Still, they lived apart from the Latin American Peruvian society and tended to reside in all-Japanese ethnic enclaves. Some Japanese eventually became Peruvian citizens, but many held on to their Japanese citizenship. With the U.S. entry into World War II, Latin American countries allied themselves with the United States and other Allied nations, and cooperated with the U.S. government in the removal of Japanese from their countries because of "military necessity."

Thus, U.S. Justice Department camps housed 2,260 so-called dangerous persons of Japanese ancestry who were from twelve Latin American countries. They were arrested and deported to the United States and held without trial at Department of Justice camps, run by the Immigration and Naturalization Service at Kenedy, Seagoville, and Crystal City, Texas; Fort Missoula, Montana; and Santa Fe, New Mexico. Among them were approximately 1,800 Japanese Peruvians. The U.S. government had hoped to use the Japanese Latin Americans as potential exchanges for hostages/prisoners of war held by Japan.

In 1945, the Japanese Latin Americans being held at Immigration and Naturalization Service camps were told that they were "illegal aliens" and subject to deportation. Peru did not want to readmit those Japanese, even if they were Peruvian citizens or married to a Peruvian citizen. After the war, 1,400 of these people were prevented from returning to their homes in Peru. Some were deported to Japan, and 365 decided to stay in the United States. In 1946, attorney Wayne Collins recognized the plight of the Japanese Peruvians, who were being detained against their will. He eventually negotiated the release of 110 men, women, and children who were "paroled" and allowed to move to Seabrook Farms, New Jersey.

In 1953, Congress suspended deportation orders for the Japanese Latin Americans, and by 1954, they become eligible for U.S. citizenship. The situation of the Japanese Latin Americans in the Department of Justice detention centers has been overshadowed by the mass relocation program operated by the War Relocation Authority. Nonetheless, it should be recognized as a distinct part of the Japanese experience with wartime internment because the individuals arrested and deported to the United States were detained for precisely the same reason as West Coast people of Japanese ancestry: for being under suspicion as potentially dangerous enemy aliens.

CONCLUSION

The removal and incarceration of more than 120,000 people of Japanese ancestry from the West Coast area was not a simple task. How could such a large population be moved with little protest, violence, or disruption? It required not only military intervention and management of a large civilian population, but also the general cooperation of the individuals being evacuated. It has been more than fifty years since this happened, and there is still much controversy within the Japanese American community over how the community was forced to evacuate and endure uncomfortable and extreme conditions, and whether there should have been greater protest and resistance to the evacuation and internment orders. Although the majority of the population complied with the government orders, there were those who did not. As the war progressed, there were many people within the camps who began to protest and question their conditions. Tensions begin to arise between different groups, and the reality of incarceration brought about real consequences. Individuals were forced to make difficult choices when the government decided to institute a "loyalty" test to separate potential troublemakers from the general population and when the draft was reinstated for the Nisei. These events, combined with the psychological pressures of being incarcerated, presented challenges to all those who were behind barbed wire and not free to leave.

NOTES

1. During the period in which the Japanese lived at the assembly centers, I will refer to them as *evacuees*. When residents are moved to the relocation centers (also referred to as internment centers or camps), I will refer to them as *residents* or *internees*.

2. Poston was on the Colorado River Indian Reservation and was first admin-

istered by the Office of Indian Affairs (OIA). It was later transferred to the WRA at the end of 1943. Most of the 11,000 residents of Poston did not go through assembly centers, but were sent directly to the camp after the West Coast evacuation orders were issued. Poston was different from other camps in that it was geographically divided into three subcamps units, which made for the development of different communities and administrative complexities. See Lane Ryo Hirabayashi's introduction to Richard Nishimoto's *Inside an American Concentration Camp: Japanese American Resistance at Poston, Arizona* (Arizona: University of Arizona Press, 1995). Hirabayashi describes the location and unique conditions of the Poston relocation center.

3. Vivian McGuckin Raineri, *The Red Angel: The Life and Times of Elaine Black Yoneda, 1906–1988* (New York: International Publishers, 1991), p. 211.

4. Historian Roger Daniels (1981: 108) describes the Manzanar riot and lists a number of sources for information about the event: Dorothy S. Thomas and Richard S. Nishimoto, *The Spoilage* (Berkeley: University of California Press, 1946), pp. 49–52; Allan R. Bosworth, *America's Concentration Camps* (New York: Norton, 1967), pp. 157–62; Bill Hosokawa, *Nisei: The Quiet Americans* (New York: Morrow, 1969), pp. 361–2; Audrie Girdner and Anne Loftis, *The Great Betrayal* (New York: Macmillan, 1969), pp. 263–6; and the War Relocation Authority, *WRA: A Story of Human Conservation* (Washington, D.C.: U.S. Government Printing Office, 1946), pp. 49–51.

4

The Question of Loyalty: Japanese Americans in the Military and Draft Resisters

Throughout the war, the U.S. government consistently maintained that the loyalty of people of Japanese ancestry was in question and that their internment was based on military necessity. Once the population was confined to internment camps, and the war was in full operation, the government began to address the loyalty issue. The loyalty review process was used as a mechanism to weed out so-called "loyals" from potential "disloyals."

This chapter examines the loyalty review program and the consequent problems the program created: a segregation facility at Tule Lake Relocation Center, renunciation and repatriation, and draft resisters. Despite the problems with the loyalty review program, it led to the reinstitution of the draft for Japanese Americans. This chapter also examines how loyalty tied into the military service of Japanese Americans. Most of the more than 33,000 Japanese Americans who served in the U.S. military during World War II were in one of three military units: the 100th Battalion, which originated in Hawaii; the 442nd Regimental Combat Team, comprising volunteers and draftees from the ten mainland internment camps; and the Military Intelligence Service (MIS), consisting of Nisei and Kibei, who worked in the Pacific Theater.

THE LOYALTY REVIEW PROGRAM

The War Relocation Authority was concerned about creating a dependent incarcerated population of the interned Japanese. They feared that some Issei and Nisei would not ever want to leave the camps and began to explore the necessity for keeping Japanese Americans there. The

WRA also wanted to find a way for Japanese Americans to participate in the war effort and to relieve the wartime labor shortages in the Midwest and East.

On February 1, 1943, the army announced the formation of the 442nd Regimental Combat Team. They first looked for volunteers to man this unit, but eventually began to consider reinstating the draft for Nisei. The task fell upon the WRA to consider implementing a plan that would assess the trustworthiness of the Japanese population and allow for the army's desire to reinstate the draft.

As the head of the Western Defense Command, General DeWitt was opposed to any plan that would involve the release of Japanese from the camps and felt it was impossible to distinguish the loyal from the disloyal. But Assistant Secretary of War John J. McCloy was more positively inclined to allowing Nisei into the army. His opinions were influenced by Hawaii's commanding officer, Delos Emmons. Emmons was favorably impressed by his experiences with the Japanese in Hawaii, their performance in the Hawaii National Guard (later to become the 100th Battalion) as they trained at Camp McCoy, Wisconsin, and the success of the Nisei and Kibei already in the Military Intelligence Language School at the Presidio of San Francisco. Despite DeWitt's reservations, the War Department proceeded with a plan for loyalty review.

Interestingly, President Roosevelt also supported such a program to reinstate the draft and an all-Japanese combat unit. He stated:

No loyal citizen of the United States should be denied the democratic right to exercise the responsibilities of his citizenship, regardless of his ancestry. The principle on which this country was founded and by which it has always been governed is that Americanism is a matter of mind and heart; Americanism is not, and never was, a matter of race or ancestry. A good American is one who is loyal to this country and to our creed of liberty and democracy. Every loyal American citizen should be given the opportunity to serve this country wherever his skills will make the greatest contribution—whether it be in the ranks of our armed forces, war production, agriculture, government service, or other work essential to the war effort. (CWRIC, 1982: 191)

The loyalty review program would be administered as a part of the Application for Leave Clearance. A questionnaire would be used to determine whether an individual would be "at risk" if released from the relocation center (Document 4). The answers of adult respondents would be used to determine their eligibility for enlistment into the military (either volunteer or draft) and work in any war-related industry. The questionnaire asked about family background, education, and employment. Following the administration of the questionnaire, a Joint Board consisting of representatives from the navy, War Relocation Authority, military intelligence and the provost marshal general would decide the disposition of each adult internee. Some would be allowed to work in war production facilities, serve in the army, or be released for other work outside the internment camps.

The two critical questions in this form were numbers 27 and 28. Question 27 asked, "Are you willing to serve in the armed forces of the United States on combat duty, wherever ordered?" This was followed by the so-called "loyalty question," question 28: "Will you swear unqualified allegiance to the United States of America and faithfully defend the United States from any or all attack by foreign or domestic forces, and forswear any form of allegiance or obedience to the Japanese Emperor, or any other foreign government, power, or organization?"

For Issei, question 28 was difficult. It was unfair for them to answer because any response left them few choices or options. A "no" answer meant their loyalty was in question. A "yes" answer meant they would have been made "stateless citizens" or citizens without a country. It required them to forswear allegiance to the country of their birth, Japan, and yet, as "aliens" they were ineligible for citizenship in the United States. Many were not sure of how their responses would be used. Since the questionnaire was called Application for Leave Clearance did this mean they would be forced to leave the camps if they were given clearance? If so, where would they go if they had lost their homes and property and were prohibited from returning to the West Coast? One evacuee summed it up this way:

One can understand a situation of the head of a household, his livelihood taken away, having to face the possibility of earning a living for his family in some strange city. The temptation to declare a "no" "no" position [to questions 27 and 28] just to maintain a dependent life style in the camps was very strong indeed. In such cases the issue is survival, not loyalty. (CWRIC, 1982: 193)

The vast majority of Japanese answered the questionnaire with affirmative responses to questions 27 and 28. Those who did not were dubbed "no-no" and were separated from the so-called loyals or "yes-yes" respondents. The no-no respondents were removed and transferred to Tule Lake Relocation Center, which had now been designated as a segregation center.

Because of the loyalty questions, many Issei were unable to complete the questionnaire. Nisei also felt that their loyalty was being challenged because it assumed that they were automatically loyal to Japan. Although the WRA ultimately declared the loyalty review program a success, it was not without its problems. At Tule Lake, there was a great deal of resistance to registering. More than 3,000 refused to register, and the process was never completed.

TULE LAKE SEGREGATION CENTER

Although the loyalty review program was used as a tool to distinguish so-called loyals from disloyals there had already been plans to create a segregated camp for special "security risk" individuals. By spring 1943, Tule Lake was selected for its size and because it already housed many of those who were in this category. Among those to be sent to the Tule Lake facility were:

[T]hose who had applied for expatriation or repatriation to Japan and not withdrawn their application before July 1, 1943; those who answered "no" to the loyalty question or refused to answer it during registration and had not changed their answers; those who were denied leave clearance due to some accumulation of adverse evidence in their records; aliens from Department of Justice internment camps whom that agency recommended for detention; and family members of segregants who chose to remain with the family. (CWRIC, 1982: 208)

In addition to these categories of individuals, the WRA also included those who had indicated that their loyalties were with Japan and not with the United States.

The internee population already living at Tule Lake had the choice of either staying at the camp or being transferred to another relocation center. About 6,000 stayed, 6,200 moved out, and more than 11,000 evacuees were moved to Tule Lake during the fall of 1943 (CWRIC, 1982). The Tule Lake population grew to more than 18,000 individuals. This was a much larger population than what the facility was built for, and housing was cramped. The population demographics also changed. Tule Lake once housed evacuees from distinct communities in Sacramento, southwestern Oregon, and western Washington. Under segregation, Tule Lake was populated with individuals and families from throughout California, Hawaii, Washington, and Oregon. They were many single male farm laborers as well as families from rural and urban areas.

Because Tule Lake housed a largely disaffected population, there were a number of incidents that increased the possibility of conflict between the internee population and the administration. There were labor disputes between the administration and workers. An industrial accident killed one worker and injured several others, leading to a larger-scale work strike within the community.

Following these incidents, there was a riot protesting the conditions of the camp and the observation of Caucasian workers stealing food from the internees' rations. This was how it was described by one internee, Tokio Yamane:

It was on November 4th, 1943, as I recall, that the Tule Lake Food Warehouse Disturbances occurred. A Mr. Kobayashi, a Japanese American on security patrol, discovered several WRA Caucasian personnel stealing food from the Internee Food Warehouse during the night and loading the food on their own truck which was parked alongside the warehouse. Mr. Kobayashi, who had the authority of a warder, remonstrated with the WRA personnel because they were taking the internees' food. Mr. Kobayashi was attacked by the Caucasian WRA personnel and a scuffle ensued.

During this time, the Organization for the Betterment of Camp Conditions was meeting. Yamane and Koji Todorogi were asked to go to the scene to help get the situation under control and bring back the internees who had gathered there.

As Mr. Koji Todorogi and I were heading toward the warehouse area, several Caucasian WRA personnel suddenly appeared out of the darkness and attacked the two of us, without any provocation on our part, with pistols, rifles, and bats, and finally took us to the WRA office.

As the two of us were being interrogated, Mr. Kobayashi, the warder, was brought in by another group of Caucasians. During his interrogation Mr. Kobayashi was hit on the head with such force that blood gushed out and the baseball bat actually broke in two. . . . From about 9 P.M. that evening until daybreak, we were forced to stand with our backs against the office wall with our hands over our heads and were continuously kicked and abused as we were ordered to confess being the instigators of the disturbance. We denied these accusations but our protestations of innocence were completely ignored by our tormentors. The beatings continued all night long and at day break the three of us were turned over to the Military Police and we were thrown into the stockade for confinement. (CWRIC, 1982: 21)

Leaders of the disturbances and strikes at Tule Lake were placed in detention centers within the camp known as the "stockade." Because Tule Lake contained more "at-risk" people, security at the camp was increased. A double eight-foot fence was constructed surrounding the compound, and there was a prominent display of military tanks. The WRA did not retain full control of the facility; rather the army and the military police were responsible for maintaining security and order within the camp. These changes along with the increased population made Tule Lake seem more like a prison. Along with this came the mentality of "prisoner" and "jailer" between the Japanese internees and the Caucasian personnel.

Resegregationists, Renunciation, and Repatriation

Over time the outbursts and strikes declined, but there was continued distrust among the internees. Within the population there were strong pro-Japanese groups who wanted to have an even more segregated population, dubbed the "resegregationists." The resegregationists constituted a type of "cultural resistance" group in the camp. These individuals preferred a strictly Japanese way of life within the camp, with their children educated in Japanese and activities conducted in Japanese. Taeko Okamura was a child at Tule Lake and described her experiences this way:

My sister and I were enrolled in a Japanese school in preparation for our eventual expatriation to Japan. Our teachers were generally pro-Japan and taught us not only how to read and write in Japanese but also to be proud as Japanese. Their goals were to teach us to be good Japanese so that we would not be embarrassed when we got to Japan.

We were often asked to wear red or white headbands and do marching exercises. We were awakened early, hurriedly got dressed and gathered at one end of the block where a leader led us in traditional Japanese calisthenics. As the sun rose, we bowed our heads to the east. This was to show our respect to the Emperor. (CWRIC, 1982: 248)

Because of the volatile situation at Tule Lake with the pro-Japanese resegregationists, there was an effort to remove extremist pro-Japanese groups from the population. A bill was passed that would allow for the voluntary renunciation of U.S. citizenship. Those who chose this route would be removed from Tule Lake to one of the Department of Justice internment camps (Table 3.3). On July 1, 1944, Congress passed Public Law 405, which allowed individuals to renounce their citizenship. The WRA and Department of Justice worked on a procedure for renunciation, and this was announced in October 1944. An internee would have to make a written request to the Department of Justice for renunciation. A hearing would be held and then a formal renunciation, in which the attorney general would grant his approval.

Among the evacuees were a number of citizens and aliens who filed for repatriation or expatriation to Japan. (The term *repatriation* was used for those Issei who were aliens, but still citizens of Japan who wished to return; the term *expatriation* was used for those Nisei or Kibei who held U.S. citizenship but wished to give it up.) Earlier in the war, approximately 2,000 Japanese nationals had been repatriated to Japan in a prisoner of war exchange. They were mostly Issei who were being held at Immigration and Naturalization Service detention camps.

The Commission on Wartime Relocation and Internment of Civilians report (1982) suggests that these individuals were probably discouraged by their prolonged detention in the internment camps. In late 1942, early in the evacuation process, the WRA had received only 2,255 applications for repatriation. About 58 percent of the applicants were Japanese aliens; 23 percent were American citizens under the age of eighteen. By 1943, more than 9,000 applications were on file. Applications came mainly from American citizens. The increase in applications was probably a result of the pressure from the loyalty questionnaire, which caused many to question whether they should stay in the United States or return to Japan. Most of the applicants for repatriation were from all the camps, except for Granada (Colorado) and Minidoka (Idaho), which had few problems with the loyalty registration.

In 1944, the numbers of applications requesting repatriation again increased. The WRA recorded more than 19,000 applications, more than 75 percent of which came from the Tule Lake Segregation Center. By the end of 1945, more than 20,000 requests for repatriation had been made, representing another increase and 16 percent of the total number within the evacuee population.

Renunciation meant fully giving up U.S. citizenship. Individuals did it for a variety of reasons, but a common theme was the feeling that America had somehow betrayed them through the forced internment. One Nisei who was fully disillusioned with his incarceration and treatment by the U.S. government was Joe Kurihara. He was born in Kauai, Hawaii, and was a successful businessman and World War I veteran. After moving to the mainland United States, he eventually settled in California until the evacuation and internment. Kurihara was sent to Manzanar and was involved with a resistance movement of the pro-Japanese group called the Black Dragons. He was arrested after the beating of Fred Tayama, another Manzanar inmate, which sparked the Manzanar riot. He was taken to Department of Justice prison camps, and then later to Tule Lake Segregation Center.

At Tule Lake he renounced his citizenship and returned to Japan in 1946. He wrote, "It is my sincere desire to get over there as soon as possible to help rebuild Japan politically and economically. The American Democracy with which I was infused in my childhood is still unshaken. My life is dedicated to Japan with Democracy as my goal" (quoted in Thomas and Nishimoto, 1946).

In summary, there was probably a range of loyalty and feelings on the part of the segregated population. At one end the resegregationists and renunciants were seen as extremists, yet many others were at Tule Lake because they simply did not want to be separated from members of their family. Indeed, although the movement for renunciation was quite strong at Tule Lake, there were many who regretted making that decision and fought against their deportation to Japan. Attorney Wayne Collins represented these renunciants and worked to reverse their renunciation and return their U.S. citizenship.

THE CALL FOR MILITARY SERVICE

At the outbreak of the war, about 5,000 Japanese Americans served in the army. As the evacuation program on the mainland took place, the War Department would not accept any Nisei for military service, except for special, exceptional cases. They were also deemed unsuitable for the draft. But in Hawaii, the situation was different because of the large population of Japanese Americans living on the islands. There would be no evacuation and internment program, and in addition, Japanese Americans served in the Hawaiian National Guard.

The Hawaii Boys: The 100th Battalion

The manpower shortage on the islands prevented Nisei from being discharged from active service, and Japanese Americans were already employed in positions in the army and the Territorial National Guard. The 100th Battalion was formed from the 298th and 299th Regiments of the Hawaiian National Guard. While Japanese Americans on the West Coast were being ordered into assembly and relocation centers, the Hawaiian 100th Battalion was being trained and shipped off to the European front.

In June 1942, they reported to Camp McCoy, Wisconsin, for training. When they arrived they were assigned a unit name: the 100th Battalion (Separate). They were a battalion without any attachment to other military regiments. Later, the men of the 100th chose the nickname "One-Puka-Puka." In Hawaiian, a puka is a round shell with a hole in it. It looks like the number zero. Translated, their unit name was the number one, followed by two zeros.

In the Midwest, the Hawaiian Nisei were an unusual sight. Midwesterners had had very little exposure to Japanese or Japanese Americans, and they did not have the same anti-Japanese hostility as the West Coast population. As a consequence, the 100th were welcomed into the local community. The men made the best of their mainland experience. For the first time, many of them experienced snow and tried skiing and ice skating. They made friends easily with the local population with their generous "aloha" spirit. Still, with war declared on Japan, soldiers of the 100th were closely watched by army officials and the FBI.

The soldiers of the 100th viewed themselves as Americans of Japanese ancestry. They felt they could prove their loyalty to America through their service in the American military. The officers of the 100th were white (*haole*), and a handful of Japanese American and Korean American officers. Some of the officers were born in Hawaii, and other had lived there so long that they were considered *kamaaina*, a Hawaiian term for "local" longtime residents. Despite the racial differences between the officers and their men, there was also a great deal of trust and mutual respect for one another (Crost, 1994). After training in Wisconsin, the 100th moved south and trained with the newly formed 442nd Regimental Combat Team at Camp Shelby, Mississippi.

The battalion was finally called to join the 34th Infantry Division in

North Africa, where they arrived in September 1943. The 34th Infantry Division was comprised of a Midwest National guard unit that had a long history of volunteer military service going back as far as the Civil War. The soldiers had had little exposure to Americans of Japanese ancestry, and they were told by the commanding officer, Colonel Ray C. Fountain: "They are not Japanese, but Americans born in Hawaii. They aren't asking for any special consideration and we won't give them anything that isn't given all the other units. They'll be in there taking their turn with all the rest. And tell your men not to call them 'Japs' or there'll be trouble" (Crost, 1994: 71).

The 100th Battalion fought in some of the most difficult and bloody military campaigns in Europe. From their landing in North Africa they traveled to Italy, suffering heavy casualties. They were a highly decorated unit, earning more than 900 Purple Hearts and nicknamed the Purple Heart Battalion. In June, the 100th joined the 442nd RCT with they had trained with at Camp Shelby. They continued to be called the 100th because of their distinguished battle record that they had already established.

The 442nd Regimental Combat Team

Many Nisei on the mainland and in Hawaii were frustrated by their situation, unable to join the army because of their draft board status. By mid-1942, the army changed its mind about having Japanese Americans in the military with the activation of the 100th. By February 1, 1943, the 442nd Regimental Combat Team was formed.

The 442nd was recruited from volunteers from the ten relocation camps on the mainland United States, as well as volunteers from Hawaii.[1] It included the following units: 442nd Infantry Regiment, 522nd Field Artillery Battalion, 232nd Combat Engineer Company, 206th Army Ground Forces Band, Antitank Company, Cannon Company, Medical Detachment, and Service Company.

In training, the Nisei had a strong group affiliation and spirit. As infantry soldiers, they were expected to train and participate in all types of army maneuvers. Despite their small stature—the average height was 5 feet, 4 inches—they were exemplary soldiers. Because there was such strong group loyalty, they worked together as a tight team. It was said that if a soldier had a difficult time completing the training with a full fifty pounds of fighting gear, each member of his team would carry a piece of his gear to lighten the load, and if need be, carry the individual to the finish.

At Camp Shelby, the 442nd came into contact with Hawaiian-born Nisei and the men of the 100th. Although both groups were of Japanese ancestry, they could not have been more different from each other, and frequent fights broke out between the two groups. Most of the Nisei of the mainland Nisei grew up as a minority ethnic group and experienced much anti-Japanese hostility. They had been drafted and/or had volunteered from the relocation centers where most of their parents and families were still being held under armed guard. They looked down upon the Hawaii-born Nisei, whom they felt were uneducated because they spoke the local Hawaiian dialect of pidgin English. In contrast, the Hawaiian Nisei had come from a place where one-third of the population was of Japanese ancestry, and they had the experience of associating with many different Asian minority ethnic groups. The culture of the islands, especially the "aloha" spirit of generosity and goodwill, permeated their interactions with one another and with others they met, except when it came to the mainland Nisei. They thought the mainlanders were "stuck up" because of their reserved manner and their use of proper English. They had a nickname for the mainland born Nisei: they were called "kotonks," which was the sound a coconut made when it fell to the ground, and the same sound a mainlander's head made when it was hit against the barracks floor. The mainlanders called the Hawaiian Japanese "Buddhaheads," which was a play on the Japanese word *buta* or pig.

The enmity between the groups gradually disappeared. One of the major events that shifted their relationship was when the Hawaiian Nisei were taken to visit an internment camp near Camp Shelby. The South was still deeply segregated, and although the Japanese American soldiers were allowed into the white USO Club in Hattiesburg, the white girls would not dance with them. The staff at the Jerome Relocation Center in Arkansas heard about this and organized a Camp Jerome USO. At first they chartered buses so that girls from Jerome could visit the soldiers at Camp Shelby, but many girls' parents were reluctant to let them do this.

So both mainland and Hawaiian Nisei traveled to Jerome for social events at the camp. When the Hawaiian soldiers visited Jerome, they saw how the mainland Japanese lived during much of the war: inside a compound, built much like an army base, with a wire fence, soldiers, and guards in a tower watching over them. There they saw what the mainland Nisei had experienced and had a better understanding of why the mainlanders were so reserved in their actions. They saw that the mainland Nisei had lost most all of their possessions in the move to internment camps. Their families were now imprisoned, left behind, yet they still volunteered for the war. The Hawaiian Nisei understood the importance of family and community and realized what a difficult decision the mainland Nisei had to make when joining the army.

Still, when looking at the overall numbers of Nisei who volunteered for the military, the effects of the evacuation and internment program cannot be overlooked. One might speculate that there would be more

Table 4.1

100th Infantry Battalion and 442nd Regimental Combat Team: Major Campaigns in Europe

Location	Date	Unit
Naples-Foggia, Italy	Sept. 9, 1943 to Jan. 21, 1944	100th Infantry Battalion
Anzio, Italy	Jan. 22, 1944 to June 5, 1944	100th Infantry Battalion
Rome-Arno, Italy	June 6, 1944 to Sept. 1944	100th Infantry Battalion
Southern France	Aug. 15, 1944 to Sept. 14, 1944	100th/442nd Antitank Company
Northern Apennines	Sept. 10, 1944 to April 4, 1945	100th/442nd RCT*
Rhineland	Sept. 15, 1944 to Mar. 21, 1945	100th/442nd RCT*
Central Europe	Mar. 22, 1945 to May 8, 1945	522nd Field Artillery Battalion
Po Valley	April 5, 1945 to May 8, 1945	100th/442nd RCT*

*Regimental Combat Team

Source: Crost, 1994: 311.

volunteers from the relocation camps because individuals might have felt more of a need to prove themselves and their loyalty. But there was not. From the mainland relocation camps, a little over 1,200 volunteered for the all-Japanese military unit; from Hawaii, slightly over 2,600 volunteered. Nonetheless, the total numbers of volunteers and draftees of Japanese descent that became the 442nd RCT became one of the most highly decorated units for its size and length of service in the U.S. army. That accomplishment is not easy to ignore.

The 100th/442nd fought in eight major campaigns in the European Theater of Operations (see Table 4.1). They were well known for their abilities, often surprising the German and Italian armies, and were viewed as heroes in the towns and small cities they liberated.

Among their many campaigns, three war battles stand out: the liberation of the city of Bruyeres in France, the rescue of the Lost Battalion in Italy, and the liberation of the Dachau concentration camps in Germany.

Bruyeres, France

In October 1944, the 100th/442nd were ordered to take the town of Bruyeres in France. According to war correspondent Lyn Crost, Bruyeres was an important rail center and road intersection on the way to Saint-Die, an important industrial and communications center for the Germans. Nisei soldiers fought to recapture the town from German occupation. On October 15, 1944, the 100th/442nd with support troops moved to free the town of Bruyeres. Fighting in France was different from their earlier campaigns in Italy. Bruyeres was in a valley surrounded by hills studded with mines, and the landscape was heavily wooded. Four days later, on October 19, the last Germans were captured, and Bruyeres was free.

In the process of taking the town, the Japanese Americans made life-long friends with its citizens. The civilians of Bruyeres had been trapped in their homes with few supplies when the U.S. army moved in. The French were surprised by whom they saw. Many thought the Japanese army had invaded. The soldiers shared with them the few supplies they had, and the Nisei of the 100th/442nd were seen as heroes to the town.

The Rescue of the Lost Battalion

Shortly after the liberation of Bruyeres, on October 26, 1944, the 100th/442nd's 2nd Battalion found themselves in the wooded forests and heavy fog and rain in the Vosges mountains on the way to rescuing the "Lost" Texas Battalion: the 1st Battalion, 141st Infantry Regiment of the 36th Texas Division. They had been trapped behind enemy lines for several weeks. Attempts to rescue them had failed, and the 442nd was brought in to assist with the rescue. The three battalions battled their way up a hill to the fortress where the Lost Battalion was trapped. It took more than five days to rescue the Texas Lost Battalion, and there were high casualties among the ranks of the 442nd. They suffered almost 800 casualties to rescue 211 Texans (of the original 275 that were entrapped). One company was left with only seventeen riflemen, another with eight. There were no officers left in either company. All of the battalions in the 442nd were awarded Distinguished Unit Citations for their work in rescuing the Lost Battalion, but the real tragedy was in the number of casualties suffered by the unit overall.

The battle of Bruyeres and the rescue of the Lost Battalion have not been forgotten by the people of the city. Every October, they gather to remember, celebrate, and honor the Japanese Americans who helped liberate their town. A road called The Avenue of the 442 Infantry Regiment leads to a granite memorial dedicated to the Nisei soldiers of the 442nd Regimental Combat Team. A bronze plaque says in both English and French:

To the men of the 442nd Regimental Combat Team, U.S. Army, who reaffirmed an historic truth here—that loyalty to one's country is not modified by racial origin.

These Americans, whose ancestors were Japanese, on October 30, 1944, during the battle of Bruyeres broke the backbone of the German defenses and rescued the 141st Infantry Battalion which had been surrounded by the enemy for four days. (Crost, 1994: 201)

Liberation of Dachau Concentration Camps

The 522nd Field Artillery Battalion was a division of the 442nd Regimental Combat Team. This unit was responsible for the maintenance and transportation of field artillery and ammunition, and wire and radio communications. It included a medical detachment and personnel organization that maintained the service records for the men of the unit.

The men of the 522nd were not at the front lines of combat, but they had unique experiences that have only recently come to light. After the Battle of Bruyeres and the rescue of the Lost Battalion, they were separated from the 442nd and became a roving battalion, moving to whatever unit needed their help. By the end of their tour, they had traveled throughout central Europe and taken every objective of more than fifty different assignments. During the last week of April 1945, the 522nd was one of the lead units of the U.S. 7th Army troops. While pursuing the German army, they came across the scattered camps of Dachau. Originally a small town and place for German artists, the town of Dachau had been transformed to industry to produce ammunition for the German army. The concentration camp consisted of a main camp and more than 140 smaller subcamps, which provided workers for the munitions factory. These held Jewish prisoners and French prisoners of war. According to U.S. military history records, there is some controversy over which divisions of the army opened the main Dachau camp gates. The 522nd was one of the first units to reach the Dachau camps and was involved with the liberation of at least one of the camps in the area. Personal testimonials made by concentration camp survivors state that their liberators were of Japanese descent (*Fire for Effect*, 1998).

Jewish concentration camp internees could hardly believe their liberators were Japanese Americans. Some thought they were members of the Japanese national army invading Germany. Soldiers of the 522nd report that they were told not to give their rations to the prisoners. They ignored this and shared what little food and medicine they had with the Jewish prisoners they encountered. For years following this event, soldiers of the 522nd were silent about what they had seen. Many were struck by the horror of the Nazi death camp, and the inhumanity and prejudice that fed the camps. This image remained imprinted on their minds for years, but they never spoke about it. In recent years, Jewish concentration camp survivors have confirmed the presence of Japanese American soldiers liberating the camps, and the 522-Dachau connection has become known throughout the American Jewish and European Jewish community (Crost, 1994).

In recognition of their liberating at least one of the many Dachau camps, the 522nd Field Artillery Battalion has officially been listed as a concentration camp liberator by the Holocaust Museum in Washington, D.C.

The Military Intelligence Service Language School (MISLS)

Japanese American work in military intelligence had its origins at the Presidio of San Francisco, the headquarters of General DeWitt and the

Western Defense Command. Army Captain Kai Rasmussen saw the necessity of training army intelligence in Japanese language instruction and developed a program that would later become a key factor in winning the Pacific Theater war. In November 1941, Captain Rasmussen and Lieutenant Colonel John Weckerling opened the first language training facility on the West Coast in an abandoned hangar at the Presidio of San Francisco's Crissy Field. It was called the Fourth Army Intelligence School. The first class consisted of sixty individuals, fifty-eight of whom were Japanese Americans, Nisei and Kibei.

One of the main problems in finding personnel to teach at the language institute was that although Nisei might be fluent in Japanese, they were not familiar with the formal forms of Japanese military vocabulary and writing. Weckerling and Rasmussen finally found an individual uniquely qualified to direct their school. John Aiso was educated at Brown University, held a doctorate in jurisprudence from Harvard, and studied legal Japanese at Chuo University in Japan. When they found Aiso, he was working for the U.S. army as a mechanic in the motor pool. He became the most important and influential academic leader at the school because of his language skills. He understood the unique circumstances of Nisei and Kibei, who were of Japanese ancestry, born in the United States. They were challenged to prove themselves as Americans, and he helped to develop a class of Japanese American military intelligence specialists that helped to win the war.

The school had already been in session for more than a month when Pearl Harbor was bombed. After the mass evacuation was ordered, the Japanese Language School was moved to Camp Savage, Minnesota, and renamed the Military Intelligence Service Language School (MISLS). In the Midwest, the first group of Military Intelligence Service (MIS) trainees were joined by sixty-seven men from the 100th Battalion. The first group to complete their training was sent to Guadalcanal and the Aleutian Islands.

The MISLS trained more than 6,000 men to serve as translators, working in military intelligence, later to be referred to as the Military Intelligence Service. Early in the war, the military was not sure how to use their skills and expertise. But as the war progressed, the army saw the value of their training and they served in strategic intelligence gathering and translating efforts throughout the Pacific. In addition to their duties with intelligence, they took part in combat, interrogated enemy prisoners, and conducted psychological warfare, persuading Japanese soldiers to surrender. Japanese prisoners of war were often surprised to see their interrogators: ethnic Japanese in American military uniforms, speaking to them in fluent Japanese.

Graduates of the MIS language school were not segregated into one division within the military. They were often assigned singly or in pairs to a military unit, and served in every military unit and campaign in the

Pacific Theater. Most were either in the army or stationed with an air force unit in the Philippines, Hawaii, New Guinea, Okinawa, India, Burma, China, the Aleutians, Marianas, Guam, and other Pacific islands (Crost, 1994). Their work was extremely important to the strategic defense and in gathering military intelligence for the United States during the war. They were involved with Japan's surrender and treaty agreement, and in the eventual post-wartime occupation of Japan by U.S. forces.

The Nisei in the MIS were an extremely important part of winning the war. General Willoughby, General MacArthur's chief of intelligence, said that the Nisei MIS helped to shorten the war in the Pacific by two years. Yet their accomplishments have often gone unnoticed because of the classified nature of their activities. The highly publicized campaigns and success of the 100th Battalion and the 442nd Regimental Combat Team in Europe drew the most attention and served as examples of Nisei loyalty to America.

OTHER MILITARY SERVICE

Although the 442nd RCT was the most well known of the Nisei military units, Nisei were involved with other aspects of the war. Military policy was to segregate African Americans, whereas the Nisei were not fully segregated. Although the 442nd was an all-Nisei unit, Nisei served in other combat units as well. Ben Kuroki was born in Nebraska and was the son of a potato farmer. After Pearl Harbor was bombed, he tried to enlist in the armed forces but was turned down. He was finally accepted and became the first Nisei to serve in the army air force in the Pacific Theater. Kuroki was a turret gunner on a B-29 bomber that flew several missions over Japan. Another group of Nisei served with Merrill's Marauders in Burma, and others were involved with the surrender of China.

Nisei were instrumental as medics, mechanics, and clerks in the Quartermaster Corps. Nisei women served in the Women's Army Corps. Issei and Nisei served as language instructors and with the Office of Strategic Services and Office of War Information.

The Boys on the Home Front: The Varsity Victory Volunteers and the 1399th Engineer Construction Battalion

Hawaii was a critical military staging area for the United States. Although there was no full-scale evacuation and internment of citizens and aliens, people of Japanese ancestry supplied the essential manpower and labor that was important to the success of the United States military in the Pacific Theater.

The Varsity Victory Volunteers were Japanese Americans who were in the Reserve Officer Training Corps at the University of Hawaii. After Pearl Harbor was bombed, they became a part of the Hawaii Territorial Guard for military defense and civilian protection. Because of strong concerns from the government in Washington, they were honorably discharged in January 1942. They still fought to serve in the military and petitioned the military governor of Hawaii to continue with their service. They were reorganized and became a part of the 34th Combat Engineers Regiment, involved with numerous construction projects to support Hawaii's military arsenal (Kitano, 1993).

The 1399th Engineer Construction Battalion was based in Hawai and provided the manpower needed to maintain the military bases and for the infrastructure construction of other military facilities. More than 1,000 Japanese American men served in this unit, which comprised a core group of soldiers from the 370th Engineer Battalion (men who were inducted before February 1942). They built more than fifty major defense projects on Oahu during the war. They constructed and maintained roads, bridges, ammunition storage facilities, barracks, and airfields. Besides this, they built jungle-simulation training sites where military personnel were trained in jungle war fighting.

They were not a combat unit, and were known as "castoffs" and "spare parts." They were given uniforms that did not fit them, were harassed by their superiors, and assigned to do the dirty work for the military. Their primary responsibility was in the maintenance of Hawaii military facilities. Many of them felt they were at the lowest rung of the army. As Shiro Matsuo said,

You can't blame the boys. They had been treated like dogs, doing all the menial jobs. We didn't have rifles. No training, No rank. No nothing. We were supposed to go with the 100th, but the military (didn't have) laborers and that's why we were kept [in Hawaii]. We were under the jurisdiction of whatever outfit that needed us. So our boys went up to the rock quarry, dug ditches, cleaned up rubbish. At that time I was in charge of the latrines. (Chang, 1991: 133)

The men prided themselves as skilled artisans: carpenters, engineers, and workers who knew how to build and repair almost anything. The most difficult part of their assignment was the racial intolerance they felt as Japanese Americans working under *haole* officers from the mainland. For a while, there were Japanese, German, and Italian prisoners of war held at camps in Hawaii. Soldiers of the 1399th felt that the only difference between them and the POWs were their uniforms.

Nisei Women in the Armed Forces

Much of the material on Japanese Americans in the military during World War II has focused on the men. Fewer than 100 Nisei women joined the Women's Army Corps (WACs). They served in a variety of positions at military bases throughout the United States and worked for the Public Information Office and Military Intelligence. Although they were largely clerical workers, as were most women in the military at that time, there was also a group of more than 200 Nisei women in the U.S. Cadet Nursing Corps.

Many women joined the military for the same reason that Nisei men joined: to prove their loyalty. Sue (Ogata) Kato was from the Midwest and her family was not interned during World War II. Still she felt that it was important for her to join the WACs. "I joined the WACs—and this may sound like flag-waving—to prove my Americanism" (Nakano, 1990: 170). Another Nisei described her reasons in this way: "I felt the Nisei had to do more than give lip service to the United States and by joining the WACs I could prove my sincerity. . . . After all, this is everybody's war and we all have to put an equal share into it" (Nakano, 1990: 169).

Military Awards and Accolades

The 100th/442nd earned the nickname The Purple Heart Battalion for the numerous Purple Heart medals awarded to its soldiers. Their motto was "Go for Broke." It meant, "shoot the works" coming from a Hawaiian pidgin phrase used in gambling (O'Brien and Fugita, 1991). They suffered an extremely high casualty rate, and their numbers had to be replaced by other enlistees.

The distinguished battle record of the 100th/442nd is evident in the number of awards and medals they received. There were 9,486 Purple Hearts, one Medal of Honor, 52 Distinguished Service Crosses, 1 Distinguished Service Medal, 560 Silver Stars, 28 Oak Leaf Clusters in lieu of second Silver Stars, 22 Legions of Merit, 4,000 Bronze Stars, 1,200 Oak Leaf Clusters representing second Bronze Stars, 15 Soldier's Medals, 12 French croix de guerre, 2 palms representing second croix de guerre awards, 2 Italian crosses for military merit, and 2 Italian medals for military valor (Crost, 1994).

REINSTATING THE DRAFT

After the start of the war, individual draft boards were allowed to make their own decisions as to whether to accept Nisei for the draft. But as the evacuation program on the mainland took place, the War Department stopped allowing the induction of Nisei into the army. By September 1942, all draft-eligible Nisei were reclassified as IV-C or enemy aliens. (Originally, if they were classified as I-A, draft eligible, their status was changed to IC-F, unsuitable for military service.) In January 1944, almost a year after the activation of the 442nd Regimental Combat Team and following the government's loyalty review program, the local Selective Service Boards were permitted to consider eligible Nisei for the draft. Although many complied with the draft orders, there were some who questioned the validity of being drafted when their families were still left in the camps.

PROTEST: HEART MOUNTAIN DRAFT RESISTERS

Among the thousands of Nisei who proclaimed their "loyalty" and served in the military during World War II were a group of men who protested the process of loyalty review and refused to be drafted into the army. Their story has largely been invisible, overshadowed by the experiences of the 100th and 442nd. Because they refused to be drafted, they were branded as traitors, referred to in derogatory terms as draft dodgers and troublemakers. For many years following their resistance, the Japanese American community refused to acknowledge the validity of their protest, and many of the draft resisters spent their lives in obscurity. For many of the resisters, their form of protest was not a question of loyalty, but of principle. They would not compromise their rights as U.S. citizens and their beliefs in justice and civil liberties. Many of them chose not to be drafted because of what they saw as injustices in their own and their family's experiences with internment.

The most organized resistance came from the Heart Mountain, Wyoming, relocation center. The Heart Mountain Fair Play Committee was active in organizing and encouraging Nisei to avoid the draft. Frank Emi was in his twenties, married with two children, at the Heart Mountain internment camp. He protested the loyalty questionnaire with the following statement: "Under the present conditions and circumstances, I am unable to answer these questions" (Takaki 1989: 398). Emi, along with Kiyoshi Okamoto and six other Nisei, formed the Heart Mountain Fair Play Committee. They were supported by James Omura, editor of a Japanese American newspaper called the *Rocky Shimpo*, based in Denver, Colorado. Omura was supportive of Emi and others of the Fair Play Committee, publishing statements issued by the committee and writing editorials in their support.

The government authorities were worried about the Fair Play Committee and moved quickly to keep their activities under control. Emi and others were arrested and charged with conspiracy to violate the Selective Service Act—that is, resisting the draft. At their trial they declared, "We, the members of the FPC [Fair Play Committee] are not afraid to go to war—we are not afraid to risk our lives for our country. . . . We would gladly sacrifice our lives to protect and uphold the principles and ideals of our country as set forth in the Constitution and the Bill of Rights, for on its inviolability depends the freedom, liberty, justice, and protection of all people including Japanese-Americans and all other minority groups" (quoted in Takaki, 1989: 3º9).

Heart Mountain relocation center had the largest group of draft resisters. There, sixty-four Nisei refused their pre-induction physicals. They were indicted and tried as a group in one of Wyoming's largest trials. Sixty-three of the men were found guilty and sentenced to three years in a federal penitentiary, included among those men were Frank Emi and members of the Fair Play Committee. Nisei at other relocation centers also refused to be inducted into the army. All totaled, 315 men refused to be inducted into the army; 263 were convicted of avoiding the draft and served prison sentences.

After prison, the men who served time for refusing to be drafted into the army returned to their lives as ordinary citizens. In 1947, President Truman granted a pardon to the Japanese Americans who resisted the draft during World War II, including those who were a part of the Heart Mountain resistance group. However, because they refused to serve in the army, they were branded as unpatriotic and disloyal by many in the Japanese American community. It would take many years before their story would be told and understood as another response to the wartime stress of incarceration.

CONCLUSION

The Nisei who served in the military did so not only because of their sense of patriotism and the desire to show their loyalty to the United States, but also because they were driven by a distinctly Japanese code of honor and sense of duty to one's country. Perhaps one of the best ways to describe this Japanese sense is the social norm called *on* (pronounced "own"). According to sociologists, a social norm provides a guide for how an individual is to behave, an acceptable form of interacting with others. Translated, *on* means ascribed obligation, that is, an obligation one has to another individual or group as a matter of fact in their relationship with each other.

When Senator Daniel Inouye (Hawaii) volunteered for the army during World War II, his father told him that it was his duty and obligation to serve his country during this time of war—and if necessary, to die for his country. Inouye's father asked him if he knew what *on* meant. Inouye responded that he understood that *on* had everything to do with Japanese culture and the repayment of debt at every opportunity without reservation. His father told him:

The Inouyes have great *on* for America.... It has been good to us.... I would never have chosen it to be this way—it is you who must try to return the goodness of this country. You are my first son and you are very precious to your mother and to me, but you must do what must be done. If it is necessary, you must be ready to—Do not bring dishonor on our name. (Inouye, 1967: 85)

Daniel Inouye's father's message was clear: despite their experiences with racism and discrimination, Nisei soldiers had a duty and obligation to fight for the country that had given them and their parents opportunities.

Inouye was one of the many soldiers who was awarded a Distinguished Service Cross for his bravery and valor during the war. Because there were so many Japanese American soldiers who were injured and died during the war, many have often wondered if the 100th/442nd were used as cannon fodder. That is, were they used because they were Japanese and considered expendable? Or were they used in some of the most difficult and challenging battles because they could be counted on to get the job done? There is, perhaps, no easy answer to these questions. Depending on whom one asks, there could be a number of different responses. Some of the higher ranking officers of the 100th/442nd would argue that the units were known for getting the job done. When the army wanted a mission accomplished, they knew they could count on the 442nd. One also wonders if their distinguished record and individual medals went unrecognized because of continued prejudices toward Americans of Japanese ancestry.

In 1998, the army decorations review board began to evaluate a number of Asian Americans who had received the Distinguished Service Cross, the second highest-ranking medal of military valor, for military medal upgrades to the Medal of Honor. The Medal of Honor is reserved for soldiers who distinguished themselves "by gallantry and intrepidity at the risk of life, above and beyond the call of duty." In June 2000, twenty Japanese Americans who served in the 100th/442nd received the medal upgrade from President Clinton. One of the recipients was Senator Daniel Inouye, who had lost his arm in combat during the war.

The Heart Mountain draft resisters chose to make their point in a different way. Educated in the United States, they felt that the government should not have to force them to "prove" loyalty through military action when the government had abrogated their rights as U.S. citizens by their evacuation and detention in internment camps. They professed their loyalty but refused to be drafted unless their rights as citizens had been restored. Thus, although their actions might call their loyalty into question, they held to the principles of the United States as a nation: liberty, freedom, and equality. While loyal to the United States, they were concerned for the welfare and status of their families who would remain incarcerated if they were to serve in the military. Their protest drew attention to the moral and ethical dilemmas of the internment and loyalty review programs.

The "no-no" respondents to the loyalty review program is yet another example of the difficult situation the U.S. government put people of Japanese ancestry in. The Commission on Wartime Relocation and Internment of Civilians has suggested that the loyalty review program pushed the evacuees into two different directions. For those who complied and answered affirmatively to the loyalty questions, their lives could move on to more productive dimensions, especially for those who left camp. For those who challenged the loyalty questions, their segregation and isolation at Tule Lake created even more hostility and uncertainty directed toward the government and one another. They had to contend with issues over their loyalty. Because of their no-no responses, they did not know how they would be treated in the long term. Thus repatriation and renunciation were two responses that might allow them to leave the confines of internment, even if it meant returning to Japan during the war, or losing rights as a U.S. citizen.

Japanese Americans were not a monolithic group in terms of their responses to the wartime internment. Individuals had to make decisions under great pressure and duress during the war. Given their collective experiences prior to evacuation, that is, anti-Japanese hostility and discrimination, these were difficult and trying times. Decisions were made based on their past experiences. No one could foresee the consequences that each of the groups faced. Those who served in the military certainly paid for the proof of their loyalty, many with their lives. The draft resisters, renunciants, and repatriators also lived with the stigma of being branded as "disloyals." Those negative labels are still ingrained in many Japanese Americans' minds and continue to be a source of conflict within the community. At the 2000 Japanese American Citizens League National Convention, the organization voted to give formal recognition to the Heart Mountain draft resisters, calling them "Resisters of Conscience." Although there was protest at the convention, many felt that the resisters were acting according to their conscience. Such action by the national organization recognizing the past issues has been important to healing the wounds and rifts between and among Japanese Americans over the issues of loyalty.

NOTE

1. There were a few Nisei in the 442nd who did not join from the internment camps. They were living outside of the camps, but once they were drafted or decided to join the army, they were assigned to the 442nd.

5

Legal Challenges to the Evacuation and Internment

The vast majority of people of Japanese ancestry, citizen and alien, complied with the orders of the federal government and obeyed the curfew and evacuation orders. Yet there were those who challenged whether such actions were constitutional and legally within the rights of the U.S. government. In three different states, California, Oregon, and Washington, three men knowingly violated the government's orders. This chapter discusses the history, backgrounds, and court cases of three U.S. citizens, Minoru Yasui, Gordon Kiyoshi Hirabayashi, and Fred Toyosaburo Korematsu. For different reasons they refused to obey the military orders, and were arrested, tried, and convicted. Min Yasui was convicted of violating the curfew order, Gordon Hirabayashi was convicted of curfew violation and refusing to report for evacuation, and Fred Korematsu was convicted for failure to report for evacuation. Each continued to pursue his case by appealing to the U.S. Supreme Court. Together, their cases have set important legal and constitutional precedents regarding civil rights and liberties. In addition, the Supreme Court decisions reinforced the role and power of the legislative and executive branches of the government during wartime.

One other case was also of great importance. Mitsuye Endo, a U.S. citizen and employee of the state of California, complied with the government evacuation orders. Her case brought before the U.S. Supreme Court questioned whether it was legal to detain individuals who had not been charged with breaking the law.

MINORU YASUI

Minoru (Min) Yasui was born in 1916 in the small farming community of Hood River, Oregon, sixty miles east of Portland on the Columbia River gorge. He was the second-oldest of seven children of Masuo and Shidzuyo Yasui. His father was a prominent Japanese American community leader who owned farm property and a store in town. Yasui grew up in a close family, was raised in the Methodist church, attended public schools, and was encouraged to pursue higher education, as were all of his brothers and sisters. He entered the University of Oregon in 1933. While there he volunteered for Army Reserve officer training and received his commission as a second lieutenant in the Army Infantry Reserve. He then attended the University of Oregon Law School, graduating in 1939, and passed the Oregon state bar examination later that year.

Jobs were scarce for attorneys, especially Japanese Americans, so with the help of his father, Yasui obtained a job working for the Japanese consulate in Chicago. The law required U.S. citizens working for a foreign government to register that they were an agent employed by a foreign nation, which he did. Although he has described his work as primarily clerical, he did have to give speeches about Japan and its policies to American service clubs and organizations as directed by the consulate.

The day after Pearl Harbor was bombed, Yasui immediately resigned from his position and tried to return home to Portland. His return trip was difficult because the railway agent in Chicago refused to sell him a ticket. Within a few days he had received orders from the army ordering him to report for duty, which allowed him finally to buy a ticket to the West Coast. When he tried to report for duty, he was told that he was unacceptable for service and ordered off the military base. Despite the fact that he had the prerequisite military training and was commissioned as an Army Reserve officer, Yasui felt that he was being turned away because he was of Japanese ancestry. Unwillingly, he returned home to Hood River.

Within a few days after his return, his father was arrested and sent to a Department of Justice camp in Missoula, Montana. Masuo Yasui was not allowed to be represented by a lawyer during his loyalty hearing, but Min traveled to Montana to observe the proceedings. Lawyers for the government questioned the elder Yasui about pictures of the Panama Canal they had found in his house that had been drawn by a child. They intimated that these could possibly indicate a plot to blow up the canal. Min Yasui thought the indictments and the entire hearing absurd. Department of Justice officials classified his father as a potentially "disloyal" alien because of an award he had received from the emperor of Japan before the war. Masuo Yasui remained jailed at Fort Missoula, Montana. Later, he was transferred to another Department of Justice camp in Santa Fe, New Mexico.

Min Yasui was clearly disillusioned by what he saw during his father's hearings, and by his rejection by the army for military service. As a lawyer, he was trained in understanding the issues surrounding civil liberties and rights, and the U.S. Constitution. What happened to him and his father made him question the events surrounding the forced evacuation and curfew orders issued by the military. Yasui believed that the executive order, curfew, and evacuation were unconstitutional. He hoped to challenge these orders. He consulted with lawyer Earl F. Bernard, a conservative yet leading Portland attorney, who advised Yasui that it would make sense to challenge the orders only if there were criminal penalties for disobeying, of which there were none yet. Public Law 503, which provided penalties and incorporated the authority of E.O. 9066, had not yet been passed by Congress. He offered to represent Yasui, should the situation arise.

Yasui decided to challenge the government's orders when General John DeWitt ordered Military Proclamation 3. This required all enemy aliens and Japanese American citizens to be in their homes between 8 P.M. and 6 A.M. The curfew restricted the movement of Japanese Americans to a five-mile radius from their homes to places of work during noncurfew hours. According to Yasui, the general's proclamation was wrong because it made distinctions between citizens based on ancestry. Placing restrictions on Japanese Americans and not on other U.S. citizens violated the "equal protection" clause of the U.S. Constitution.

On March 28, 1942, he decided to disobey the curfew order and to walk the streets of Portland after curfew. About 11 P.M., Yasui later recollected, he got tired of walking. He stopped a Portland police officer, showed him the military order and his birth certificate that verified his Japanese ancestry, and asked to be arrested. To his surprise, the officer told him to go home. Instead of going home, Yasui turned himself in at the police station and argued himself into jail. He was finally arrested and waited out the weekend in the drunk tank of Portland city jail.

While Yasui was awaiting trial in Portland, military orders were posted for the evacuation of all residents of Japanese ancestry in the area. He notified the military authorities that he would not comply with the orders, and told them he was returning to Hood River. Since he was already testing the curfew orders, he thought he could also test the evacuation orders (Tateishi, 1984).

In Hood River, he was notified that the military police would come to get him, and on May 12, 1942, they escorted Yasui to the North Portland

Livestock Pavilion, which was the assembly center for the Portland area. After spending time there, still awaiting trial, he was moved to the Minidoka Relocation Center in Idaho.

Min Yasui's trial was held in federal court Portland with Judge James Alger Fee presiding. Yasui had waived his right to a jury trial and wanted the judge to deal directly with the issue of constitutionality of the military jurisdiction (Western Defense Command) over a civilian population (Japanese, both citizen and noncitizen). One of the main issues that surfaced at Yasui's trial was whether he had given up his U.S. citizenship by working for the Japanese consulate in Chicago, and second, whether Public Law 503, which was signed into law on March 21, 1942, was constitutional as it applied to U.S. citizens.

Judge Fee's decision took a long time. For several months he deliberated on the case while Yasui awaited his decision and continued to live at Minidoka. Yasui was brought out of camp and escorted back to Portland when the judge issued his decision. Fee ruled that Public Law 503 was not constitutional as it applied to U.S. citizens. He based his decision on the Supreme Court majority in the 1866 *Milligan* case, which had to do with the rights of citizens under martial law during the Civil War. The Supreme Court ruled that "martial law can never exist, where the courts are open, and in the proper and unobstructed exercise of their jurisdiction . . . [military rule] cannot arise from a threatened invasion. The necessity must be actual and present; the invasion real, such as effectively closes the courts and deposes the civil administration" (*Ex Parte Milligan*, 71 U.S. 2, 127 [1866]). Yasui was challenging whether the military could enforce curfew orders on people of Japanese ancestry, citizen and noncitizen. Martial law had never been declared, yet there was clear military power being exercised over a civilian population. Under *Milligan*, the courts ruled that martial law could not exist when the courts were open. This meant that the curfew order was not legal to enforce on U.S. citizens, just as Yasui had argued. But in one quick decision Judge Fee stripped Yasui of his U.S. citizenship. He decided that Yasui had forfeited his citizenship because he had worked for the Japanese consulate in Chicago shortly after his graduation from law school. Therefore, the curfew order was legal as it applied to him at the time he disobeyed it. Yasui was sentenced to one year in jail and a $5,000 fine. He appealed his case immediately, believing he had not given up his U.S. citizenship. Because Yasui was now considered an "enemy alien" he was kept in isolation. For nine months he lived in solitary confinement in Portland at the Multnomah County jail.

On May 10, 1943, Min Yasui's case was argued before the Supreme Court along with Gordon Hirabayashi's case. The court issued their opinion on June 21, 1943. In *Yasui* v. *U.S.* 320 U.S. 115 (1943), the justices reversed Judge Fee's lower court decision on Yasui's forfeiture of citizenship because of working for the Japanese consulate. Because of their decision in the Hirabayashi case, they upheld Yasui's conviction for curfew violation and returned the case to the lower court to have him resentenced for that.

Back in Portland, Judge Fee considered the time spent in the county jail as sufficient punishment and suspended the $5,000 fine. Yasui was "free" to return to live with his family at Minidoka. While there, Yasui became involved with efforts to persuade Japanese American draft resisters to change their minds.

Yasui's training as an attorney was the backdrop for his challenges to the curfew and evacuation orders. He believed that the orders were unconstitutional as applied to U.S. citizens. He believed it was his responsibility to take measures to show the rights and wrongs of the government. In an interview conducted with him later, he stated,

It was my feeling and belief, then and now, that no military authority had the right to subject any United States citizen to any requirement that does not equally apply to all other U.S. citizens. Moreover, if a citizen believes that the sovereign state is committing an illegal act, it is incumbent upon that citizen to take measures to rectify such error. . . . [I]t seemed to me then and now that if the government unlawfully curtails the rights of any person, the damage is done not only to that individual person but to the whole society. If we believe in America, if we believe in equality and democracy, if we believe in law and justice, then each of us, when we see or believe such errors are being made, has an obligation to make every effort to correct them. (quoted in Tateishi, 1984: 70–71)

GORDON KIYOSHI HIRABAYASHI

Gordon Hirabayashi was born in Auburn (near Seattle), Washington, in 1918. His father ran a roadside produce store. As a Nisei, Hirabayashi lived between the culture of his Japanese-born parents and American society. He was educated in American schools, was a senior patrol leader, and achieved the rank of Life Scout in the Boy Scouts. His parents belonged to a Japanese pacifist religion called Mukyo-kai. Translated it meant "Nonchurch Movement." It was a nontraditional unorthodox movement that had beliefs similar to those of the Religious Society of Friends, or Quakers. This group worshipped without ministers and were pacifists. He once said that he felt that his parents' religious beliefs were too strict, so he began to explore other different religious perspectives (Irons, 1989). Nonetheless, his parents' religion strongly influenced his attitudes and feelings about war.

Hirabayashi entered the University of Washington in 1937 and was an active, involved student. He participated in a number of different student religious and social-action groups, and was a student leader in the

YMCA and the Japanese Students' Club. He also joined the Seattle chapter of the Japanese American Citizens League. With an active student social life, he also sought spiritual and religious solace in different organized religious groups near campus, such as the University Temple, the Unitarian Church, and finally, the University Friends Meeting, whose beliefs lay close to his own religious upbringing.

Hirabayashi was a senior at the university when the war broke out. At the end of March 1942, he found out that the Bainbridge Island Japanese American community was to be evacuated, he joined the American Friends Service Committee in Seattle, a social-service branch of the Quakers. Although his family had not yet been ordered to evacuate, he helped other Japanese Americans store their belongings and move them to the Puyallup Assembly Center. During this time, he began to question the necessity of curfew and several times knowingly violated the 8 P.M. curfew orders. He discussed with his friends the possibility of disobeying the evacuation orders, worried about the effect it would have on his family. In the end, he followed his moral convictions and decided to disobey the evacuation orders.

Hirabayashi refused to report and register for evacuation. Before he made this decision, he consulted with attorneys and prepared a statement of his reasons for disobeying the orders. In eloquent prose he stated,

This order for the mass evacuation of all persons of Japanese descent denies them the right to live. It forces thousands of energetic, law-abiding individuals to exist in a miserable psychological and a horrible physical atmosphere. . . . Over sixty percent are American citizens . . . [their rights] are denied on a wholesale scale without due process of law and civil liberties which are theirs. . . . I must maintain my Christian principles. I consider it my duty to maintain the democratic standards for which this nation lives. Therefore, I must refuse this order for evacuation. (quoted in Irons, 1983: 88)

Hirabayashi carefully planned his arrest and turned himself into the FBI in May 1942. He had the support of the local chapter of the American Civil Liberties Union, many of whom were concerned about the issues of civil liberties and rights of the Japanese in the United States. They organized a committee to raise money for his bail and discussed possible legal strategies for his case once he was arrested.

Gordon Hirabayashi remained in jail for five months before his case was brought to trial in October 1942. Hirabayashi's attorneys argued that the curfew and evacuation orders were in violation of the due process and equal protection under the law. In other words, the U.S. Constitution guarantees citizens and noncitizens certain equal rights under its laws.

To have those laws apply only to people of Japanese ancestry, whether citizen or not, was in violation of their being treated equally in comparison with the rest of the population in the country.

Hirabayashi was represented by attorney Frank L. Walters. After only ten minutes' deliberation, the jury returned a verdict of guilty in the Hirabayashi trial. Judge Floyd Black sentenced him to two ninety-day sentences to be served concurrently, with no credit for time already served in jail. Hirabayashi asked to serve his time working on a roadside prison work crew which the judge granted him. While he served his time his case was being appealed. It was argued before the Supreme Court on May 10, 1943.

Gordon Hirabayashi's case was decided on June 21, 1943, along with Min Yasui's case. According to legal scholar Peter Irons, the Court decided to look at the case from a very narrow perspective, assuming a unanimous court decision and thus avoiding the question of evacuation and concentrating its decision on whether the curfew was legal. The basis for the Hirabayashi decision lay with the use of war powers granted to the executive and legislative branches of the government by the Constitution. The Court felt that it was appropriate for the military to set curfew orders in the interest of national security and in light of the fact that the United States was at war with Japan.

Although the justices were unanimous in their decision regarding the legality of the curfew order, there was a hint of dissension within their ranks. Justice Frank Murphy had initially intended to dissent in the Hirabayashi decision, but changed his mind at the last minute. Clearly, he felt there were issues of discrimination by singling out one ethnic or ancestry group for differential treatment. He wrote,

Under the curfew order here challenged no less than 70,000 American citizens have been placed under a special ban and deprived of their liberty because of their particular racial inheritance. In this sense it bears a melancholy resemblance to the treatment of members of the Jewish race in Germany and other parts of Europe. The result is the creation in this country of two classes of citizens ... to sanction discrimination between groups of United States citizens on the basis of ancestry. In my opinion this goes to the very brink of constitutional power. (*Hirabayashi* v. *U.S.*, 320 U.S. 81, 111 [1943]).

Despite the Court's unanimous decision, Hirabayashi always believed in his rights as an American citizen. He stated, "It was my feeling at that time, that having been born here and educated and having the culture of an American citizen, that I should be given the privilege of a citizen— that a citizen should not be denied privileges because of his descent" (quoted in Irons, 1983: 157).

FRED TOYOSABURO KOREMATSU

Fred Korematsu was born in Oakland, California, in 1919. His father ran a nursery in Oakland. He graduated from Oakland High in 1938, and briefly attended Los Angeles City College. He later attended the Master School of Welding in Oakland and was trained as a shipyard welder and belonged to the Boiler Makers Union. After Pearl Harbor, the union expelled all of its members of Japanese ancestry. When he tried to register for the draft, he was turned down because of a medical condition. Out of work and unable to serve in the military, he made his living at short-term welding jobs.

On May 9, 1942, his parents were evacuated from their Oakland home and moved to the Tanforan Assembly Center near San Francisco. Korematsu told them he was going to Nevada and did not report. At this time it was still possible to voluntarily evacuate and leave the prohibited areas of the West Coast. Part of the reason he did not want to go was because he wanted to be with his Italian American girlfriend, Ida Boitano. They wanted to leave California and move to the Midwest or East where he could avoid being interned and they could get married. He had minor cosmetic surgery to change his appearance to look "less" Japanese and tried to pass as Chinese. He thought that by doing this he and his girlfriend would be less noticeable when they moved out of state. But within weeks, his girlfriend realized that it would be difficult for both of them and ended the relationship.

Because he had not reported for evacuation, Korematsu was in violation of the law. On May 30, 1942, police responded to a tip of his whereabouts and arrested Korematsu while he was waiting for his girlfriend in San Leandro, California. Initially, he gave his identity as Clyde Sarah and claimed to be of Spanish-Hawaiian origin. Police noted that he could not speak Spanish and that his draft card had been altered. Someone in the police station recognized him. His cover failing, he soon identified himself and told his reasons for failing to report and avoiding evacuation.

While in jail awaiting trial, Korematsu was visited by Ernest Besig, a lawyer from the American Civil Liberties Union who was looking for a volunteer to serve as a test case for the legality of the evacuation orders. Besig had met with other Japanese Americans who had violated the evacuation order, but they had declined legal representation. Fred Koremastu appeared to be more willing to test the constitutionality of the orders. Unlike Min Yasui and Gordon Hirabayashi, he appeared to be motivated by different, more personal reasons: a romance he did not want to leave. His blue-collar background did not prevent him from expressing his feelings. In a prepared statement Korematsu gave to Ernest Besig, he expressed his outrage over the evacuation and detention of Japanese in the United States.

Assembly Camps were for: Dangerous Enemy Aliens and Citizens: These camps have been definitely an imprisonment under armed guard with orders shoot to kill. In order to be imprisoned, these people should have been given a fair trial in order that they may defend their loyalty at court in a democratic way, but they were placed in imprisonment without any fair trial! Many Disloyal German and Italians were caught, but they were not all corralled under armed guard like the Japanese—is this a racial issue? If not, the Loyal Citizens want fair trial to prove their loyalty? (quoted in Irons, 1983: 99)

Fred Korematsu was eventually represented by attorneys Wayne Collins and Clarence E. Rust. The Korematsu case raised a number of issues, the most critical one was whether Korematsu's due process rights were being violated by his being forced to evacuate. His trial in the lower federal court moved quickly compared with Min Yasui's. On September 8, 1942, Korematsu was found guilty and sentenced to five years of probation, but in an unusual move, the judge did not impose the sentence. Technically, he was a free man. While the lawyers stated their intent to appeal, the judge imposed a bail that was posted by Ernest Besig. Korematsu was still a free man, but because of the exclusion and evacuation orders, he was escorted by military police to Tanforan Assembly Center, where he joined the rest of his family. Korematsu's attorneys appealed the decision to the U.S. Supreme Court.

In May 1943, Korematsu's case went before the U.S. Supreme Court at the same time as Yasui's and Hirabayashi's. The first Korematsu case dealt with the sole legal question of whether a conviction without a sentence is appealable to the Supreme Court. The Supreme Court sent Korematsu's case back to the Court of Appeals where it was decided it was appealable. The case was remanded back to the Supreme Court for the constitutional question in December 1944. The Court in a 6–3 majority decision upheld the validity of the evacuation orders because of wartime necessity. The Court ruled that race was not the reason why Korematsu or any other person of Japanese ancestry were placed into confinement. The majority opinion for the Court stated,

To cast this case into outlines of racial prejudice, without reference to the real military dangers which were present, merely confuses the issue. Korematsu was not excluded from the Military Area because of hostility to him or his race. He was excluded because we are at war with the Japanese Empire, because the properly constituted military authorities feared an invasion of our West Coast and felt constrained to take proper security measures, because they decided that the military urgency of the situation demanded that all citizens of Japanese ancestry be segregated from the West Coast temporarily, and finally, because Congress, reposing its confidence at this time of war in our military leaders, as inevitably it must, determined that they should have the power to do just this. (323 U.S. 214, 223 [1944])

There were three dissenting opinions, however. Justices Owen J. Roberts, Robert H. Jackson, and Frank Murphy were in the minority. In their opinion, there were issues of whether there was denial of due process of law because of an individual's ethnic ancestry. Justice Murphy wrote, "Being an obvious racial discrimination [Executive Order 9066], the order deprives all those within its scope of equal protection of the laws as guaranteed by the Fifth Amendment. It further deprives these individuals of their constitutional rights to live and work where they will, to establish a home where they choose and to move about freely" (323 U.S. 214, 234 [1944]).

Murphy's dissent continued,

I dissent, therefore, from this legalization of racism. Racial discrimination in any form and in any degree has no justifiable part whatever in our democratic way of life. It is unattractive in any setting but is utterly revolting among a free people who have embraced the principles set forth in the Constitution of the United States. All residents of this nation are kin in some way by blood or culture to a foreign land. Yet they are primarily and necessarily a part of the new and distinct civilization of the United States. They must, accordingly, be treated at all times as the heirs of the American experiment, and as entitled to all the rights and freedoms guaranteed by the Constitution. (323 U.S. 214, 242 [1944])

All three Supreme Court cases were essential to bolstering the government's claim of military necessity for the evacuation and internment program. Korematsu's case has been one of the most important cases central to the teaching of constitutional law in the United States. The decision of the Supreme Court gave the power to the military that in turn exercised its power over citizens and noncitizens of the country during a national crisis, even though no martial law had been declared. This decision raises serious questions about the rights and civil liberties of all people of this country if and when "military necessity" becomes the dictates of governance.

MITSUYE ENDO

The case of Mitsuye Endo is different from the Yasui, Hirabayashi, and Korematsu cases. Whereas they had various reasons for deliberately disobeying the evacuation and curfew orders and knowingly did so, Mitsuye Endo was already at Tanforan Assembly Center and was approached by attorneys to test whether it was legal for the government to detain her.

Mitsuye Endo was born in Sacramento, California, in 1920. She was educated in the United States, raised as a Methodist, had never been to Japan, and did not speak or read Japanese. After attending high school, she went to work for the state of California as a clerical worker for the Department of Motor Vehicles. Once the war broke out, she was terminated from her job because of her Japanese ancestry. As she puts it, "We were given a piece of paper saying we were suspended because we were of Japanese ancestry. We were accused of something, but I can't even remember the allegations" (quoted in Tateishi, 1984: 61).

At the outbreak of World War II, all Nisei who worked for the state of California were dismissed from their jobs. The state personnel board questioned their loyalty and charged then with "failure of good behavior, fraud in securing employment, incompetency, inefficiency, and acts incompatible with and inimical to the public service" as grounds for dismissal. Despite the requirement of being a U.S. citizen for state employment, they were falsely accused of being citizens of Japan (Irons, 1983: 101).

The concerns of the dismissed state employees were brought to the attention of lawyer Saburo Kido, president of the Japanese American Citizens League. He enlisted the support of a Caucasian lawyer, James Purcell, to try to get the personnel board to rescind their actions. But before Purcell and Kido had a chance to file their case, General DeWitt's exclusion orders went into effect, and their clients were moved to the assembly centers.

Endo had reported as was required by the military orders and was interned at Tanforan Assembly Center near San Francisco. When Purcell visited the center, he was appalled by the conditions. Center officials forced him to meet with clients in their living quarters, which were whitewashed horse stalls still smelling of horse manure. As he remarked, "I grew up in Folsom prison [California]. . . . My father was a guard there. I know a prison when I see it, and Tanforan was a prison with watchtowers and guns" (quoted in Irons, 1983: 101). His visit to Tanforan made him aware of the injustices suffered by the Japanese Americans and influenced how he would focus his case.

Purcell interviewed several potential candidates for a test case for the American Civil Liberties Union. Endo was selected because her "life" credentials held the most appeal. She was selected because she had the "best background" for a test case: she was a U.S. citizen, she did not speak Japanese, her parents had never returned to Japan, and she had a brother serving in the U.S. army. She could be presented as a "loyal" citizen who despite her ancestry was clearly a model U.S. citizen.

In July 1942, Purcell filed a writ of habeas corpus petition on behalf of Mitsuye Endo. The term *habeas corpus* comes from the Latin "[that] you have the body." This legal procedure is used to free individuals who are being detained and is a protection against arbitrary imprisonment. Mitsuye Endo had complied with the evacuation orders, she had answered affirmatively to the loyalty questionnaire, and she had never been charged with any crime. The petition requested her release. Both federal and state constitutions provide that the privilege of habeas corpus shall not be suspended in cases of rebellion or invasion.

Endo was an unusual plaintiff in that she never appeared in court and rarely met with her lawyers. Even she herself admits that it was difficult for her to think of becoming a "test" case before the Supreme Court. Endo recalled, "I was very young and I was very shy, so it was awfully hard to have this thing happen to me. It was awfully hard for me. . . . I never imagined it would go to the Supreme Court. . . . While all this was going on, it seemed like a dream. It just didn't seem like it was happening to me" (quoted in Tateishi, 1984: 61).

Although Endo has downplayed her role as a plaintiff, her case was very important because it affected all Japanese Americans who were still being held in internment camps. Usually habeas corpus cases are to be heard immediately, but it took almost a year before the federal courts decided on her case. A defendant in a case is allowed to post bail and be released while the case is pending. Initially she was denied the right to leave the camp because she was of Japanese ancestry. After the government attorneys became aware of the habeas corpus petition, they offered to release Endo if she promised not to enter the restricted West Coast area. The government wanted to avoid a Supreme Court test case. Her habeas corpus petition was denied, and it was appealed. It took another year before the case was forwarded to the Supreme Court in 1944. Endo heroically refused to abandon the legal case and remained in camp for two more years (Irons, 1983).

In October 1944, Endo's case moved forward to the Supreme Court, along with the second Korematsu hearing. While the justices had already decided in the earlier cases of Hirabayashi and Yasui, their decisions in these cases were more complex and divided because it looked like the war was going to end soon. On December 18, 1944, the Supreme Court reached its decision in *Ex parte Endo* (323 U.S. 283 [1944]). In their unanimous decision, they stated that the government had no authority to detain Mitsuye Endo or other admittedly loyal citizens in internment camps. The court wrote,

We are of the view that Mitsuye Endo should be given her liberty. In reaching that conclusion we do not come to the underlying constitutional issues which have been argued. For we conclude that whatever power the War Relocation Authority may have to detain other classes of citizens, it has no authority to subject citizens who are concededly loyal to its leave procedure. (323 U.S. 283, 297 [1944])

This decision was the necessary turning point needed to close the internment camps. Any Japanese American who signed the loyalty questionnaire was free to leave the camp. Of course, for many, there were difficult questions of where they would go, what they would do, and how they would be accepted. Already, the two Arkansas camps had been closed, with residents being transferred to other camps. After the *Endo* decision, all of the other camps, with the exception of Tule Lake, closed between October and November 1945. Tule Lake was the last, closed in March 1946 because it was a segregation center and continued to house a large proportion of those who answered "no" to the loyalty questionnaire.

OTHER JAPANESE AMERICAN CASES

The cases of Min Yasui, Gordon Hirabayashi, Fred Korematsu, and Mitsuye Endo are the most highly publicized of the Japanese American internment cases. There were, however, other Japanese Americans who challenged the internment orders, but whose cases are not well known. One Nisei couple, Ernest and Toki Wakayama of Los Angeles, felt that the evacuation orders were discriminatory. They approached the American Civil Liberties Union for advice about whether they should challenge the orders. They were advised to report to the assembly center or risk arrest. Their only other option was to report and use a habeas corpus petition to gain their release from the assembly center on the grounds that they had been detained without cause.

In many ways, the Wakayamas were an ideal couple to test the legality of the evacuation. They were both American born, Nisei. Ernest Wakayama was a former postal worker, World War I veteran, and former officer of a local chapter of the American Legion. But their case was never pursued by the American Civil Liberties Union. Shortly after the Wakayama family reported to camp, authorities arrested Ernest Wakayama along with others for conducting a meeting in Japanese (which was forbidden in the camps) to organize a protest against the camp conditions. After being held in the Los Angeles County Jail, he was finally released and moved to the Manzanar Relocation Center with his family. The time spent in jail for Wakayama made him disillusioned with the American system of justice. In 1943 he applied for repatriation and went to live in Japan.

In another lesser-known case, a habeas corpus petition was filed in Seattle on behalf of Mary Asaba Ventura, a Japanese American married to a Filipino national. Her petition for release was based upon the curfew order violating her freedom of movement with the threat of arrest. Judge Lloyd L. Black issued the opinion that her habeas corpus petition was improperly used because she was technically not being held in custody against her will. Her lawyers argued that curfew was "constructive custody" because Japanese Americans were being required to stay in their homes against their will during the curfew hours. But Black defended DeWitt's curfew orders, arguing his concern over potential loyalty of people of Japanese ancestry, and Ventura's petition was dismissed (Irons, 1983).

AN EVALUATION OF THE LEGAL CHALLENGES AND SUPREME COURT DECISIONS

The Japanese Americans who challenged the legal system did so as a symbol of protest and resistance, whether for personal reasons as in the case of Fred Korematsu, or moral or legal reasons as in the cases of Gordon Hirabayashi and Min Yasui. Mitsuye Endo chose to stay in camp and proceed with her legal case. Each Supreme Court case had slightly different outcomes locally, but at the top level, the justices were largely unanimous in their decisions.

These cases have had important significance in the legal arena, particularly as they apply to the Fourteenth Amendment and issues of race and ancestry. The Supreme Court decisions reinforced the use of racial characteristics or ancestry as criteria for singling out a particular group or population. Even though the courts went out of their way to say that racial classification is wrong and discriminatory, they deferred to the military authorities' arguments that national security was at stake. In *Korematsu*, the Court said that it was all right to disadvantage a group for reasons of pressing public necessity, but not because of racial motivation. Thus, reinforcing racial stereotyping was legitimate in the interest of national security. Because of the *Korematsu* decision, the courts must now look carefully at laws that restrict a certain group because of racial characteristics. Laws must pass the "strict scrutiny" test to ensure that when racial classifications are used, there must be a strong "compelling state interest" such as national security or war.

The justices also responded to the complex wartime "hysteria." Their decisions showed that the Court was very much influenced and motivated by a claim of "military dangers" rather than racial prejudice. Thus, the constitutionality of the relocation program was viewed in the interest of national security.

In the *Endo* decision, the justices did not address the constitutional issues as they applied to the Japanese internment cases or the Fourteenth Amendment. The Fourteenth Amendment contains the equal protection clause designed to protect all citizens in the United States. The rights of

Japanese Americans were violated because the government on the basis of race and national ancestry singled them out for evacuation and internment. As a group, they were deprived of their liberty and property when they were forced to leave their homes and places of employment to live within guarded centers and camps.

In summary, all of these cases indicate the complexity of the wartime decision to evacuate and remove people of Japanese ancestry from the West Coast. In the United States, the executive, legislative, and judicial branches are the bodies to ensure that government actions are not made without some form of checks and balances. The president was responsible for the executive order that allowed the military to enforce curfew and the evacuation of Japanese Americans. Congress was responsible for putting forward the public laws that validated the president's executive order. The Supreme Court bore the responsibility of interpreting the laws and their constitutionality. Nonetheless, it was still individual people who were involved with making these decisions. Their actions have to be understood within the context of their own personal beliefs and experiences that may have dictated the decisions they ultimately made.

REVISITING KOREMATSU, YASUI, AND HIRABAYASHI: THE CORAM NOBIS CASES

In most cases, the Supreme Court decisions are final and establish important precedent-setting case law. The Japanese American Supreme Court cases would not disappear after the *Korematsu* decision in 1944. Instead, they resurfaced forty years later, after a long period of silence from Japanese Americans over their wartime experience. In the early 1980s, a rare chance finding by a legal scholar researching the Hirabayashi, Koremastsu, and Yasui cases, and a changed social climate, brought about the opportunity to revisit these cases and challenge the government's claims of "military necessity."

In 1981, attorney Peter Irons was doing research on the Japanese American Supreme Court cases of Gordon Hirabayashi, Fred Korematsu, and Min Yasui. During his research he found formerly classified documents that were released under the Freedom of Information Act. These documents showed that the government had suppressed evidence and presented information to the Supreme Court that contained "lies" and "intentional falsehoods" regarding the necessity for military evacuation of people of Japanese ancestry from the West Coast. Irons also discovered military files that showed that the War Department destroyed and altered key material to these cases.

Irons contacted the three defendants immediately. They were all interested in pursuing their cases again, hoping that this new evidence could overturn their former convictions. At the time, Gordon Hirabayashi was a professor emeritus of sociology at the University of Alberta in Canada. Min Yasui was executive director of the Denver Commission on Community Relations, and Fred Korematsu was retired and living in San Leandro, California, only blocks away from where he was arrested in 1942.

Using a very obscure provision in the law, Fred Korematsu, Minoru Yasui, and Gordon Hirabayashi filed to have their cases reopened and their convictions removed. In a procedure called writ of *error coram nobis* they asked the courts to look at their convictions again. The term *coram nobis* comes from the Latin "the error before us." It is related to the writ of habeas corpus used in Mitsuye Endo's case. Whereas habeas corpus is designed to protect people from being unlawfully detained, *coram nobis* is used after there has been a conviction and final judgment. These ancient writs descended from English common law practices designed to protect people against arbitrary and unlawful action. *Coram* allows people who has been convicted to challenge that conviction once they have already served their sentence. It is done only when the original trials had some "fundamental error." In these cases, Irons had found that the government had deliberately concealed, altered, and suppressed evidence that was favorable to the defendants.

The decision to reopen the three cases using the *coram nobis* procedure was walking on new legal territory. There had never been a Supreme Court decision that had been successfully challenged in this manner. A legal team was assembled for each of the defendants. The teams consisted of Sansei lawyers in San Francisco, Portland, and Seattle. Finally, in 1983, lawyers for Fred Korematsu, a group that included many Sansei whose parents had been interned, filed a petition to seek the reversal of Korematsu's original conviction. Two weeks later, identical petitions were filed in Portland and Seattle, the original cities of Min Yasui and Gordon Hirabayashi's cases.

These three cases originally tried in three different lower federal district courts, with three different judges, were being reviewed again. As might be expected, three somewhat similar, yet different results were rendered by the judges in the 1980s. Fred Korematsu's conviction was the first to be decided. In 1984, U.S. District Court Judge Marilyn Hall Patel vacated Korematsu's previous conviction, and ordered an evidentiary fact-finding hearing. Judge Patel, a strong civil rights advocate, stated in her opinion,

Korematsu remains on the pages of our legal and political history. As a legal precedent it is now recognized as having very limited application. As historical precedent it stands as a constant caution that in times of war or declared military necessity our institution must be vigilant in protecting constitutional guarantees. It stands as a caution that in times of distress the shield of military necessity and national security must not be used to protect governmental actions from close scrutiny and accountability. It stands as a caution that in times of international hostility and antagonisms our institutions, legislative, executive and judicial, must be prepared to protect all citizens from the petty fears and prejudices that are so easily aroused. (quoted in Irons, 1989: 243)

In the case of Minoru Yasui, Judge Robert C. Belloni vacated the conviction, but declined to make a ruling on the evidence because more than forty years had passed since the case was first heard. In addressing the court, Yasui said, "It is true that I am but an insignificant individual, but this case does not involve me as a person, nor does it involve just Japanese Americans, all Americans, who believe in the dream of equality and freedom and justice" (quoted in Kessler, 1993: 272). Yasui and his attorney wanted the judge to order an evidentiary hearing so that other material could be introduced into the record that would show that the government's restrictions were not based upon military necessity. Yasui appealed the judge's ruling, but died in November 1986 before his case could be heard, rendering his case moot. His lawyer and Yasui's family continued to press his case, taking it before the Ninth Circuit Court of Appeals and the Supreme Court, where both times, the case was dismissed.

Gordon Hirabayashi's case in Seattle was the last to be heard. Judge Donald S. Voorhees vacated Hirabayashi's earlier conviction for refusing to be evacuated, but upheld his conviction for curfew violation. Similar to Supreme Court Justice Owen J. Roberts, he felt that the curfew restriction that singled out Hirabayashi because he was of Japanese ancestry was reasonable for that time. Hirabayashi appealed and Voorhees was instructed to vacate the conviction for curfew violation, which he did in 1988.

Since none of the *coram nobis* cases reached the U.S. Supreme Court in the 1980s, the constitutional interpretation of the wartime cases remains the law of the land. However, by vacating the convictions of Korematsu, Yasui, and Hirabayashi, the federal courts questioned the very facts that the wartime cases relied on. Any future court will take notice of these cases. The courts must be vigilant during times of public hysteria and must not accept claims of military necessity as cause for government action toward a civilian population.

Despite the differences in how these cases fared in the courts in the 1980s, all three stand as challenges to the U.S. judicial system. They were brought by individuals who were educated in the American system of education and understood both the privileges, freedoms, and protections guaranteed by the U.S. Constitution. Each sought to remedy his particular situation through the judicial system, and continued to believe in his rights, even when he lost his fight in the highest court of the land.

They returned to their cases forty years later to challenge the impropriety of the government and its false claim of military necessity as the basis of their original convictions. Their perseverance and willingness to take a stand is an example of their strength and their belief in their cause.

6

After the War: Resettlement and Redress

The decision to end the internment program and open up the formerly restricted areas of the West Coast drew much controversy among the ranks of the War Department, the Department of the Interior (War Relocation Authority), and the Justice Department. The findings by the Commission on Wartime Relocation and Internment (1982) suggest that the logical ending of exclusion and the closing of the camps would be based upon some change in the *reasons* for exclusion. In other words, if people of Japanese ancestry were being excluded from the West Coast because of suspected issues of loyalty, there would no longer be any need for exclusion once loyalty was assured. Unfortunately, the reasons for exclusion were complicated by different individuals within the government agencies who held opinions about the nature of "loyalty" among people of Japanese ancestry. Thus, there was a prolonged debate in different departments of the government about when the exclusion orders for the West Coast should be lifted.

Since the War Relocation Authority was the government agency designated to manage the civilian population within the camps, one might expect that it had substantial influence on whether the camps should continue to operate. Yet it was the War Department and military arms of the government that wielded considerable power over whether exclusion should be ended. The chief concern of the War Department was that if so-called loyals were allowed to return to the West Coast, they would be criticized over the issue of whether the evacuation should have occurred in the first place. General DeWitt was always firmly on the side of evacuation and the continued operation of the internment camps. He subscribed to the belief that "ethnicity determined loyalty" and did not believe that Japanese, citizen or alien, could be trusted during the time of war because they would be loyal to Japan. Part of DeWitt's loyalty argument appears in his *Final Report* (1942) in which he alludes to the culture and belief system of the Japanese people being alien to American culture and beliefs. He believed most Japanese in America to be loyal to Japan and, thus, could not be trusted. Consequently, his position throughout the war and afterward was that the evacuation and internment program was justified.

The War Department in general took a more generous stand on the loyalty issue. They felt that loyalty was a matter of individual choice and that it would be possible to distinguish the loyal from the disloyal. Once loyalty could be determined, there would be no reason for the Japanese to be excluded from the West Coast. It was the government's responsibility to assess the loyalty of the evacuated population and then return them to a normal life outside of confinement once loyalty was assured. Thus, the loyalty review program (discussed in this volume, Chapter 4) and the Application for Leave Clearance was the vehicle through which to address this issue.

There was also much concern over the timing of the loyalty review program. Why had the War Department waited until all people of Japanese ancestry had been moved to the relocation centers, rather than conducting loyalty review in the assembly centers? If the War Department had decided to conduct loyalty reviews earlier in the evacuation process, they would have been subjected to a great deal of criticism for allowing the "loyal" Japanese Americans to return to the West Coast so early during the war. This especially concerned the government after millions of dollars had been spent in constructing the internment camps. It was not an easy decision either way.

By early 1944, there were hints that the exclusion orders for Japanese on the West Coast might be lifted. Secretary of War Stimson proposed to end exclusion at a cabinet meeting in the spring of 1944. His suggestion was supported by Secretary of the Interior Harold Ickes and Undersecretary of State Edward Stettinius. However, this was an election year, and it was doubtful whether Roosevelt, who was up for reelection, would support such a measure. Military authorities had a difficult time maintaining the same arguments for exclusion as they did at the outbreak of the war.

At the executive level, there was concern over ending internment because of Roosevelt's election campaign. Roosevelt's memos to his aides during this period indicate that he believed in taking a slower, cautious course in lifting the ban on Japanese living on the West Coast. It was not until the first cabinet meeting following the November election that it was decided to remove the exclusion order. This was announced to the public in November 1944, after Roosevelt had won the election. The government's move to end exclusion roughly coincided with the Supreme Court's decision in Mitsuye Endo's habeas corpus case. That both occurred about the same time suggests that the government was having difficulty continuing to justify the internment of Japanese Americans.

Finally, on December 17, 1944, Public Proclamation 21 was issued. General DeWitt's mass exclusion orders were rescinded. The proclamation stated,

The people of the states situated within the Western Defense Command, are assured that the records of all persons of Japanese ancestry have been carefully examined and only those persons who have been cleared by military authority have been permitted to return. They should be accorded the same treatment and allowed to enjoy the same privileges accorded other law abiding American citizens or residents. (quoted in *Personal Justice Denied*, CWRIC, 1982: 235–6)

Instead of mass exclusion, the government now prohibited entry into "sensitive" areas of the Western Defense Command of certain individuals—who were ones that were determined to be potential security risks based upon criteria established by the Justice and War Departments. The loyalty questionnaire (discussed in Chapter 4) was the basis for receiving security clearance. Those who did not answer affirmatively to the questionnaire were already held at the Tule Lake Segregation Center in California. Individuals who were interned at Justice Department and Immigration and Naturalization Service camps were also still considered potential "risks" for loyalty, and were not immediately released.

RESETTLEMENT

Much of the discussion about resettlement focuses on the time period from when people began to leave the camps until, ultimately, all the camps closed. In reality, resettlement began much earlier than this during the period prior to the evacuation with *voluntary* resettlement. In other words, prior to actual evacuation and movement into assembly centers, people of Japanese ancestry had the opportunity to voluntarily move themselves from the West Coast restricted areas to zones outside of the restricted areas, generally areas east of California, Washington, and Oregon, although portions of eastern Washington and eastern Oregon were not within the restricted zones.

Public Proclamation 21 had provisions that intended for the relocation centers to be closed within one year. Those who chose to leave the camps knew that it would be challenging, if not difficult, to live outside of the camps, since the United States was still at war with Japan. At first, they could not return to their West Coast homes, so they moved to the Midwest and East in the hopes of having greater freedom and choice in their lives. Those most likely to leave the camps were young, between the ages of fifteen and thirty-five (CWRIC, 1982). Confined to camp, these people's choices were limited, and given the opportunity to leave, they did. Also, many of the young people were in the college relocation program. More than likely, these young people knew English and had some skills or training that would help in their resettlement. By 1945, only the very young and the very old were left in the camps.

The case of three returnees to Hood River, Oregon, is one example of how some Japanese were received when they tried to return to their former homes on the West Coast. Located east of Portland, Oregon, Hood River had a sizable Japanese population working in agriculture. In January 1945, three Nisei men—Min Asai, Sat Noji, and Ray Sato— decided to return. After they had been in camp for a short period of time, they received permanent clearance to leave and were working in the Midwest. After the West Coast exclusion orders were lifted, they decided to return to Oregon because that was the only home they had ever known.

They were to arrive by train early in January, but were delayed. Several local residents who were known to be anti-Japanese were going to "meet them" at the train station to tell them they were not welcome. But the men never arrived—only their baggage. They had been delayed and arrived a few days later. One sympathetic farmer from the valley, Avon Sutton, met them and took them to Ray Sato's house. The three decided to stay together during the returnees' first days back in town, feeling that might be safer for them (Kessler, 1993).

Over time, other Nisei farmers came back into town. The hostility toward the Japanese did not subside. Vigilantes vandalized farm equipment, broke windows, and generally harassed Japanese in whatever way they could. In the town of Hood River, signs were posted stating "No Japs Wanted, No Japs Allowed." Japanese Americans were ostracized and prevented from entering many public places: movie theaters, restaurants, and stores. They found that no one in town would sell anything to them, and they had to depend on sympathetic neighbors to help them out. Children who returned with their parents faced the same social ostracism in the schools as they were singled out and harassed. It was a difficult time for those who chose to return to Hood River.

What brought the most national attention to Hood River were the actions of the local American Legion Post No. 22. The post had created an "honor roll" plaque that listed the names of Hood River residents who served in the military during the war. The honor roll was prominently displayed near the county courthouse. On it were the names of sixteen Nisei servicemen, two of whom had been killed in action. Ten of the men had received the Purple Heart for being wounded in action. The post voted to remove the names of all sixteen Nisei from the honor roll.

The post's actions drew national criticism, and the national head-quarters ordered that it reinscribe the names on the honor roll or face expulsion from the American Legion. With much resistance, the post restored the names, publicly stating that it "does not change the senti-ment of the Post on the question of the Japanese returning to Hood River" (Kessler, 1993: 244).

The incidents in Hood River represented only a fraction of the varying experiences Japanese had during the resettlement period. There were in many cases supportive and sympathetic individuals who helped and aided Japanese who returned to their homes.

Dave Tatsuno was from San Francisco, interned at Topaz Relocation Center. He had rented his home to Caleb Foote, a sympathetic Quaker who published articles in favor of Nisei before the war. Foote invited Tatsuno to stay with him as he explored the possibility of moving back to San Francisco. Tatsuno was impressed by the friendliness of the Af-rican American businessmen and bankers who had settled in the former San Francisco Japantown. He decided to bring his entire family back from Utah, and they were able to start their family store with a small amount of savings they had managed to keep after their last store had been liquidated (Taylor, 1993).

The Japanese Americans' experiences moving back to their hometown communities and living in new communities were varied. With few financial resources when they left camp, many had difficulty finding housing and work. Some cities with substantial Japanese American pop-ulations before the war were able to establish community support net-works immediately. In San Jose, California, the Buddhist church served as a "hostel," housing single young people and families. So did the his-toric Kuwabara Hospital in the city's Japantown. Families that had once lived close together were now separated by geographic distances as young couples with their families forged new lives away from Japanese American communities. People now had to adapt, by attempting to as-similate into non-Japanese communities, and by forming their own sup-port networks and organizations.

COMPENSATION FOR LOSSES

Whether returning to their previous homes or starting to rebuild their lives in new places, it was not an easy transition for most Japanese Amer-icans. After all, they had spent at least a year or more confined to deserts and swamplands; they did not know how they would be accepted once they left camp and returned home. Moreover, they did not know what would remain of their possessions they had stored, or what might have happened to the land they once had. Almost everyone experienced some form of material loss and had limited resources to pick up the pieces of their lives that they left before evacuation. In 1948, Congress passed the Evacuation Claims Act to allow people of Japanese ancestry to seek compensation from the U.S. government for losses they incurred as a result of their incarceration. Their claims were limited to "damage to or loss of real or personal property," which was not covered by insurance and was a reasonable consequence of the evacuation and exclusion.

It is difficult to make estimates about the total property and income loss of the West Coast Japanese population during the period of evacuation. One amount frequently cited is $400 million, although this is not substantiated by any research. A 1949 study by Broom and Riemer suggests a loss of about $77 million, and this figure appears to be the best scientific guess at the probable value of the losses.

The story of Tomoye Takahashi exemplifies the losses that families incurred at the time of evacuation. She and her family were first evacuated to Tanforan Assembly Center, and later moved to Topaz Relocation Center in Utah. When they left San Francisco, they rented their home, fully furnished, for $45 a month. They locked all of their possessions they could not take with them in one room of the basement of their house. Included among these were Japanese kimonos, silk parasols, jewelry, records, dolls, and family photographs. When they returned they found that the room had been opened and vandalized, and that all of their personal family letters and photographs were strewn about. Most of their valuable family heirlooms were gone. Later, the Takahashis noticed that some of their neighbors were using their furniture and appliances. They reported their losses to the Golden Gate Park police, who said, "Have you ever heard of a Chinaman's chance? You don't have a Chinaman's chance. No court will listen to you and no lawyer would take your case" (quoted in Taylor, 1993: 277).

Although 26,568 claims were filed for an amount totaling $148 million, the government paid only $37 million in compensation. Only a small percentage of people actually received compensation for their losses. The government paid about ten cents for every dollar of property lost because former internees had to have documents proving their losses. For example, by 1948 when the Evacuation Claims Act was passed, the Internal Revenue Service had already destroyed most of its 1939 to 1942 income tax records. This made it difficult to assess the dollar value, in prewar terms, of the property anyone might have held or their earnings from that period prior to evacuation (CWRIC, 1982).

The Japanese American Citizens League knew that it would be difficult for those seeking compensation to prove their losses with physical documentation. They felt,

It was the exception and not the rule when minute and detailed records and documents were retained. In the stress and tension of 1942, when one could only take to camp what could be hand carried, when one did not know how long he would be detained or whether he would ever be allowed to return, it would be unreasonable to expect that emotion-charged men and women would have chosen to pack books and records instead of the food, the medicines, and the clothing which they took with them to war relocation centers. The whole community was moved, and so books and records could not be left with neighbors or even friends. And, today 12 years later, with all the great changes that have taken place particularly on the west coast, it is almost impossible to secure even remotely accurate appraisals and evaluations of the homes, the businesses, the farms and the properties of more than a decade ago, a decade of war and upheaval.

To add further difficulties, under Federal and State codes, most of the government records of 1942—which might have been of value as cross-references—have been destroyed pursuant to law. (quoted in CWRIC, 1982: 119)

The process of filing a claim and receiving compensation was lengthy and burdensome. Once a claim was filed, the attorney general was required to review each claim. Between 1949 and 1950, only 232 claims were adjudicated out of 26,000 filed. Later, claims in the amount of $2,500 or less were settled without the formal procedure. Thus by 1955, 22,000 claims had been settled. Now only the larger claims remained, and the Evacuation Claims Act was amended to allow the attorney general to settle those up to $100,000. Out of all of these, only fifteen cases were ever taken to the Court of Claims. This is a small number of court cases, considering the probable amount of the losses sustained by the evacuated Japanese American population.

Arthur and Estelle Ishigo were an interracial couple who had lived in Los Angeles before the war and were interned together at Heart Mountain, Wyoming. Estelle was an artist, and Arthur, an aspiring actor. They stayed at Heart Mountain until the very last day. Leaving with barely $25, they took the bus back to Los Angeles, where they lived in a trailer park. Arthur took janitorial work wherever he could find it, and Estelle worked in the fish canneries at Terminal Island. When time came to apply for compensation, they meticulously documented all the possessions they had lost when they were uprooted from their home. The government offered them $102.50 as a settlement. For years, and after numerous appeals, they accepted the paltry sum as settlement for their losses.[1]

Although the losses are reported in terms of individual, family, and small business holdings, the Japanese evacuation also impacted the gross productivity of the West Coast states. Forty-five percent of all people of Japanese ancestry who were living in the evacuation area were involved with agriculture. Eighteen percent were involved with the wholesaling, retailing, and transportation of food products. The value of the 6,118 farms operated by people of Japanese ancestry was estimated at

$72,600,000, with another $6 million worth of equipment (CWRIC, 1982: 122). Although the Japanese farmers were a smaller percentage of all farmers in the West Coast states overall, the value and productivity of their farms outpaced all other farms for that time period. Japanese farmers were engaged in productive, labor-intensive crops, and the evacuation came at the time of peak harvest for the spring crops, especially strawberries and flowers in California. It is difficult to estimate how many Japanese farmers did not return to their land after the war, or suffered setbacks caused by loss of equipment or rundown property.

The second major area of losses was in Japanese American businesses. Hotels, shops, and service-oriented businesses all had to be liquidated, sold, or rented to someone else. Shops had to liquidate their inventory quickly at fire sale prices, often with goods sold for a fraction of their cost. More often, Japanese-manufactured goods were disposed of because no one wanted to buy things made in Japan.

IMMEASURABLE LOSSES

The compensation for losses could not ever replace certain items of sentimental or emotional value. Social or psychological losses or trauma caused by the evacuation and incarceration are also difficult to measure. Without a doubt, after the war Japanese Americans suffered some social stigma as a result of being singled out because of their race. Other losses that cannot be measured include the deprivation of liberty, and health-related illnesses that resulted in premature death or physical injury caused by the events.

How did they cope with such a heavy burden of losses, especially those who might have lost family members who died in camp or were killed serving in the military? One way to look at this is by understanding the unique culture and values held by the Issei and then Nisei in America. A number of cultural explanations have tried to account for the behavior of Japanese Americans during and after the war. Sociologist Harry Kitano (1993) suggests that certain Japanese values served as coping mechanisms and help to explain how and why Japanese Americans behaved as they did in their situation. Japanese norms such as *gaman* (which means internalization of, and suppression of anger and emotion, but also can be construed as strength and perseverance), *shi-ka-ta-ga-nai* (it cannot be helped), *haji* (shame), *on* (ascribed obligation), and *enryo* (deference, obsequiousness) served as rational, emotional handles to deal with the stresses of evacuation and internment (Kitano, 1993). In addition, the Japanese cultural emphasis on conformity and obedience meant following the orders of those in power—the president and the U.S. army. These worked to gain cooperation among the Japanese population. Accordingly, these Japanese cultural norms, ingrained and transported from Japan, were adapted to the U.S. situation and also help to explain why Japanese Americans responded to the evacuation and internment the way that they did.

REBUILDING COMMUNITY

In the decades following World War II, Japanese Americans struggled to rebuild their lives and communities. After the war, the Issei were still considered aliens ineligible for citizenship. But in 1952, the McCarran-Walter Immigration Act was passed. This was the first major change in immigration legislation since the 1924 Immigration Act. The law allowed a small quota of immigration from Japan, but more importantly, Issei were now eligible for naturalized U.S. citizenship.

For the most part, Japanese Americans attempted to blend into the mainstream of American society, raising children and families and pursuing their version of the "American dream." They encouraged their children to assimilate, do well in school, and become professionally educated. Perhaps their children's successes would compensate for the discrimination they had experienced in the past. Japanese American institutions and organizations, such as the JACL, and the Buddhist and Japanese Protestant churches, continued to flourish in many West Coast communities, although the *"Nihon-machi"* Japantowns of prewar years never grew to the same size they were before the war. After camp, the mainland Japanese American community was forced to disperse. Resettlement meant that Japanese Americans were no longer geographically concentrated on the West Coast.

Nisei adjustment after the war took many different paths. Most simply chose to forget about the experience and put it behind them. Other Nisei continued to distrust white society because of what had happened, and instead chose to associate with other Japanese Americans. At the other end, there were those Nisei who thought assimilation was the best path toward acceptance. In other words, they thought it best to become less Japanese, to not associate with anything Japanese or Japan's institutions, and to attempt to blend into mainstream American society. In fact, the government's resettlement policies seemed to encourage this mode of adaptation. After they were released from the confines of camp, the WRA told the Japanese not to congregate as a group in public, and to avoid living next door to another Japanese American family (CWRIC, 1982).

In addition to the geographic dispersal of the community, there were also ideological splits that continued to resonate throughout the community. The responses on the loyalty questionnaire, finding out someone was a "no-no" or a draft resister, or even interned at Tule Lake, caused many in the Japanese American community to turn away from that person. According to one person, "[E]ven to this day, there are many amongst us who do not speak about that period for fear that the same harsh feelings might arise up again to the surface" (CWRIC, 1982: 301).

The Nisei veterans returning from the war encountered a mixed reception. They were lauded by President Harry S. Truman, who told them, "You fought prejudice, and you won." They received presidential unit citations, but all at a cost of losing several thousand men. As decorated veterans, they still encountered anti-Japanese prejudice when they returned home. In his uniform, Daniel Inouye, who served in the 100th Battalion and who lost his arm in battle, tried to get his hair cut but was turned away. He described it this way:

[A] day or so before the troopship left, I went to this barbershop in one of the towns ringing San Francisco—and got as far as the door.

"Are you Chinese?" the man said to me.

I looked past him at the three empty chairs, the other two barbers were watching us closely. "I'm an American," I said.

"Are you Chinese?"

"I think what you want to know is where my father was born. My father was born in Japan. I'm an American." Deep in my gut I knew what was coming.

"Don't give me that American stuff," he said swiftly. "You're a Jap and we don't cut Jap hair."

I wanted to hit him. I could see myself—it was as though I were standing in front of a mirror. There I stood, in full uniform, the new captain's bars bright on my shoulders, four rows of ribbons on my chest, the combat infantry badge, the distinguished unit citations—and a hook where my hand was supposed to be. And he didn't cut Jap hair. To think that I had gone through a war to save his skin—and he didn't cut Jap hair.

I said, "I'm sorry. I'm sorry for you and the likes of you." And I went back to my ship. (Inouye, 1967: 207–8)

After the war, many Nisei veterans struggled with the loss of close friends in their unit. No one was immune to this; everyone seemed to know someone who died. But within their ranks, they were told to *ga-man*, to endure and press on, once they returned. The men in the Military Intelligence Service could share little of their wartime victories since their work was highly classified. Today the stories of the Nisei vets have been brought to the forefront of the Japanese American experience with the knowledge that there were high casualties in the 100th and 442nd units.

For many Japanese Americans, though, the postwar years were ones in which the memories of camp were silenced, but not forgotten. There was certainly selective amnesia about the events, and individuals chose to remember or forget, depending on the emotional and social tie they had to the memory. One fact still remained, however: Japanese Americans may have been silent about the wartime experience, but they did not forget. The memories would go into hiding but continue to linger.

REDISCOVERING THE PAST:
SANSEI AND THE QUEST FOR HISTORY

The social movements and activism of the 1960s were influential in the lives of third-generation Japanese Americans: the Sansei. Most Sansei were born after the war and had very little knowledge of their parents' and grandparents' experiences. As a part of the baby boom generation, they are in a unique group of individuals who experienced the socially turbulent 1960s. As their Nisei parents came of age before and during the time of internment, the Sansei were largely influenced by the civil rights, anti–Vietnam War, and women's movements of the 1960s through the 1970s. The rise of civil rights and concurrent emphasis on ethnic and racial identity as well as the historical racism experienced by American ethnic minorities caused Sansei to ask questions and pursue their own ethnic group's history. This led to the uncovering and recovering of Japanese American history, particularly the World War II internment camp experience.

The camp experience had a definite effect on the way many Sansei were raised. Although most Sansei were not old enough to have actually been in camp, they were certainly indirectly affected by their parents' experience:

[M]y father [a Nisei] always told us, "Get a good education, for it is something no one could take away from you." . . . He said we should assimilate, for any cultural deviation from the mainstream would hold us back. (quoted in CWRIC, 1982: 300)

Within the civil rights movement was a component that helped to galvanize young college-age Sansei to question the version of history that they had learned growing up. The interest in ethnic identity and recovering of lost history was a large part of the movement for ethnic studies at colleges and universities throughout the nation.

Uncovering the "silent past" for Sansei also meant taking social and political action on what they had learned. Beginning in the early 1970s, the first Manzanar pilgrimages occurred. Bridging the generations, Issei, Nisei, and Sansei joined together to make a trip to the site of Manzanar in the eastern Sierra Nevada mountains in California. The Tule Lake Relocation Center in Northern California, near the Oregon border, also became the site of pilgrimage activities. Here, former residents recall the harsh, desolate living conditions, as well as the strength of those incarcerated to bring humanity into their day-to-day lives. These activities became a chance for generations to talk to one another about the events that transpired during World War II. They have become a focal point for a living history lesson, combining deep personal reflections with learning experiences at the internment camp sites. Ann Muto of Cupertino, California, reflected upon her experience at the Tule Lake pilgrimage in 2000. The event brought:

[L]asting impressions of the pilgrimage include the courage of the older Niseis [sic] who were willing to go back into their past and share their memories, painful or not, with others. Their willingness to open up made it easier for others to share some of their own pain. I was impressed with the commitment of the younger members of the pilgrimage, who were unwilling to let the sacrifices of their parents and older generations be forgotten. Being in their presence made me proud to be a *Nikkei*. (Japanese American Resource Center/Museum *Newsletter*, August 2000 p. 3)

Ann's poem "Missing Pieces" captures the spirit of the pilgrimage:

> There are missing pieces in my life
> Not simply forgotten memories
> But unspoken words
>
> I wish my parents were still alive
> And willing to take the step back
> To explore what comes up
> To share who they were when it all happened
> They died silent
> Their stories untold
>
> This pilgrimage helped me with my healing
> and by hearing the accounts of others
> I am able to assemble a story
> That could have been theirs
> That could be mine
>
> Those are the missing pieces
> That I need
> To make myself whole

THE CAMPAIGN FOR REDRESS[2]

According to Roger Daniels (1991), it is difficult to date the precise beginnings of the movement toward compensating Japanese Americans for their wartime losses. Some protests occurred at the time of the evacuation that could be interpreted as statements of disaffection. Later, the 1948 Evacuations Claims Act could be construed as some sort of partial compensation. Neither represented the full sentiment of reparations toward the Japanese American community. It was not until the late 1960s that groups of Japanese Americans in Seattle, San Francisco, and Southern California began to discuss some type of compensation. The word *reparations* was often used, but over time, the term *redress* became the accepted term describing the movement to seek a government acknowledgment and apology, and monetary compensation for Japanese Americans.

As in any social movement, the campaign for redress needed to have a significant population that supported and believed in the goals of the movement. Japanese Americans needed not only group support, but also support from outside, from non-Japanese Americans. There was also a need for leadership and institutional/organizational structure to support and sustain a redress campaign/movement. This came from the leaders within the JACL, and the JACL served as the organization that pushed forward the redress agenda.

The campaign for redress began in the early 1970s at the national JACL conventions. The issue of redress was raised in San Francisco in 1970, then later at the Chicago JACL convention; every two years at the national meeting, redress resolutions were brought up. Finally the JACL established a National Committee for Redress and successfully introduced a redress platform at the 1978 JACL convention in Salt Lake City, calling for a $25,000 compensation sum (Daniels, 1991). Much of the documentation on compensation indicated that Japanese Americans were never fully compensated for the losses they incurred as a result of the government's forced evacuation.

The National Committee for Redress considered the JACL resolutions and eventually decided to pursue legislative action through Congress to achieve some type of compensation, rather than a court lawsuit. They knew it would be a difficult struggle to get legislation that would appropriate more than $3 billion in funds for redress, but chose to work through Congress, hoping that they could at least achieve some recognition for the wrongs that the government committed against people of Japanese ancestry during World War II. One of their main goals was to pursue the formation of a fact-finding commission that would investigate the primary reason for the evacuation and relocation program, that is, the oft-cited government belief that military necessity lay behind the evacuation.

Finally, with support of Japanese American members of Congress, including Senator S.I. Hayakawa (who was, incidentally, Japanese born in Canada, but a naturalized U.S. citizen), a bill was introduced to form a commission investigating the wartime relocation and internment program. In 1980, Congress passed Public Law 96–317 that established the Commission on Wartime Relocation and Internment of Civilians (CWRIC).[3] The commission was directed to

1. review the facts and circumstances surrounding Executive Order Numbered 9066, issued February 19, 1942, and the impact of such Executive Order on American citizens and permanent resident aliens;

2. review directives of the United States military forces requiring the relocation and, in some cases, detention in internment camps of American citizens, including Aleut citizens, and permanent resident aliens of the Aleutian and Pribolof Islands; and

3. recommend appropriate remedies. (CWRIC, 1982:1)

In 1981, the commission held more than twenty days of hearings throughout the United States in Washington, D.C., Los Angeles, San Francisco, Seattle, Anchorage, Chicago, New York City, and Cambridge, Massachusetts. They heard oral testimony from more than 750 witnesses. These people were evacuees, former government officials, public figures, interested citizens, and historians and others who had studied the wartime internment of civilians, specifically, people of Japanese ancestry. The commission also researched the vast federal archival holdings of the internment during World War II. The results of the research are reported in the commission's report, *Personal Justice Denied* (1982).[4] The commission's report is extensive and exhaustive. In addition to reporting on the evacuation and removal of people of Japanese ancestry from the West Coast, it discusses the removal of 1,875 residents of Japanese ancestry from Hawaii, the removal and internment of German and Italian aliens, the exclusion of German American and Italian American citizens, and the detainment of Japanese from Latin America.

The commission's final report contained several recommendations to redress the injustices of the internment. Among these were recommendations for a full government apology to the people who were incarcerated against their will, replacing the entitlements that they may have lost as a result of their incarceration; to establish a fund to educate people about the injustices of the wartime; and to have Congress appropriate money to provide a one-time per-capita payment of $20,000 to each surviving internee to compensate them for their losses. Although the commission's recommendations received unanimous support, Congressman Daniel Lungren (California) was not in favor of the monetary compensation or redress payment of $20,000. He believed that such a payment might set a precedent for other groups who had experienced discrimination who would then request redress. According to him, an apology was enough.

Beginning in 1983, legislation was introduced to have Congress appropriate the funds for the redress payments. In 1987, legislation passed the U.S. House of Representatives, followed in 1988 by passage in the U.S. Senate. Key to the passage of the House and Senate bills were bipartisan support and the strategic work of elected Japanese American senators and congressman: Senator Daniel Inouye (Hawaii), Senator Spark Matsunaga (Hawaii), Congressman Norman Y. Mineta (California), and Congressman Robert Matsui (California). The Civil Liberties Act of 1988 was signed into law by President Ronald Reagan. The law provided for a $20,000 redress payment to about 60,000 individuals of Japanese ancestry who were interned during World War II. The estates of those who had already died before the bill was signed into law were not eligible for the payment.

Perhaps more important than the monetary payment itself was the formal apology that Congress made on behalf of the U.S. government and the American people. In a dramatic yet poignant ceremony, the first redress payments were made at the Department of Justice by Attorney General Richard Thornburgh. Five of the oldest survivors were more than 100 years of age and were in wheelchairs and walkers, as they received their check from the government. Their payments were accompanied by a letter signed by President George H. Bush (see this volume, Document 6).

At the close of the last century, the Office of Redress Administration, which operated under the Civil Rights Division of the U.S. Department of Justice declared that 82,219 persons received the full $20,000 in redress payments.

One final chapter of the internment cases remained with the Japanese Latin Americans. Approximately 1,500 were found ineligible for redress payments; most of these were the cases of Japanese Latin Americans who were brought into the United States as deportees from other countries. Their case took another direction to compensate and settle. Because they were not originally U.S. citizens, and were brought to the United States as deportees of another country, they were in a kind of "legal no-man's land" when it came time to decided whether they were eligible for redress payments. There were Japanese Peruvians who were deported from Latin America and were being detained in the United States during the war, children born in the United States of Japanese Peruvian descent who were American citizens, and other Japanese Latin Americans who applied for U.S. citizenship once it became available for them. These categories of individuals did not fit the criteria for redress payments under the Civil Liberties Act of 1988.

A lawsuit was brought on behalf of those Latin American Japanese who remained in the United States after the war (*Mochizuki* v. *United States*, No. 97–294C) to deem them eligible for redress payments. The Court of Federal Claims granted approval for a partial settlement of claims made by the Japanese Peruvians. Three hundred and ninety-six Japanese Latin Americans were eligible for $5,000 payments under the *Mochizuki* settlement.

The movement for redress was not a unified national cause within the

Japanese American community. There were those who did not support the formation of a national commission investigating the internment and the campaign for redress through Congress. As in many social movements, different groups can emerge, especially those that seek a different course of action. One group that formed in 1979 was called the National Council for Japanese American Redress (NCJAR). Comprised of Japanese Americans in Seattle, they organized support for a national redress bill to be sent to Congress. NCJAR worked with Congressman Mike Lowry of Washington State to sponsor a redress bill in Congress. Although that bill ultimately failed to garner support for a variety of reasons, the supporters of NCJAR proceeded in a class action lawsuit against the U.S. government on behalf of the more than 120,000 people of Japanese ancestry interned during World War II (*William Hohri et al.* v. *United States,* U.S. District Court for the District of Columbia, March 16, 1983).

William Hohri's class action lawsuit was dismissed on technical grounds by a federal judge in the District of Columbia shortly after it was filed in May 1983. But as lawsuits are frequently drawn out over time, the case went to several different courts of appeals and to the Supreme Court, until in 1988 it was finally denied any further judicial action.[5]

CONCLUSION

For the Japanese American community, World War II represents a significant historical marker. The events that occurred are deeply embedded within the memories of all those who experienced the disruption in their lives. Although the Issei and Nisei attempted to move on with their lives, to forget the past, it was not the same for the Sansei. The Sansei would have to do their own searching as a generation, to find out about the silent pasts of their parents. "Camp" would still have a significant meaning for the generation. Sansei activist Warren Furutani stated before the Commission on Wartime Relocation and Internment of Civilians that camp has affected even those generations who were born after the war. It has and will be a constant point of reference for Japanese Americans because of the social and historical meaning people have given to the event.

The years that followed the war were a long struggle to achieve recognition and an acknowledgment that civil rights were violated and that the evacuation and incarceration were unnecessary. The government's claim of military necessity was used as a convenient handle, and worked as a cover-up for the racism that dominated the social atmosphere before, during, and after the war. The struggle to achieve redress was truly a victory for the entire community, although it was too late for the many thousands of Japanese Americans who did not live to see the reparations and receive an apology.

Today, Japanese Americans continue to remember the significance of what happened to their community and families during World War II. Every February, throughout the United States, Day of Remembrance events are organized. These have become a ritualized day of reflection and memory of the signing of Executive Order 9066. The Manzanar and Tule Lake pilgrimages are other reminders of the camp history. One phenomenon of the 1980s and 1990s was the organization of "camp reunions" where former internees came together to renew acquaintances and friendships. These probably would not have occurred had it not been for the work of the redress movement and the opening to allow Issei, Nisei, and Sansei to talk about the war years. The significance of these events is not lost in the face of success in redress. In fact, they have heightened the awareness of anyone who was involved, or those who have just learned about the camps.

Social scientists David J. O'Brien and Stephen S. Fugita suggest that the community has been incredibly resilient in the face of the trauma it experienced. They ask the question, "Why did the Japanese American community survive as well as it did?" The wartime internment experience has had a paradoxical effect on the meaning of "community" for Japanese Americans. Before the war, the community was concentrated geographically in both rural and urban areas on the West Coast. The wartime experience of incarceration had the effect of separating and dispersing the community from the West Coast after the camps closed. After the war, there was still some clustering of the Japanese population on the West Coast, but areas outside the West also grew (see Table 6.1).

The sense of community changed as people left the camps and moved into urban and suburban areas where there were fewer Japanese Americans. The geographic dispersal of the community forced a type of assimilation, so that many, but not all, third-generation Japanese Americans grew up away and isolated from traditional Nisei community networks. On the other hand, the network of organizations and community became even more important for the community after the war.

Despite the positive bearing within the community to rebuild and move forward, there are probably many stories of sadness and tragedy, where lives were torn apart and never returned to normal. When individuals and communities experience a dramatic change, catastrophe, or other devastating event, they often become disorganized and dysfunctional because of the lack of support that is usually present. This was no different for the Japanese American community. For some, the wartime experience traumatized the community as a whole such that continued

Table 6.1
Japanese American Population in the United States, 1950–1990

Census Year	1950	1960	1970	1980	1990
Region/State					
Total U.S.	326,276	463,568	587,246	716,331	847,562
Hawaii	184,598	203,455	217,175	239,734	247,486
Pacific Coast	98,310	178,985	240,532	306,328	361,217
Mountain	14,231	17,549	20,318	29,471	34,254
North Central	18,734	29,318	42,670	46,254	63,210
South	3,055	16,245	28,504	47,631	67,193
Northeast	7,348	18,016	38,047	47,913	74,202

Source: Adapted from Spickard (1996: 162–3).

psychological and social problems continue to exist within the community, largely hidden and not talked about.[6]

Part of the answer to this lies in cultural explanations. A certain part of community survival is *gaman* or perseverance, bearing up, much of what sociologist Harry Kitano suggests. But more than "culture" Japanese Americans have continued to find ways to maintain a meaningful community despite the disruptions. Thus, the friendships and family relationships, as well as the social activities (athletic leagues, churches, Japanese cultural schools) of the Japanese American community provided meaning to being Japanese American, and that was derived within the context of the camp experience and later, outside the camp experience.

Along those lines, the community has survived because it has been able to retain the memory of the camp experience. It has done so through much struggle and emotional catharsis. Doing so has allowed other generations of Japanese Americans to experience and understand the historical significance of the internment camps. Thus, the community has a sense of commonality and collective identity because of the past, and continues to bring that memory into the present and future. Japanese Americans today do not want anyone to forget what happened during the war. They understand how the social and political climate of the country can affect the way that laws and policies are made and how they can affect any individual or group. Keeping these memories alive remind Japanese Americans, and all Americans, of the mistakes and faltering of ordinary men and women. They also remind us of human survival and dignity under global and international stress and strain of war.

NOTES

1. See Steven Okazaki's award-winning documentary *Days of Waiting* for a poignant portrayal of the life of Estelle Ishigo during her days at Heart Mountain, Wyoming.

2. For a more detailed analysis of the political and social processes of Japanese American redress legislation see Leslie T. Hatamiya's *Righting a Wrong: Japanese Americans and the Passage of the Civil Liberties Act of 1988* (Stanford, Calif.: Stanford University Press, 1993).

3. The commission members included nine appointed individuals: Joan Bernstein, former general counsel of the Department of Health and Human Services, chair of the committee; Congressman Daniel Lungren, vice-chairman former senator Edward Brooke; former congressman Father Robert Drinnan; Dr. Arthur Flemming, chairman of the U.S. Commission on Civil Rights; the Honorable Arthur Goldberg, former justice of the Supreme Court; Father Ishmael Gromoff of the Pribilof Islands, Alaska; Judge William Marutani, Court of Common Pleas of the state of Pennsylvania; former senator Hugh Mitchell (Daniels, 1991: 193).

4. Selected portions of the Los Angeles (August 4–6, 1981) and San Francisco (August 11–13, 1981) testimonies can be found in *Amerasia Journal* 8 (1): 1981; and in William Minoru Hohri's *Repairing America: An Account of the Movement for Japanese-American Redress* (Pullman, Wash.: Washington State University Press, 1988).

5. Although Hohri's lawsuit was dismissed, his account of the redress movement is documented in his book *Repairing America: An Account of the Movement for Japanese-American Redress* (Pullman, Wash.: Washington State University Press, 1988).

6. The Sansei Legacy Project is one such group that has dealt with intergenerational relations and memories of camp. It is currently housed at the Buena Vista United Methodist Church in Alameda, California. Satsuki Ina's film *Children of the Camps* also documents the intense psychological and emotional pressures felt by individuals who were young children while in camp.

Photographic Essay

The photographs in this section capture a small segment of the Japanese American internment camp experience. They are stored at the National Archives and Records Administration at College Park, Maryland. They are from Record Group 210, Series G, titled Central Photographic File of the War Relocation Authority, 1942–1945. Professional photographers were commissioned by the WRA to document the daily life and treatment of Japanese Americans during World War II. More than 7,800 photographs are stored with the National Archives. More than 4,000 of these are digitized and can be viewed at the National Archives Research Room Web site. Other photographic material on the Japanese American internment can be found at the Bancroft Library at the University of California, Berkeley, the National Japanese American Historical Society in San Francisco, and the Japanese American National Museum in Los Angeles.

These photographs show Japanese Americans at home and at work immediately prior to evacuation; evacuees at assembly centers where they were processed before being assigned to relocation centers; and agricultural, vocational, educational, recreational, religious, and internal political activities at each of the ten relocation centers. In addition, the photos show WRA personnel and local officials, Nisei resettled in their former homes or at work after releases from a relocation center, Nisei servicemen and women at awards ceremonies or on leave, and the arrival and departure of evacuees who were transferred from one of the relocation centers to the Tule Lake Segregation Center in September 1943. Other photos show repatriated Japanese Americans embarking for Japan; and property formerly owned by Japanese Americans but vandalized, deserted, or taken over by others.

As with all photos, they are taken from the perspective of the individual photographer, whether or not they were sympathetic to the circumstances of internment for Japanese Americans. There is always a certain element of "staging" that takes place in the photographs, because many of the pictures were used for public relations purposes. Thus, one has to view them as subjective snapshots of the particular event and time period.

Exclusion Order posted at First and Front Streets, San Francisco, California. Photographer: Dorothea Lange. National Archives photo no. 210–G–A39. Courtesy of the National Archives.

This store was at 13th and Franklin Streets in Oakland, California. The owner was a University of California graduate of Japanese descent. On December 8, the day after Pearl Harbor, he placed the I AM AN AMERICAN sign on the storefront. Photographer: Dorothea Lange. National Archives photo no. 210–G–C519. Courtesy of the National Archives.

These barracks were former horse stalls and served as family living quarters at Tanforan Assembly Center in San Bruno, California. Each door enters into a family unit of two small rooms. Each living quarter is equipped with a bed and mattress for each person. Residents had to build their own benches, chairs, tables, and shelves from scrap lumber. Photographer: Dorothea Lange. National Archives photo no. 210–G–C28. Courtesy of the National Archives.

Evacuees board a bus to take them to Manzanar Relocation Center in Lone Pine, California. Photographer: Clem Albers. National Archives photo no. 210–G–A290. Courtesy of the National Archives.

View of Granada Relocation Center looking northwest from the water tower, Amache, Colorado. Photographer: Joe McClelland. National Archives photo no. 210–G–A753. Courtesy of the National Archives.

Mealtime at Manzanar Relocation Center. Every effort was made to keep family groups together in the dining halls and living quarters. Photographer: Clem Albers. National Archives photo no. 210–G–A17. Courtesy of the National Archives.

A typical interior of a barracks home. Note the curtain partition separating the sleeping area from the family living area. With the exception of sleeping cots provided by the army, furniture had to be built from local products. Photographer: Tom Parker. National Archives photo no. 210–G–E291. Courtesy of the National Archives.

A Boy Scout group flies the colors and marches in the Amache Summer Carnival Parade, Granada Relocation Center (Colorado). Photographer: Joe McClelland. National Archives photo no. 210–G–B672. Courtesy of the National Archives.

Against the backdrop of the eastern Sierra Nevada mountains, the American flag flies in front of barrack homes at Manzanar Relocation Center in California. Photographer: Dorothea Lange. National Archives photo no. 210–G–C840. Courtesy of the National Archives.

President Truman presents the 7th Presidential Unit Citation to the 100th/442nd Regimental Combat Team on the White House lawn, July 15, 1946. National Archives photo. Courtesy of the National Japanese American Historical Society and the National Archives.

Biographies: The Personalities behind the Japanese American Internment Program

INTRODUCTION

The biographies in this section characterize a diverse range of individuals who were inextricably linked to the Japanese American wartime experience. There were many key individuals in the Japanese internment experience during World War II. It is difficult to select only those who had major political, social, economic, or cultural influence on this time period. Those presented below portray the complexity of that experience.

In general, the biographies can be roughly categorized into four areas. The first group consists of those individuals at the elected and appointed levels of the government who were responsible for and upheld legal interpretations of the decision to evacuate and relocate more than 120,000 people of Japanese ancestry. They include people such as President Franklin Delano Roosevelt, Lieutenant Colonel John DeWitt, and Colonel Karl R. Bendetsen; members of Roosevelt's cabinet, Secretary of War Henry Stimson, Assistant Secretary of War John McCloy, Attorney General Francis Biddle, Justice Department Attorney Edward Ennis; Supreme Court Justices Frank Murphy and Owen J. Roberts; and War Relocation Authority directors Milton S. Eisenhower and Dillon S. Meyer. The second group of individuals are Japanese Americans whose names are recognized as key figures (whether by choice or by circumstance) during the evacuation and internment period. They are leaders of the JACL Mike Masaoka and Saburo Kido; media opinion makers James Omura and James Sakamoto; Lieutenant Colonel John Aiso of the Military Intelligence Language School; and Japanese Americans who legally challenged the evacuation orders, Mitsuye Endo, Fred Korematsu, Gordon

Hirabayashi, Minoru Yasui (profiled in Chapter 5). A third group of individuals consists of both Japanese and non-Japanese who provided a viewpoint and analysis of the camp experience from a scholarly point of view. They include the principal investigator for the Japanese American Evacuation Research Study (JERS) Dorothy Swaine Thomas, and the research assistants who worked on the study, Charles Kikuchi, Richard Nishimoto, Tamie Tsuchiyama, and Rosalie Hankey Wax; WRA photographer Dorothea Lange; and attorney Wayne M. Collins, who fought numerous, complex legal challenges presented by the evacuation and internment.

History has often overlooked those individuals who gave meaning in the form of literary and cultural contributions. The final group consists of those who produced works that were representative and influential of the camp experience: artists Chiura Obata and Mine Okubo, and writer John Okada. As with any list, there are always omissions and some errors. Consider this list a foundation to the Japanese American experience during World War II. Further biographies can be found by consulting *Japanese American History: An A-to-Z Reference from 1868 to the Present* edited by Brian Niiya (New York: Facts on File, 1991).

John Fujiu Aiso (1909–1987)

John Aiso was a key figure in the establishment of the Military Intelligence Language School in San Francisco. He was born in Burbank, California, and educated in Southern California. His educational experiences were marred by the prejudices of the time. He was elected as school president in the ninth grade, but there were parents of other students who were unhappy with his election, which forced the student government to disband for the year. He also received the distinction of being the valedictorian of Hollywood High School and winner of a local oratorical contest. But his achievements were usurped by having to choose between the valedictory honor or participating in an oratorical contest he had won, which would have given him the chance to compete at the national finals. He finally decided to withdraw from the contest. After his high school graduation he attended Saijo Gakuen in Tokyo, Japan, and studied Japanese. After one year, he returned to the United States to attend Brown University. He graduated cum laude in 1931, attended Harvard Law School (1934), and followed this with postgraduate law studies at Chuo University in Japan in 1936.

Returning to the United States after his studies in Japan, he was drafted in December 1940 and ordered to report for duty in April 1941. He was a private second class and assigned to a company that repaired trucks. At this time, the army was considering forming a school that would focus on training intelligence officers in Japanese language. Lieutenant Colonel John Weckerling and Captain Kai Rasmussen began a search for Army soldiers who had knowledge of the Japanese language. Aiso was recruited to the school as a student and was later promoted to assistant instructor and finally head instructor.

He became the most important and influential academic leader in the school, not only because of his language skills and legal training, but because he understood the unique circumstances of the Nisei and Kibei who were recruited for the program. He knew they were challenged to prove themselves as Americans because their loyalty was in question. His early experiences with prejudice made him build a class of language specialists that would help to win the war. More than 6,000 students attended and graduated from this school. They later served as translators and interpreters in the Pacific Theater during World War II. When Aiso left active duty in 1947, he had attained the rank of lieutenant colonel.

Aiso's career trajectory took him back to the legal field, where he practiced general law and was appointed commissioner of the Los Angeles Superior Court in 1952, followed by an appointment as a judge of the municipal court a year later. Shortly afterward, in 1953, he was appointed judge of the Superior Court of Los Angeles County. He was appointed by California governor Ronald Reagan as an associate justice of the California Court of Appeals for the Second Appellate District. After leaving the courts in 1972, he joined as special counsel the law firm of O'Melveny and Myers. Tragically, Aiso was killed by a mugger in 1987.

Sources: Tad Ichinokuchi, ed., *John Aiso and the M.I.S.: Japanese-American Soldiers in the Military Intelligence Service, World War II* (Los Angeles: Military Intelligence Service Club of Southern California, 1988), pp. 4–35; Brian Niiya, ed., "John Fujio Aiso," in *Japanese American History: An A-to-Z Reference from 1868 to the Present* (New York: Facts on File, 1991).

Karl R. Bendetsen (1907–1989)

Karl Robin Bendetsen was appointed by General John DeWitt, commander of the West Coast Defense Command, to direct the evacuation of Japanese from the West Coast. He played an instrumental role in the evacuation process and the formation of the relocation centers.

Bendetsen was born in Aberdeen, Washington, in 1907. He was educated at local public schools and later attended Stanford University and Law School in California, graduating with a B.A. in 1929 and an LL.B. in 1932. He returned to Washington State to practice general corporate, tax, and real estate law. Later, his law practice turned to the logging, lumber, and mining industries. He was a member of the Washington State National Guard from 1921 to 1924 and the field artillery branch of the U.S. Army Officers' Reserve Corps from 1929 to 1940. In 1941, he was called into active serve as a captain in the field artillery, and later became a special assistant of the U.S. secretary of war to Douglas Mac-Arthur.

Bendetsen describes his role in the evacuation as one in which he "conceived method, formulated details and directed evacuation of 120,000 persons of Japanese ancestry from military areas." He believed that the problem with enemy aliens in the United States was limited to the Japanese, not Germans or Italians, and that both citizens and enemy aliens were suspect. He stated, "[B]y far the vast majority of those who have studied the Oriental assert that a substantial majority of Nisei bear allegiance to Japan, are well controlled and disciplined by the enemy, and at the proper time will engage in organized sabotage, particularly, should a raid along the Pacific Coast be attempted by the Japanese" (CWRIC, 1982: 78).

Bendetsen's first orders were for the Bainbridge Island (Seattle) Japanese American community. After this group was removed, there was a period of "voluntary evacuation," which allowed people of Japanese ancestry to move from the restricted area of the West Coast Defense Command to areas inland. During the "voluntary" resettlement period of evacuation, he felt it was not the army's responsibility to provide food and housing for these voluntary resettlers; otherwise too many might take up the opportunity for free food and living. He was quoted as saying that the army's primary job "is to kill Japanese not to save Japanese." If the army was involved with the resettlement issues, it would divert much-needed resources away from winning the war (CWRIC, 1982: 101).

Although Bendetsen may have had a distinguished military career, and was a successful businessman and lawyer, he left his legacy with the evacuation and internment program of 1942. Unlike some of the other government and military officials who supported the decision to evacuate the Japanese and later regretted their decision, Bendetsen firmly believed that it was the right thing to do and that there was no loss of liberty or civil rights by the government's decision to forcibly remove and intern people of Japanese ancestry. In a 1984 letter to historian Sandra C. Taylor, Bendetsen continued to defend the government's decisions:

Executive Order 9066 of President Roosevelt interned no one. Persons of Japanese ancestry were excluded from remaining in the military frontier of the Pacific Coast. All such people were free to relocate any place they chose in the United States (other than in the frontier). Thousands did so relocate themselves. The Army helped them to do so. Any and all persons of Japanese ancestry in relocation centers were free to move anywhere in the United States they chose other than the war frontier. Many of them remained in the relocation centers wholly by choice. They could leave during the day to work for compensation in private employment. Thousands did so. They had free board and room. They had free medical care. Their children were educated, many through college degrees. They were not interned. (quoted in Daniels et al., 1991: 215–6)

Sources: Roger Daniels, Sandra C. Taylor, and Harry H. L. Kitano, "Letter from Karl R. Bendetsen to Sandra C. Taylor" in *Japanese Americans from Relocation to Redress*, rev. ed., (Seattle: University of Washington Press, 1991); *Who's Who in America, 1946–1947* (Chicago: A. N. Marquis Company, 1946), p. 73.

Francis Beverley Biddle (1886–1968)

Frances Biddle was U.S. attorney general under President Roosevelt at the time of the Japanese American evacuation and internment. He was born in Paris, France, son of an upper-class Philadelphia family, and educated at The Haverford College Grammar School and graduated from Groton Academy. He entered Harvard and graduated in 1909, followed by a law degree in 1911. His first job was as the personal secretary to Associate Justice Oliver Wendell Holmes for the 1911–1912 Supreme Court. Holmes profoundly influenced Biddle's political and social leanings.

After his work with the justice, Biddle entered the family law practice. Politically, he was a Republican, but he grew increasingly disenchanted with the party's politics. He campaigned for Progressive Party candidate Theodore Roosevelt in 1912 and was a delegate to the 1916 Progressive Party convention. But the Progressive ticket did not hold Biddle for long, as it endorsed the Republican candidate, and Biddle left.

Biddle received training as an artillery officer during World War I, but the armistice was signed and he was discharged before he saw any fighting. He went back to his law practice, representing a number of different clients, including the Dionne quintuplets and the Pennsylvania Railroad. He even found time to write a novel about Philadelphia's high society.

As the United States entered the Great Depression, Biddle was disillusioned by the Republicans' ability to pull the nation out of its economic troubles. He campaigned against Herbert Hoover. Now a devotee of the Roosevelt administration, he was appointed as the first chairman of the National Labor Relations Board. Throughout the 1930s Biddle moved in and out of public service, serving as legal counsel for a committee investigating the Tennessee Valley Authority, the U.S. Court of Appeals for the Third Circuit, U.S. Solicitor General, and finally, U.S. attorney general in 1941. As part of Roosevelt's team of advisers, Biddle was reluctant to implement the wartime evacuation orders of Japanese Americans from the West Coast of the United States, but did not actively seek to prevent the military orders from being issued. In his biography he wrote,

American citizens of Japanese origin were not even handled like aliens of the other enemy nationalities—Germans and Italians—on a selective basis, but as untouchables, a group who could not be trusted and had to be shut up only *because* they were of Japanese descent.

I thought at the time that the program was ill-advised, unnecessary, and un-necessarily cruel, taking Japanese who were not suspect, and Japanese Americans whose rights were disregarded, from their homes and from their businesses to sit idly in the lonely misery of barracks while the war was being fought in the world beyond. (Biddle, 1962: 212–3)

Although Biddle might have disagreed with the intent of the evacuation orders, he nonetheless, did not take an active role in preventing the mass incarceration of people of Japanese ancestry. In the end, he concluded that public opinion played a large role in the decision to evacuate the Japanese, and that individuals both in the War Department and the military were largely influenced by these attitudes.

Source: Frances Biddle, *In Brief Authority* (New York: Doubleday 1962); "Frances Beverley Biddle" in *Dictionary of American Biography* (New York: Charles Scribner's Sons, 1996).

Wayne M. Collins (1900–1974)

Wayne Mortimer Collins was a lawyer whose work spanned a number of different, yet related, challenges to the Japanese American evacuation and internment. He was a strong and passionate supporter of civil rights and pursued cases for those he felt had been wronged. He represented Fred Korematsu in his challenge of the government's evacuation orders. Collins was brought on to Fred Korematsu's case by Korematsu's original attorney, Edward Besig. He also represented Iva Ikuko Toguri D'Aquino, also known as Tokyo Rose. Finally, he was also the attorney for those Japanese Americans who renounced their citizenship and were being held at the Tule Lake Segregation Center, and Japanese Peruvians who were brought into the United States and held without trial at Justice Department prison camps during the war.

Collins was born in Sacramento, and raised and educated in San Francisco. Among his work with Japanese Americans during the war, Collins was instrumental in getting the stockade at the Tule Lake Segregation Center closed. The stockade was a "prison within a prison" and used as a form of punishment to house "troublemakers"—anyone who disbeyed camp policies—preventing any form of protest against the camp administration or authorities. Also at Tule Lake were a number of renunciants, Nisei who had decided to give up their U.S. citizenship and would be repatriated back to Japan. Collins believed that many of them did this under pressure from pro-Japan segregationist groups within the Tule Lake Center, that the center administration did nothing to stop this coercion, and that the conditions of the Tule Lake Center forced people to make decisions when they did not actually want to give up their U.S. citizenship. Against the objections of the National American Civil Liberties Union (for whom he worked), he decided to represent the renunciants. Collins worked for fourteen years to get the renunciants' citizenship rights restored.

Following the war, Collins worked on behalf of 365 Peruvian Japanese who were to be deported to Japan. They were in a terribly difficult international situation: they had been brought to the United States as prisoners and held as hostages at Justice Department camps to be used as potential bargaining chips for American prisoners of war. After having been detained in U.S. Department of Justice internment camps, they were not allowed back into Peru. Collins worked to get their release, and eventually several hundred were allowed to leave the camp and resettle in Seabrook Farms, New Jersey.

Author Michi Weglyn, who wrote *Years of Infamy: The Untold Story of America's Concentration Camps*, writes in her dedication, "Wayne M. Collins: Who Did More to Correct a Democracy's Mistake Than Any Other One Person."

Sources: Brian Niiya, ed., "Wayne M. Collins" in *Japanese American History: An A-to-Z Reference from 1868 to the Present* (New York: Facts on File, 1991); Michi Weglyn, *Years of Infamy* (New York: William Morrow, 1976).

John Lesesne DeWitt (1890–1964)

General John L. DeWitt was commander of the Fourth Army at the time of Pearl Harbor and became head of the Western Defense Command. He was the top military official in charge of the evacuation and internment of Japanese Americans from the West Coast. He was born in 1880 at Fort Sidney, Nebraska. A career military man, he left Princeton University to join the army in 1898, serving in the Spanish-American War. While in the army, he established himself as a supply officer, working in the office of the quartermaster general in Washington, D.C., from 1914 to 1917, and later as the director of supply and transportation for the First Army in France during World War I. He was not a combat soldier, but had a solid, undistinguished career, finally leading to his appointment as quartermaster general in 1930. He did several tours of the Philippines. Following his fourth tour of duty there, he held an administrative post as a commandant of the Army War College. His post to the Presidio of San Francisco as commander of the Fourth Army in 1939 were to be his final years before retirement.

Once the United States entered the war, DeWitt's position and influence as head of the Western Defense Command became critical. This area housed the largest numbers of people of Japanese descent outside the Hawaiian Islands. As early as December 19, 1941, DeWitt recommended that there be some form of removal or evacuation of enemy aliens from the Western Defense Command. Initially, he did not distinguish between different enemy aliens of Japanese, German, or Italian origin, but over time, it became clear that he felt it was necessary to restrict and contain both aliens and American citizens of Japanese ancestry. The result was the evacuation and internment program directed and carried out by the army, later to be administered by the Department of Interior's War Relocation Authority.

Source: Peter Irons, *Justice at War* (New York: Oxford University Press, 1983).

Milton S. Eisenhower (1899–1985)

Milton Stover Eisenhower was the first director of the War Relocation Authority, the civilian agency under the Department of Interior designed to administer the ten Japanese American relocation centers or internment camps. He came from working in the Department of Agriculture and was the brother of Dwight D. Eisenhower, a ranking military official during the war. This close relation made his appointment to the position as director of the WRA seem appropriate.

Before the movement to assembly centers began, the WRA supported a "voluntary resettlement" plan to move Japanese Americans from the West Coast areas. When voluntary resettlement was ended by Public Proclamation 4 on March 27, 1942, Eisenhower's plan was to have a more organized flow of Japanese move from the West Coast restricted areas to inland settlements and have them work on agricultural projects as a means of sustaining the population. He needed the support of government officials from the receiving states to accept Japanese resettlers. Governors from these states protested these plans, including military official Colonel Karl R. Bendetsen, who believed the Japanese could not be trusted. The alternate proposal was to move Japanese into the "relocation centers" and build sustainable communities with agriculture and other industries, where the population could be monitored and controlled.

Regretting the entire evacuation and relocation programs, Eisenhower wrote in his 1974 memoirs, "I have brooded about this whole episode on and off for the past three decades, for it is illustrative of how an entire society can somehow plunge off course." He was never in full agreement with the army official's ideas regarding the Japanese evacuation and was WRA director for only three short months, leaving before the opening of all the permanent relocation centers.

Sources: Milton S. Eisenhower, *The President Is Calling* (New York: Doubleday, 1974); Peter Irons, *Justice at War: The Story of the Japanese American Internment Cases* (New York: Oxford University Press, 1983).

Edward J. Ennis (1907–1990)

Edward Ennis was an attorney assigned to the U.S. Department of Justice and head of the Alien Enemy Control Unit. His role in the evacuation and internment programs was twofold. As the lawyer for the Justice Department, he, like Attorney General Francis Biddle, opposed the formation of internment camps, believing that they were unconstitutional. Unfortunately, his viewpoint was overshadowed by the more powerful presidential cabinet members from the War Department, Henry Stimson and John J. McCloy. He did not have the power to keep the president from signing Executive Order 9066.

Although opposed to the camps, he was head of the Justice Department's program to detain enemy aliens in the United States. Immediately after Pearl Harbor, the Justice Department arrested alien (noncitizen) Japanese, Germans, and Italians living in the United States, without evidence of any wrongdoing on their part. These individuals were granted hearings to determine their "loyalty" to the United States. More than half of the Germans and Italians were released following the hearings. Most of the Japanese continued to be detained during the war.

After working with the Justice Department, Ennis worked for the American Civil Liberties Union as general council from 1955 to 1969, and from 1969 to 1977 he served as president.

Source: Brian Niiya, ed., "Edward Ennis" in *Japanese American History: An A-to-Z Reference from 1868 to the Present* (New York: Facts on File, 1991).

Saburo Kido (1902–1977)

Saburo Kido was one of the founding members of the Japanese American Citizens League (JACL) and an instrumental leader during the period of the Japanese American internment. He was president of the JACL when Pearl Harbor was bombed. Kido was born in Hilo, Hawaii, and educated in Hawaii, but at the age of nineteen, he went to San Francisco to attend Hastings College of Law, earning his degree in 1926. He began practicing law in San Francisco's Japantown.

In 1926, he met another Nisei, Tom Yatabe, who founded the American Loyalty League. Both were concerned about the discrimination Nisei were subjected to, despite the fact that they were American citizens. Kido went on to co-found the San Francisco New American Citizens League in 1928. One of the first conferences in the United States for Nisei was held in 1929.

In Seattle in 1930, several Japanese American organizations merged to form the Japanese American Citizens League, or JACL. In 1940, Kido was elected president of the JACL, and he hired a young Nisei from Utah, Mike Masaoka. Together, Kido and Masaoka served in the top leadership positions in the JACL and shaped the JACL's stand on the wartime evacuation. The organization pledged their full support and co-operation to the war effort, as revealed in both their testimony before the Tolan Committee, and a letter that Kido sent to President Roosevelt immediately after Pearl Harbor.

Kido's address to the emergency JACL meeting in San Francisco on March 8, 1942, illustrates the gravity of the wartime situation for Japanese Americans (Document 2). He expressed his concern about the Japanese American population, reiterating the JACL position of cooperating with military and government authorities. By doing so, the Japanese would show their citizenship and loyalty during the time of national crisis.

Not everyone within the Japanese American community has agreed with the JACL stand of cooperation and compliance with the government during the war. Although Kido and his family could have voluntarily resettled outside of the West Coast restricted areas, he decided to evacuate with his family. They were sent to Poston, but since it was well known that he was a JACL leader, and because of the organization's stand of cooperation with the government during the evacuation and internment, he was injured in an assault by a Kibei who disagreed with him. Despite this, after the war, Kido continued to remain active in the JACL.

Sources: See Bill Hosokawa, *JACL in Quest of Justice: The History of the Japanese American Citizens League* (New York: William Morrow, 1982); and *Nisei: The Quiet Americans* (New York: William Morrow, 1969); Brian Niiya, ed., "Saburo Kido" in *Japanese American History: An A-to-Z Reference from 1868 to the Present* (New York: Facts on File, 1991).

Charles Kikuchi (1916–1988)

Charles Kikuchi is best known for his contributions as a research assistant for the Japanese American Evacuation Research Study (JERS). He was attending the University of California, Berkeley, at the time of the evacuation and was sent to live at Tanforan Assembly Center. His affiliation with Berkeley connected him with Dorothy Swaine Thomas, who was the director of JERS. Thus, while at Tanforan and later when he was transferred to the Gila Relocation Center (Arizona) he continued to collect information on behalf of JERS.

Kikuchi was born in Vallejo, California, second of eight children. Because of family problems, he grew up in a Salvation Army orphanage.

When he reached eighteen, he left the orphans home and attended San Francisco State College. He graduated in 1939, but like many college-educated Nisei, had difficulty finding a job. At the outbreak of World War II he was living in Berkeley as a graduate student in social welfare at the University of California, Berkeley.

Some of Kikuchi's work is noted in *The Kikuchi Diary* (1973), an account of his experiences before the time he and his family were evacuated to Tanforan Assembly Center. Kikuchi was one of the early "resettlers," leaving camp to live in the Chicago area in 1943. He continued his research by collecting life histories of the Nisei resettlers, which appear in the second series of the JERS study, *The Salvage* (Berkeley: University of California Press, 1952). For a brief time, Kikuchi was in the military, serving just before the bombing of Hiroshima. He was honorably discharged and continued working toward his graduate degree, enrolling at the New York School of Social Work and receiving his Masters of Social Work degree in 1947. He worked as a clinical social worker for twenty-three years for the Veterans Administration in New York.

Kikuchi's contributions to the research on internment camps has often been overlooked since he never had full authorship of any book about the internment camp experience. His diary, published in 1973, touches upon the difficulties faced by Nisei during the wartime. He collected sixty-four life histories that are highlighted in *The Salvage*. His work as a researcher was notable because he gathered information under a wide range of circumstances—in an assembly center, at a relocation center, and outside of camp in Chicago. His diary captures the social and emotional turmoil felt by many Nisei during the evacuation and internment period.

Source: Charles Kikuchi, *The Kikuchi Diary: Chronicles of an American Concentration Camp*, edited and with an introduction by John Modell (Urbana and Chicago: University of Illinois Press, 1973).

Dorothea Lange (1895–1965)

Dorothea Margaretta Nutzhorn, better known as Dorothea Lange, worked for the War Relocation Authority as a photographer and documented the evacuation and internment of Japanese Americans.

She was born in Hoboken, New Jersey, daughter of Heinrich (Henry) Martin Nutzhorn and Joanna (Joan) Caroline Lange. After her parents divorced in 1912, she lived with her mother in Manhattan's Lower East Side in New York City. This neighborhood gave her a chance to live, work, and observe an immigrant ethnic enclave. She graduated from high school in 1913 and briefly attended the New York Training School for Teachers before she finally decided she wanted to become a photographer. She apprenticed to photographer Arnold Genthe, who taught her candid and portraiture work. She was also able to study photography with Columbia University's Clarence H. White. Photography was just coming to be recognized as an artistic medium that captured images in a different way from painting and other forms of illustration. As she became further professionalized as a photographer, she adopted her mother's maiden name in 1918 and became known as Dorothea Lange.

Lange was best known for her portraiture work on displaced rural farmworkers during the Great Depression. In 1920, she married artist Maynard Dixon, twenty years older than her. She was a well-known and successful portrait photographer. On one of her many trips with her husband to the Southwest (the subject of his paintings) she began to take pictures of people with a more realistic tone and feel. Later, these became known as documentary photographs. Throughout the Great Depression she worked with several photographers focusing on documentary photography. She worked with economist Paul Schuster Taylor on farm laborers throughout California, and eventually they both went to work for the Rural Rehabilitation Division of the Federal Emergency Relief Administration (FERA). Later, Taylor and Lange married.

At the outbreak of World War II, Lange had just received a prestigious Guggenheim Fellowship for photography. She resigned and in 1942 joined the War Relocation Authority to document the evacuation and internment of Japanese Americans. Lange captured some of the most enduring images of Japanese Americans during the evacuation, relocation, and internment period. Beyond traditional portraitures, she documented the day-to-day living and activities of thousands of Japanese as they struggled to create lives confined by barbed wire. Thousands of her photographs catalog the wartime experience of Japanese Americans. Undoubtedly, her views about the mass evacuation and incarceration show up in the photographs she took. Her images often juxtaposed the human side and the courage of the people who were being moved, with their harsh living conditions and the inhumanity of living within barbed wire. Because of this, many of Lange's photos were censored by the government and never shown in a public venue.

Many years later, these photographs were exhibited in 1972 at the Whitney Museum, and then published in a book about the relocation titled *Executive Order 9066* (1973). Most of her photographic work is considered part of the public domain and can be accessed through the National Archives and Records Administration, Photograph and Print Division. Other portions of her work not dealing directly with Japanese Americans can be found at the Oakland Museum in California.

Source: "Dorothea Lange" in *Dictionary of American Biography* (New York: Charles Scribner's Sons, 1996).

Mike M. Masaoka (1915–1991)

Mike Masaru Masaoka was a Japanese American community leader and an influential member of the Japanese American Citizens League, for which he was a lobbyist. He was one of eight children born to Eijiro and Haruye Masaoka, in California in 1915. His family moved to Salt Lake City, Utah, in 1918. They owned a grocery store and fish market in the city's small Japantown. When he was nine years old, his father was killed in an accident, and the young Masaoka and his siblings were forced to grow up quickly to support their mother and the family.

Masaoka was educated in public schools and attended the University of Utah, graduating with a bachelor's degree in 1937. In 1938, he became involved with the fledgling Japanese American Citizens League (JACL). He attended the national convention in Los Angeles that year. From there he decided to form a group of Japanese Americans in Utah called the Intermountain District Council, becoming their president in 1939. Shortly afterward, the council was accepted as a chapter of the national JACL. His leadership and organizational savvy found him a job with the JACL as its first executive secretary in 1941, and he worked as a lobbyist in Washington, D.C., on its behalf.

Masaoka has been a controversial figure within the Japanese American community. During the war, Masaoka, as a representative of the JACL, agreed to fully cooperate with the authorities should the government decide to evacuate people of Japanese ancestry from the West Coast. He believed that Nisei should prove their loyalty to the United States and was one of the first to volunteer for the 442nd Regimental Combat team when it was formed. He authored the patriotic "Japanese American Creed" that has been espoused by the national JACL.

Even since his death in 1991, Masaoka has remained a controversial figure. The National Mall in Washington, D.C., is building a monument to the Japanese American experience during World War II. The monument contains inscriptions from various Japanese Americans, one of whom is Mike Masaoka. Part of the proposed inscription is taken from the "Japanese American Creed" written in 1940 for the Japanese American Citizens League. It reads, "I am proud that I am an American of Japanese ancestry. I believe in her institutions, ideals and traditions; I glory in her heritage; I boast of her history; I trust in her future."

That his name and statement will be inscribed on the monument has caused a great deal of controversy among those Japanese Americans who feel that it is inappropriate, and that Masaoka himself did not accurately represent the sentiment of all the people of Japanese ancestry incarcerated in the wartime camps.

Whatever controversy Masaoka has engendered, his life was marked by achievements and contributions as a Japanese American and to the history of Japanese in America.

Sources: Mike M. Masaoka, *They Call Me Moses Masaoka* (New York: William Morrow, 1987); Brian Niiya, ed., "Mike Masaoka" in *Japanese American History: An A-to-Z Reference from 1868 to the Present* (New York: Facts on File, 1991).

John J. McCloy (1895–1989)

John Jay McCloy Jr. was assistant secretary of war in the Roosevelt cabinet. He was born in Philadelphia and educated at Amherst College and Harvard Law School (1921). He went to New York and first joined the firm of Cadwalader, Wichersham, and Taft. By 1929, he had become partner in the firm of Carvath, Henderson and de Gersdoff. His work with this firm drew the attention of Henry Stimson, Roosevelt's secretary of war, and he was first appointed as a consultant to army intelligence. In 1941, he became Stimson's assistant secretary.

While working with Stimson, it was important that the War Department present a united front in their advising the president of the necessity for the evacuation and internment programs. After Pearl Harbor, McCloy strongly advocated for the evacuation of Japanese Americans from the West Coast, and acted to administer the program once Executive Order 9066 was signed by President Roosevelt. While McCloy actively worked to support the orders, he is also believed to have moderated the restrictiveness of the internment program by allowing for individual exemptions as well as creating work furloughs that allowed individuals to leave the camp. He was also a strong supporter of creating the all-Nisei military unit, the 442nd Regimental Combat Team.

After serving in the Roosevelt cabinet, McCloy was president of the World Bank and remained active in the public arena, serving as an adviser to both Republican and Democratic presidents following Roosevelt. He also served on the controversial Warren Commission, which issued the official investigation of President John F. Kennedy's assassination.

Throughout his lifetime, McCloy stood firmly beside his beliefs in the military necessity of the evacuation and relocation programs. In a letter to Jane B. Kaihatsu, he stated,

I firmly believe that with the knowledge we now have and which, at the time, was available to the President of the U.S. of the existence of subversive agencies along the West Coast, that the relocation method against the Japanese was a good reason why serious acts of sabotage did not occur on the West Coast after the President's order was given. I believe it was the effectiveness of the relocation order which added to the security of the West Coast and indirectly to the security of the country as a whole. (Daniels et al., 1991: 214)

Sources: Roger Daniels, Sandra C. Taylor, and Harry H. L. Kitano, eds., "Letter from John J. McCloy to Jane B. Kaihatsu" in *Japanese Americans: From Relocation to Redress*, rev. ed., (Seattle: University of Washington Press, 1991); "John Jay McCloy, Jr.," *American National Biography* (New York: Oxford, 1999).

Dillon S. Myer (1891–1982)

Dillon S. Myer was the second director of the War Relocation Authority, a division of the Department of the Interior that administered the relocation centers for Japanese Americans. He was born in Hebron, Ohio, raised in the Midwest, and attended Ohio State University, majoring in agronomy (a soil management and crop production science). He graduated in 1914 and shortly afterward began a career as a government worker in the agricultural area. He was assistant chief of the Soil Conservation Service in 1938. When Milton S. Eisenhower resigned as director of the WRA in 1942, Myer was recommended as his successor.

Myer followed a path similar to many other government officials of the time. Like Eisenhower, he was influenced by the New Deal politics. He has often been described as a man of "courageous and inspired leadership" and as a "champion of human rights and common decency" (according to the Japanese American Citizens League citation on May 22, 1946).

Recent scholarship about the chief director of the WRA has reconceptualized his role in the assimilation and Americanization process of Japanese Americans, and the questionable treatment of "troublemakers"— individuals who protested or organized around the conditions in the camps, draft resisters, or "disloyals" and pro-Japanese factions in the WRA Relocation Centers (Drinnon, 1987; Weglyn, 1976). Historian Richard Drinnon depicts Myer as someone who used various factions within the camps to keep disturbances and troublemakers at bay. Drinnon's treatment of Myer draws a comparative analysis with Myer's position as director of the Bureau of Indian Affairs, a job he had after the closing of the WRA camps. Until his death, Myer steadfastly believed that the government was justified in its actions during World War II and that the mass incarceration was necessary. Not surprisingly, then, he opposed efforts toward monetary redress after the war.

Source: Richard Drinnon, *Keeper of the Concentration Camps: Dillon S. Myer and American Racism* (Berkeley: University of California Press, 1987); Dillon S. Myer, *Uprooted Ameri-*

cans: The Japanese Americans and the War Relocation Authority during World War II (Tucson: University of Arizona Press, 1971); Michi Weglyn, *Years of Infamy: The Untold Story of America's Concentration Camps* (New York: William Morrow, 1976).

Frank Murphy (1880–1949)

Supreme Court Justice Frank Murphy wrote strong opinions in the Korematsu and Hirabayashi cases. Frank Murphy was born in Harbor Beach, Michigan, educated in public schools, and received an LL.B. from the University of Michigan in 1914. He joined a Detroit law firm that served as counsel to the city's employer association. Murphy attended Reserve Officers Training Camp and was commissioned as a first lieutenant. He served in France without seeing combat, and in Germany under occupation.

Murphy served in a number of political positions before being appointed to the Supreme Court. He served as assistant U.S. attorney for Michigan's Eastern District. He ran for Congress once in 1920, but was defeated. He was in a highly successful law practice, and also taught law at the University of Detroit and Detroit College of Law.

Murphy was Roosevelt's fifth appointment to the Supreme Court. Although his appointment was well accepted by those outside the Court, Murphy was not a legal scholar. He did bring to the Court the experience of being a trial judge. During his tenure, he was known for his decisions as well as dissents in the field of civil liberties.

Murphy's viewpoints become clear in the cases of Gordon Hirabayashi and Fred Korematsu. In the case of Hirabayashi, he had originally written a dissent, but pressured to have a unanimous court decision in the final vote, he sided with the majority. Interestingly, in his opinion, elements of his dissent were still written in, stating that the Court bore "a melancholy resemblance to the treatment accorded to the members of the Jewish race in Germany" and that the Court's decision "goes to the very brink of constitutional power." Murphy dissented in *Korematsu* v. *United States* 323 U.S. 214 (1944), insisting that the majority decision was a "legalization of racism." Murphy died of heart disease in 1949.

Source: Peter Irons, *Justice at War: The Story of the Japanese American Internment Cases* (New York: Oxford University Press, 1983).

Richard Nishimoto (1904–1956)

Richard Nishimoto was interned at Poston Relocation Center and was a researcher with the Japanese American Evacuation and Resettlement Study (JERS). He co-authored (with Dorothy Swaine Thomas) *The Spoilage,* a study of Japanese American camp life. His job as researcher for the JERS project was to conduct ethnographic and sociological observations of camp life. Born in Tokyo, Japan, he was educated through middle school there. When he was seventeen years old, he emigrated to the United States in 1921 to join his parents in San Francisco. He attended Lowell High School between 1921 and 1925, then Stanford University between 1925 and 1929. While he earned a bachelor's degree in engineering, he also took classes in economics, political science, psychology, and sociology.

Nishimoto was married to Yae Imae in 1931 and moved to Los Angeles. He first worked as a partner in a Japanese grocery store, but soon found himself an owner-operator of a fruit and vegetable market in Gardena, California. At the outbreak of the war, Nishimoto and his family were evacuated and sent to Poston, Arizona. Poston was known as the Colorado River War Relocation Center, on the California-Arizona border seventeen miles south of the town of Parker. Poston was the second largest in population of all WRA camps. Within it, there was active research conducted by sociologist Thomas, that could not have been done without the Japanese American research assistants in the field to do the observations and analyses.

Nishimoto's role as a researcher has only recently been acknowledged by academic audiences. Because he was not formally trained in sociological and anthropological research methods (although he did have a college degree), his role in the collection, analysis, and writing of the data has been underplayed. Yet he was an invaluable part of the research studies done by sociologists in the camps. His working knowledge of camp life, and Japanese American and Japanese culture, made him a valuable "insider" to the research process. Indeed, the principal researcher Dorothy Swaine Thomas relied on Nishimoto, as he was co-author of *The Spoilage*. She also relied upon his insights and knowledge for the subsequent books of the JERS series, *The Salvage* (Berkeley: University of California Press, 1952), and tenBroek et al., *Prejudice, War, and the Constitution* (Berkeley: University of California Press, 1968).

Sources: See Lane Ryo Hirabayashi's introduction and afterword of Richard S. Nishimoto's writings, *Inside an American Concentration Camp, Japanese American Resistance at Poston, Arizona* by Richard S. Nishimoto (Tucson: University of Arizona Press, 1995).

Chiura Obata (1885–1975)

Issei artist Chiura Obata founded the Tanforan Art School at the Tanforan Assembly Center and the Topaz Art School in Utah. Born in Sendai, Japan, Zoroku Obata chose the name Chiura as his artist name. He grew up as the only child of an artist, and began training in sumi (ink) painting at a young age. Chiura had a rebellious spirit and ran away from home when his father threatened to send him to military school.

He eventually apprenticed himself to a master painter in Tokyo. He came to San Francisco at the age of eighteen in 1903. He worked as a "school-boy" doing domestic work while studying English. He met Haruko Kohashi through mutual friends in San Francisco's Japantown, and they were married in 1912.

The Obatas had four children and settled in San Francisco, where Chiura continued painting and formed the East West Art Society, a group of Japanese, American, Russian, and Chinese artists. In 1928, Obata's father died, and he and his family returned to Japan. As the only son, it was his responsibility to carry on his father's legacy as an artist and teacher. Two years later, and missing California, the family returned to the United States. He taught at University of California, Berkeley, in the 1930s, first as a lecturer, then later as an assistant professor, despite the fact that he did not have a college degree and was not fluent in English.

Obata's founding of the Tanforan and Topaz art schools was guided by his belief that art and the creative mind could lift individual spirits. He said,

[T]his is wartime, and there is suffering for everyone, and one cannot think of individual well-being only. We must all work together for greater constructive peace in the future. In order to bring out such peace we must educate all the people. We feel that art is one of the most constructive forms of education. Sincere creative endeavoring, especially in these stressing times, I strongly believe will aid in developing a sense of calmness and appreciation which is so desirable and following it come sound judgment and a spirit of cooperation. In such manner I feel that the general morale of the people will be uplifted. (quoted in Hill, 2000: 38)

Today, more than 200 pieces Obata's artwork survive as creative documentation and expression of the Japanese experience with incarceration. The images show the resiliency and creativity of Japanese Americans and can be thought of as a creative lens through which we can view the perceptions and emotions of people of Japanese ancestry during the period of their forced incarceration. According to his granddaughter Kimi Kodani Hill, "Obata's artwork serves as an enduring testament to the spirit of people surviving in the face of adversity and expresses his gratitude to the natural beauty that sustained him 'as a mother heart comforts lost children.' "

Source: Kimi Kodani Hill, *Topaz Moon Chiura Obata's Art of the Internment* (Berkeley: HeyDey Books, 2000).

John Okada (1923–1971)

John Okada wrote *No-No Boy* in 1957. The novel was published by Charles Tuttle and Company and explored the controversial issue of loyalty within the Japanese American community during the war. It was not a success and was rejected by the Japanese American community. Okada was from Seattle, Washington, and was interned at Minidoka (Idaho). He left camp to attend college and afterward volunteered for the army. He was discharged in 1946 as a sergeant and later graduated from the University of Washington with a B.A. in English. He received an M.A. from Columbia University in 1949.

The novel centers around a protagonist named Ichiro. He is ostracized by his community because of his responses to the loyalty questionnaire. The novel looks at Ichiro's thoughts as he comes to terms with his decisions, but also his quest for identity and place in the United States. At the time of his death, Okada was believed to be almost finished with a second novel about an Issei protagonist. His family destroyed all of his papers following his death.

Asian American literary critics have lauded Okada for his forthrightness and dealing with an unpopular subject. They feel that his novel should be recognized as a classic in Asian American and American literature because of its important subject matter.

Sources: Brian Niiya, ed., "John Okada" in *Japanese American History: An A-to-Z Reference from 1868 to the Present* (New York: Facts on File, 1991); John Okada, *No-No Boy* (Rutherford, Vt.: Charles E. Tuttle, 1957; Seattle: University of Washington Press, 1979).

Mine Okubo (1912–2001)

Nisei artist Mine Okubo documented her experiences in camp with drawings and narrative published in her book *Citizen 13660*. Published in 1946 by Columbia University Press, hers was the first book about the camps by a Japanese American internee. She was born in Riverside, California, and educated at the University of California, Berkeley, graduating with a degree in art in 1936. In 1938, she received a scholarship that allowed her to travel and study in Europe. Sensing that war was imminent, she returned to the United States in 1939 and began painting murals for the Federal Arts Program throughout the San Francisco Bay area.

She was living in Berkeley, at the time of the evacuation. She and her brother went first to Tanforan Assembly Center in San Bruno, then later moved to the Topaz Relocation Center in Utah. At Tanforan, she joined the Tanforan Art School faculty. She must have been a popular role model for young girls at the art school, as Chiura Obata, founder of the Art School noted in his recollections:

I asked the youngest girl (six years old), "Do you like to learn to paint?" With smiles and sparkling eyes she responded, "Sure I do!" "Who is your teacher?" I asked. "Mine Okubo," she replied. The older girls standing by remarked, "Yes, she's pretty. I want to learn from her too." (quoted in Hill, 2000: 41)

Okubo's portfolio of camp drawings included more than 200 pen and ink drawings, as well as illustrations in charcoal and watercolor. In addition to being an art instructor, she drew for the Topaz literary magazine *Trek*. Staff members of New York's *Fortune* magazine saw her work, and she left camp in 1944 to resettle there and work for the magazine. She became a successful commercial artist whose work appeared in the *New York Times, Time,* and *Life*. She has had major exhibits at several galleries including the Mortimer Levitt Gallery, Image Gallery, Oakland Art Museum, and a forty-year retrospective at the Catherine Gallery and Basement Workshop in New York.

Sources: Brian Niiya, ed., "Mine Okubo," in *Japanese American History: An A-to-Z Reference from 1868 to the Present* (New York: Facts on File, 1991); Kimi Kodani Hill, *Topaz Moon* (Berkeley: Heyday Books, 2000); Mine Okubo, *Citizen 13660* (New York: Columbia University Press, 1946).

James Omura (1912–   )

Journalist James Omura was one of the few voices of opposition during the Tolan Hearings held shortly after the passage of Executive Order 9066. He was born in Seattle, Washington, and served as the English-language editor for a number of different Japanese-language newspapers in the United States. He was responsible for publishing the first Nisei magazine in the United States titled *Current Life* in October 1940. It was shortlived because of the bombing of Pearl Harbor, ceasing publication in January 1942.

Omura and his wife, Fumiko Okuma, were living in San Francisco at the time of the evacuation and voluntarily relocated to Denver, Colorado, before the evacuation order went into effect. In Colorado he worked at a number of different odd jobs, including helping to resettle other voluntary evacuees in the Denver area, and working in a munitions factory, as a gardener, and as a free-lance writer for Japanese-language newspapers in the Denver area. In 1944, he took a job with the *Rocky Shimpo* as the English-language editor.

He was best known for supporting the Heart Mountain draft resisters and their organization, the Heart Mountain Fair Play Committee, publishing controversial opinion pieces supporting their cause, and printing the committee's press releases. Because he supported the resisters, he was constantly in battle with the JACL's newspaper, *Pacific Citizen*, and the camp's newspaper, *The Heart Mountain Sentinel*. Because of his support, he was tried in 1944 along with leaders of the Fair Play Committee for counseling individuals to violate the Selective Service Act (draft). The members of the committee were found guilty, but Omura was acquitted in the charges.

Sources: Brian Niiya, ed., "James Omura" in *Japanese American History: An A-to-Z Reference from 1868 to the Present* (New York: Facts on File, 1991); also see Arthur A. Hansen, "James Matsumoto Omura: An Interview," in *Amerasia Journal* 13, 2 (1986–1987): 99–113.

Owen Josephus Roberts (1875–1955)

Owen J. Roberts was associate justice of the United States Supreme Court, ruling on the cases of Gordon Hirabayashi, Fred Korematsu, and Min Yasui. He was born in Philadelphia, Pennsylvania, and educated at the University of Pennsylvania, where he received his law degree. After law school, he joined the faculty of the university and taught bankruptcy, contracts, damages, and property, but never constitutional law. He published legal articles that drew much attention and led to his eventual appointment to a three-year term as the first assistant district attorney of Philadelphia County from 1901 to 1904. In 1930, Roberts, a Republican, was nominated by President Herbert Hoover and was unanimously confirmed to the Supreme Court.

Although generally cast as a conservative justice, he was known to be a liberal in terms of civil rights. In *Hirabayashi* 320 U.S. 81 (1943) and *Yasui* 320 U.S. 115 (1943), Roberts sided with the majority court opinion, which upheld the legality of the military curfew order. In the case of *Korematsu* 323 U.S. 214 (1944), he was one of the three justices (along with Justices Frank Murphy and Robert H. Jackson) who dissented. He stated,

I dissent, because I think the indisputable facts exhibit a clear violation of Constitutional rights. . . . it is the case of *convicting a citizen* as *punishment* for not submitting to imprisonment in a concentration camp, based on his ancestry, and solely because of his ancestry, without evidence or inquiry concerning his loyalty and good disposition towards the United States. (323 U.S. 214, 229 [1944])

Although Supreme Court appointments are lifelong until retirement, Roberts resigned from the Court to pursue other educational and philanthropic activities that were important to him. He remained in the Philadelphia area and died in 1955.

Franklin D. Roosevelt (1882–1945)

Franklin Delano Roosevelt was the thirty-second president of the United States and signed Executive Order 9066, which gave the military the power to evacuate and intern people of Japanese descent.

Born in New York, he was the only son of James Roosevelt and Sara Delano. As an only child, he grew up in a sheltered environment, protected by his wealth and class privilege. He later attended Groton Academy, a private boarding school in Massachusetts, then entered Harvard College in 1900. During his time at Harvard, he began to secretly court Eleanor Roosevelt, the niece of his distant cousin Theodore Roosevelt. They were married in 1905. Eleanor Roosevelt was known to be a champion of human and civil rights causes. Though she has often been cited as an influential first lady in her husband's domestic affairs, her role in the Japanese American internment is almost nonexistent. Whether for public relations, or out of genuine concern for the conditions of the Japanese Americans, she did, however, visit the Gila River (Arizona) camp in 1943.

Taking office in the midst of the greatest economic depression the country had ever experienced, Roosevelt pushed forward dramatic changes in legislation and government involvement that attempted to bring the country back into economic prosperity. Although often cited as a champion of the New Deal, people's rights, and bringing the nation together at a time of economic and social difficulty, his role in the mass removal and incarceration of Japanese has been downplayed. He has often been portrayed as a president concerned and struggling with the complex state of international affairs and war, with little time to think through the consequences of a mass civilian removal program. Indeed, he had surrounded himself with able politicians and military men, and he relied on them for direction and guidance in his domestic and foreign affairs. Thus, he was strongly influenced by their beliefs and viewpoints in ordering the mass evacuation, and did not see the potential negative repercussions or violations of civil liberties through his executive order. His role as chief executive officer and president in the evacuation and internment cannot be ignored. His signing of Executive Order 9066 was probably one of the few shortcomings of his presidency that overlooked and abrogated the civil rights of minorities.

Source: "Franklin Delano Roosevelt" in *Dictionary of American Biography* (New York: Charles Scribner's Sons, 1941–1945), Supplement Three.

James Y. Sakamoto (1903–1955)

James Yoshinori Sakamoto was a newspaper publisher and early founder of the Japanese American Citizens League (JACL). At the outbreak of the war, he founded the JACL Emergency Defense Council, a group formed to work with government authorities to monitor and report "subversive" activities within the Japanese American community. He testified before the Tolan Committee against the evacuation and relocation program, but in concert with other JACL leaders, agreed to cooperate with whatever the government wanted them to do.

Sakamato was born in Seattle and was a star athlete in baseball, judo, boxing, and football. He eventually moved to New York City to serve as the English editor for the *Japanese American News*. He also tried to pursue a career as a professional boxer and even fought at Madison Square Garden. In 1926, though, he suffered eye problems and began to go blind. He returned to Seattle.

As a Nisei, Sakamoto saw himself as an American. Given his beliefs and his former position as a journalist, in 1928, he founded the *Japanese American Courier*, an English-language newspaper. The *Courier* targeted a Japanese American audience and focused on local, national, and international news, and sports. Many of the editorials stressed Nisei adopting a "100 percent American" perspective, and he supported the formation of an organization composed of Japanese Americans who were U.S. citizens. Thus, he was an early supporter of the JACL and served as its national president from 1936 to 1938. The war broke out, the JACL leadership pledged their support to the government, and the *Courier* stopped publishing in 1942.

Sakamoto was evacuated to Tanforan Assembly Center. While there he was appointed as the chief supervisor and served as the liaison between the Japanese staff and the Caucasian personnel and administration. Because of this position, he and the staff who worked for him held great power within the assembly center leadership. After Tanforan, he was moved Minidoka (Idaho), where he was never able to reestablish the same power he had held at Tanforan. After camp, he returned to Seattle and was tragically killed by a car in 1955.

Source: Brian Niiya, ed., "James Sakamoto" in *Japanese American History: An A-to-Z Reference from 1868 to the Present* (New York: Facts on File, 1991).

Dorothy Swaine Thomas (1899–1977)

Sociologist Dorothy Swaine Thomas directed the Japanese American Evacuation and Resettlement Study (JERS). She was born in Baltimore, Maryland, daughter of John Knight Thomas and Sara Elizabeth Swaine. She attended Barnard College in New York City and majored in a joint program of economics and sociology, studying with William F. Ogburn. Ogburn urged her to become a quantitative social scientist. After graduating from Barnard, she attended the London School of Economics, where she received her doctorate in economics in 1924.

After her graduation, she worked for a short while at the Federal Reserve Bank, then received a postdoctoral fellowship from the Social Science Research Council. She also worked at Columbia University's Teacher College and Yale University's Institute for Human Relations. In 1926, she met sociologist W. I. Thomas and worked with him, and in 1935, they married. The Thomases collaborated on many research projects.

Thomas received tenure from the University of California, Berkeley, in 1940, just before the outbreak of World War II. As a professor of rural sociology, she was awarded a grant to study the evacuation, internment, and resettlement of Japanese Americans during World War II, later to be called the Japanese American Evacuation and Resettlement Study, or JERS. This study probably could not have been conducted if it were not for several Japanese American sociologists who were themselves interned at the relocation centers and assisted Thomas in interviewing residents and collecting oral histories. Her first book documenting and analyzing the Japanese American internment experience, *The Spoilage* (1946), is co-authored with Richard S. Nishimoto. Volume Two of the Japanese American Evacuation and Resettlement Study, *The Salvage* (1952), is written with the assistance of Charles Kikuchi and James Sakoda, two Japanese American research assistants who conducted interviews and research with her. Both of the books examine the internment and resettlement experiences of the Japanese American population using both qualitative (life histories) and quantitative (demographic) analyses. Written primarily toward an academic audience, her books capture the devastating effects of internment and reveal the struggles and difficulties that Japanese Americans underwent during the war years.

Source: Janice Roscoe, *Women in Sociology*, ed. Mary Jo Deegan (Westport, Conn.: Greenwood, 1991), pp. 400–8.

Tamie Tsuchiyama (1915–1984)

Tamie Tsuchiyama worked as a research assistant for the Japanese American Evacuation Research Study (JERS) at the Colorado River (Poston) Relocation Center in Arizona. She was the only professionally trained woman of Japanese descent trained as a fieldworker for JERS. Following her work in the field, in 1947 she became the first Japanese American woman to obtain a Ph.D. in sociocultural anthropology from the University of California, Berkeley.

Born on the island of Kauai, Hawaii, she was one of three children. After she finished high school in 1934, she enrolled at the University of Hawaii, Manoa, in Honolulu. Here she discovered her affinity for anthropology. In 1936, she left Hawaii to attend the University of California, Los Angeles (UCLA), where her sister was attending school. Unfortunately, UCLA had only one anthropologist with no formal department on the campus. Tsuchiyama left for the University of California, Berkeley, which had an established department and offered the degree she wanted. She excelled at Berkeley, studying with well-known anthropologists A. L. Kroeber, Robert Lowie, and Paul Radin. By 1941, she had completed her doctoral-level comprehensive exams. But the outbreak of war altered her path. She was hired by sociologist Dorothy Swaine Thomas to serve as a research assistant, studying the effects of the Japanese American relocation program.

Tsuchiyama moved into and lived at the Santa Anita Assembly Center, and later Poston. For two years she corresponded with Thomas about her observations and field reports from the two places. Although initially there was much collegiality between the two, by 1944, there were serious doubts within their relationship, and Tsuchiyama pulled away from the project just as Thomas was becoming critical of her work. After her falling out with Thomas, Tsuchiyama enlisted and became a private in the Women's Army Corps (WAC). She was assigned to the Military Intelligence Service at Fort Snelling, Minnesota. Her job, along with other female recruits, was to translate documents from Japanese to English. After the war, having received her doctorate in anthropology, she worked for a few years for the government in their Public Opinion and Sociological Research Division.

Dr. Tsuchiyama's work as an anthropologist and with the JERS study have largely gone unrecognized. Undoubtedly, her contributions have been overlooked because of the racial and gender-based biases of academic institutions at the time she was doing her studies. Yet her work was a vital, necessary, and important component for the large-scale studies about Japanese American internment conducted by social scientists during the war.

Source: Lane Ryo Hirabayashi, *The Politics of Fieldwork: Research in an American Concentration Camp* (Tucson: University of Arizona Press, 1999).

Rosalie Hankey Wax (1911–1998)

Anthropologist Rosalie Wax was a graduate student researcher hired by Dorothy Swaine Thomas with the Japanese American Evacuation and Research Study (JERS). Wax's job was to record and observe the effects of the so-called loyalty questionnaire on the residents of the center. She was to find out how the "loyals" felt about themselves and the so-called disloyals when the disloyals were moved out of the center to the Tule Lake Segregation Center. She began the process of participant observation in 1943, even though she had very little familiarity or knowledge about the Japanese American history, culture, and community.

She was born on November 11, 1911, in Des Plaines, Illinois. In 1930, she and her family left the Midwest and settled in a low-income Mexican American neighborhood in Los Angeles. The family struggled through the Great Depression, during which she did housework, received some public assistance, worked in Works Progress Administration jobs, and attended school. She was awarded a small scholarship to attend the University of California, Berkeley, in 1940, and graduated with a bachelor of arts in anthropology in 1942.

After the bombing of Pearl Harbor, Wax hoped to enter the military, but was rejected because of poor eyesight. She subsequently began to do graduate work at Berkeley. She was approached by Dorothy Swaine Thomas, then a professor of rural sociology, to do fieldwork on the Japanese Americans living at Gila Relocation Center in Arizona.

At first Wax found it difficult establishing rapport and gaining trust from within the Japanese American population. The "loyals" would not talk to her, so she decided to talk to the "disloyals" and how they felt about their situation. Eventually, the "disloyal" population was moved to the Tule Lake Segregation Center, and she lost contact with her informants. She visited Tule Lake throughout 1944, and finally moved there. After a year, the study ended and Wax left the center. In her book *Doing Fieldwork* (1971), she says she was sad to leave the field and felt a great sense of loss at the end of the project, especially after having developed a certain rapport with the segregated population of Japanese Americans.

After the war she moved to the University of Chicago and was a teaching assistant in the department of anthropology. In 1949, she married Murray Wax, a professor of sociology at the University of Chicago. She began work on her dissertation and received her doctor of philosophy degree in 1950. Her dissertation titled "The Development of Authoritarianism: A Study of the Japanese American Relocation Centers" was based upon her work as a participant observer in the Gila River and Tule Lake Relocation Centers.

Wax's career as an anthropologist took her throughout the United States. She was an assistant professor in the department of anthropology at the University of Chicago, the director of a series of workshops on American Indian affairs at the University of Colorado, and visiting lecturer at the University of Miami at Coral Gables. She and her husband studied education on the Oglala Sioux Indian Reservation in South Dakota, and she continued to be involved with Indian education projects throughout her career.

Although Wax made substantial contributions to the field of American Indian education, her fieldwork and research in the Japanese American internment camps has been questioned. As Japanese Americans have been revisiting the World War II period, there have been new interpretations and analyses of the role of outsiders, researchers, and government and military personnel in the social relations within the camps. In the case of Wax, her role as a participant observer was anything but neutral, but was perhaps influenced by who she was, and the difficult and sensitive situation under which the Japanese Americans were forced to live.

Sources: Sheryl J. Grana, *Women in Sociology*, ed. Mary Jo Deegan (Westport, Conn.: Greenwood Press, 1991); Peter T. Suzuki, "Anthropologists in the Wartime Camps for Japanese Americans: A Documentary Study," *Dialectical Anthropology* 6 (1981):23–60; Peter T. Suzuki, "The University of California Japanese Evacuation and Resettlement Study: A Prolegomenon," *Dialectical Anthropology* 10 (1986):189–213.

Primary Documents

Document 1
EXECUTIVE ORDER NO. 9066

WHEREAS the successful prosecution of the war requires every possible protection against espionage and against sabotage to national defense material, national defense premises and national defense utilities as defined in Section 4, Act of April 20, 1918, 40 Stat. 533, as amended by the Act of November 30, 1940, 54 Stat. 1220, and the Act of August 21, 1941, 55 Stat. 655 (U.S.C., Title 50, Sec. 104):

Now, THEREFORE, by virtue of the authority vested in me as President of the United States, and Commander in Chief of the Army and Navy, I hereby authorize and direct the Secretary of War, and the Military Commanders who he may from time to time designate, whenever he or any designated Commander deems such action necessary or desirable to prescribe military areas in such places and of such extent as he or the appropriate Military Commander may determine, from which any or all persons may be excluded, and with respect to which, the right to any person to enter, remain in, or leave shall be subject to whatever restriction the Secretary of War or the appropriate Military Commander may impose in his discretion. The Secretary of War is hereby authorized to provide for residents of any such area who are excluded therefrom, such transportation, food, shelter, and other accommodations as may be necessary, in the judgment of the Secretary of War or the said Military Commander, and until other such arrangements are made, to accomplish the purpose of this order. The designation of military areas in any region or locality shall supersede designations of prohibited and restricted areas by the Attorney General under the Proclamations of December 7 and 8, 1941, and shall supersede the responsibility and authority of the Attorney General under the said Proclamations in respect of such prohibited and restricted areas.

I hereby further authorize and direct the Secretary of War and the said Military Commanders to take such steps as he or the appropriate Military Commander may deem advisable to enforce compliance with the restrictions applicable to each Military area herein above authorized to be designated, including the use of Federal troops and other Federal Agencies, with authority to accept assistance of state and local agencies.

I hereby further authorize and direct all Executive Departments, independent establishments and other Federal Agencies, to assist the Secretary of War or the said Military Commanders in carrying out this Executive Order, including the furnishing of medical aid, hospitalization, food, clothing, transportation, use of land, shelter, and other supplies, equipment, utilities, facilities, and services.

This order shall not be construed as modifying or limiting in any way the authority heretofore granted under Executive Order 8972, dated December 12, 1941, nor shall it be construed as limiting or modifying the duty and responsibility of the Federal Bureau of Investigation, with respect to the investigation of alleged acts of sabotage or the duty and responsibility of the Attorney General and the Department of Justice under the Proclamations of December 7 and 8, 1941, prescribing regulations for the conduct and control of alien enemies, except as such duty and responsibility is superseded by the designation of military areas hereunder.

Franklin D. Roosevelt
THE WHITE HOUSE
February 19, 1942

Source: Roger Daniels, *Concentration Camps: North America Japanese in the United States and Canada during World War II* (Malabar, Fla.: Robert E. Krieger, 1981) p. 208.

Document 2
SABURO KIDO'S ADDRESS AT THE EMERGENCY JACL MEETING

SAN FRANCISCO, MARCH 8, 1942

This most likely may be the last National Council meeting we shall be able to hold for a long time to come. In a sense, this is a farewell gathering for most of us since we shall not know where we will be scattered, nor for how long. It is with a heavy heart that I say these words.

When the first ominous signs pointed to possible Japanese-American hostilities, we began to make preparations to mitigate the blows which may be directed against us because of our Japanese extraction. . . . many of us were lulled into overconfidence because of the friendly expressions extended us by our American friends. . . .

It has been our constant fear that race prejudice would be fanned by the various elements which have been constantly watching for an opening to destroy us. They included many of our economic competitors and those who believe this country belongs to the "whites." Many of them wanted to indulge in the unpatriotic pastime of using us as a political football in this hour of America's greatest peril. . . .

Today we are preparing to go into temporary exile from the homes in which we were born and raised. . . . The very foundations which have taken years to build up are being torn from under us. Many of you are wondering where our constitutional rights have flown to. Most of us still cannot believe that we, citizens of this country, have been placed ahead of "alien enemies" for evacuation from military areas. . . .

I am confident that the day is coming when those who are responsible for these outrageous violations of our rights will be ashamed of their conduct. We hope the thinking citizens will appreciate the principles which are at stake with us American citizens in this crucial test.

Source: Bill Hosokawa, *JACL In Quest of Justice* (New York: William Morrow, 1982) pp. 364–6.

Document 3
PUBLIC LAW 503–77TH CONGRESS

AN ACT To provide a penalty for violation of restrictions or orders with respect to persons entering, remaining in, leaving, or committing any act in military areas or zones.

Be it enacted by the Senate and House of Representatives of the United States of America in Congress assembled, That whoever shall enter, remain in, or leave, or commit any act in any military areas or military zone prescribed, under the authority of an Executive order of the President, by the Secretary of War, or by any military commander designated by the Secretary of War, contrary to the restrictions applicable to any such area or zone or contrary to the order of the Secretary of War or any such military commander, shall, if it appear that he knew or should have known of the existence and extent of the restrictions or order and that his act was in violation thereof, be guilty of a misdemeanor and upon conviction shall be liable to a fine not to exceed $5,000 or to imprisonment for not more than one year, or both, for each offense.

Approved, March 21, 1942

Source: *Report of the Subcommittee on Japanese War Relocation Centers to the Committee on Military Affairs United States Senate* 78th Congress (Washington, D.C.: U.S. Government Printing Office, May 7, 1943), p. 113.

Document 4
SELECTIVE SERVICE SYSTEM

STATEMENT OF UNITED STATES CITIZEN OF JAPANESE ANCESTRY

1. _____
    (Surname)   (English given name)   (Japanese given name)
    (a) Alias _____

2. Local selective service board _____
                                       (Number)

    (City)   (County)   (State)

3. Date of birth _____ Place of birth _____

4. Present address _____
                    (Street)   (City)   (State)

5. Last two addresses at which you lived 3 months or more (exclude residence at relocation center and at assembly center):
    _____ From _____ To _____
    _____ From _____ To _____

6. Sex _____ Height _____ Weight _____

7. Are you a registered voter? _____ Year first registered _____
    Where? _____ Party _____

8. Marital Status _____ Citizenship of wife _____ Race of wife _____

9. _____
    (Father's Name)   (Town or Ken)   (State or Country)

    (Occupation)   (Birthplace)

10. _____
    (Mother's Name)   (Town or Ken)   (State or Country)

    (Occupation)   (Birthplace)

In items 11 and 12, you need not list relatives other than your parents, your children, your brothers and sisters
For each person give name; relationship to you (such as father); citizenship, complete address; occupation

11. Relatives in the United States (if in military service, indicate whether a selectee or volunteer):

(a) _____
    (Name)   (Relationship to you)   (Citizenship)

(b) _____
    (Name)   (Relationship to you)   (Citizenship)

(c) _____
    (Name)   (Relationship to you)   (Citizenship)

12. Relatives in Japan (see instructions above item 11):

_____
    (Name)   (Relationship to you)   (Citizenship)

_____
    (Complete Address)   (Occupation)

_____
    (Name)   (Relationship to you)   (Citizenship)

_____
    (Complete Address)   (Occupation)

13. Education

Name   *Place*   *Years of Attendance*

_____ _____ From _____ to _____
(Kindergarten)

_____ _____ From _____ to _____
(Grade school)

_____ _____ From _____ to _____
(Japanese language school)

_____ _____ From _____ to _____
(High school)

_____ _____ From _____ to _____
(Junior college, college, or university)

_____
(Type of military training, such as R.O.T.C. or *Gunji Kyoren*) (Where and when)

_____
(Other schooling)   (Years of attendance)

14. Foreign travel (give dates, where, how, for whom, with whom, and reasons therefor):

_____
_____
_____

15. Employment (give employers' names and kinds of business, addresses, and dates from 1935 to date):

_____
_____
_____

16. Religion _____ Membership in religious groups _____

17. Membership in organizations (clubs, societies, associations, etc.). Give name, kind of organization, and dates of membership.

18. Knowledge of foreign languages (put check mark in proper squares):
    (a) Japanese   (b) Other _____
                                                        (specify)

	Good	Fair	Poor		Good	Fair	Poor
Reading				Reading			
Writing				Writing			
Speaking				Speaking			

19. Sports and hobbies _____

20. List five references, other than relatives or former employers, giving address, occupation, and number of years known:

(Name)	(Complete address)	(Occupation)	(Years known)

21. Have you ever been convicted by a court of a criminal offense (other than a minor traffic violation)? _____

Offense	When	What court	Sentence

22. Give details on any foreign investments
    (a) Accounts in foreign banks. Amount, $_____
        Bank _____ Date account opened _____
    (b) Investments in foreign countries. Amount, $_____
        Company _____ Date acquired _____
    (c) Do you have a safe-deposit box in a foreign country?
        What country? _____ Date acquired _____
        Contents _____

23. List contributions you have made to any society, organization, or club:

Organization	Place	Amount	Date

24. List magazines and newspapers to which you have subscribed or have customarily read:

25. To the best of your knowledge, was your birth ever registered with any Japanese governmental agency for the purpose of establishing a claim to Japanese citizenship?
    (a) If so registered, have you applied for cancelation [*sic*] of such registration? _____
    (Yes or no)

26. Have you ever applied for repatriation to Japan? _____

27. Are you willing to serve in the armed forces of the United States on combat duty, wherever ordered? _____

28. Will you swear unqualified allegiance to the United States of America and faithfully defend the United States from any or all attack by foreign or domestic forces, and forswear any form of allegiance or obedience to the Japanese emperor, or any other foreign government, power, or organization? _____

(Date)	(Signature)

NOTE:—Any person who knowingly and willfully falsifies or conceals a material fact or makes a false or fraudulent statement or representation in any matter within the jurisdiction of any department or agency of the United States is liable to a fine of not more than $10,000 or 10 years' imprisonment, or both.

For females question number 27 was worded:

27. If the opportunity presents itself and you are found qualified, would you be willing to volunteer for the Army Nurse Corps or the W.A.A.C.?

Source: *Report of the Subcommittee on Japanese War Relocation Centers to the Committee on Military Affairs* (Washington, D.C.: U.S. Government Printing Office, May 7, 1943), pp. 245–7.

Document 5
PROCLAMATION 4417

AN AMERICAN PROMISE
BY THE PRESIDENT OF THE UNITED STATES
OF AMERICA

A Proclamation

In this Bicentennial Year, we are commemorating the anniversary dates of many of the great events in American history. An honest reckoning, however, must include a recognition of our national mistakes as well as our achievements. Learning from our mistakes is not pleasant, but as a great philosopher once admonished, we must do so if we want to avoid repeating them.

February 19th is the anniversary of a sad day in American history. It was on that date in 1942, in the midst of the response to the hostilities that began on December 7, 1941, that Executive Order No. 9066 was issued, subsequently enforced by the criminal penalties of a statute enacted on March 21, 1942, resulting in the uprooting of loyal Americans. Over one hundred thousand persons of Japanese ancestry were removed from their homes, detained in special camps, and eventually relocated.

The tremendous effort by the War Relocation Authority and concerned Americans for the welfare of these Japanese-Americans may add perspective to that story, but it does not erase the setback to fundamental American principles. Fortunately, the Japanese-American community in Hawaii was spared the indignities suffered by those on our mainland.

We now know that we should have known then—not only was that evacuation wrong, but Japanese-Americans were and are loyal Americans. On the battlefield and at home, Japanese-Americans—names like Hamada, Mitsumori, Marimoto, Noguchi, Yamasaki, Kido, Munemori, and Miyamura—have been and continue to be written in our history for the sacrifices and the contributions they have made to the well-being and security of this, our common Nation.

The Executive order that was issued on February 19, 1942, was for the sole purpose of prosecuting the war with the Axis Powers, and ceased to be effective with the end of those hostilities. Because there was no formal statement of its termination, however, there is concern among many Japanese-Americans that there may yet be some life in that obsolete document. I think it appropriate, in this our Bicentennial Year, to remove all doubt on that matter, and to make clear our commitment in the future.

NOW, THEREFORE, I, GERALD R. FORD, President of the United States of America, do hereby proclaim that all the authority conferred by Executive Order No. 9066 terminated upon the issuance of Proclamation No. 2714, which formally proclaimed the cessation of the hostilities of World War II on December 31, 1946.

I call upon the American people to affirm with me this American Promise—that we have learned from the tragedy of that long-ago experience forever to treasure liberty and justice for each individual American, and resolve that this kind of action shall never again be repeated.

IN WITNESS WHEREOF, I have hereunto set my hand this nineteenth day of February in the year of our Lord nineteen hundred seventy-six, and the Independence of the United States of American the two hundredth.

GERALD R. FORD

Source: *Federal Register*, 41, no. 35 (February 20, 1976).

Document 6
APOLOGY LETTER FROM THE WHITE HOUSE

THE WHITE HOUSE
WASHINGTON

A monetary sum and words alone cannot restore lost years or erase painful memories; neither can they fully convey our Nation's resolve to uphold the rights of individuals. We can never fully right the wrongs of the past. But we can take a clear stand for justice and recognize that serious injustices were done to Japanese Americans during World War II.

In enacting a law calling for restitution and offering a sincere apology, your fellow Americans have, in a very real sense, renewed their traditional commitment to the ideals of freedom, equality, and justice. You and your family have our best wishes for the future.

Sincerely,
GEORGE BUSH
PRESIDENT OF THE UNITED STATES
OCTOBER 1990

Source: JACL Curriculum and Resource Guide, 1996.

Document 7
EXCERPT FROM "OKAASAN" PORTRAIT OF AN ISSEI MOTHER

Grace Eto Shibata was born and raised in Los Osos, west of the town of San Luis Obispo, in the central coast area of California. Just as she was about ready to attend college, her family was evacuated to Manzanar Relocation Center. After camp, she and her family returned to their farm and she attended the local junior college. She met and married Art Shibata and moved to the San Francisco Bay Area, where she joined him in his cut flower growing business. Most recently she graduated from college at the age of seventy-four.

The essay below is an excerpt from her memoir published in Mei Nakano's *Japanese American Women: Three Generations, 1890–1990*. The essay titled "Okaasan" (translated means "mother") gives us a descriptive, sensitive portrait of an Issei woman. The excerpt presented below details her family's experience immediately following Pearl Harbor and the confusion and turmoil they experienced before their evacuation to Manzanar.

On December 7, 1941, I was setting the table for lunch, as music flowed from the radio in the living room. Suddenly, the program was interrupted again and again by the newscaster announcing that Pearl Harbor was bombed by Japan. Was it really true? Mother could not really understand the broadcast, but was concerned. When Father came home and heard the news, there was total disbelief and bewilderment on his face. *"Sonna koto wa nai hazu da!"* (That cannot be!) But as news continued, reality sunk in, and we became somber. Mother turned pale.

Early the next morning when I came downstairs, I found Mother sitting silently by the unlit wood stove (the stove was now used as a heater), one light still on. She looked up, but did not give her usual smile. She appeared not to have slept. Her clothes were the same as the ones she had worn the day before, and her hair had not been combed. And she wasn't bustling. Mother was always bustling in the morning.

"What happened Mama?" I asked, puzzled.

"Around eleven last night, after we all went to bed, the police came and took Father away," she explained, her voice grave. "They were very apologetic and polite, saying it was the FBI orders and that they were instructed to take him in for questioning. He complied without hesitation, for he knows these men, and there was no reason to be afraid. But it's 4:30, and he still has not returned. I'm afraid something serious has happened."

"Why didn't you wake us?" I pressed.

In typical fashion, she said, "You had school, and there was no reason you should lose sleep over this. I thought he might be home by this time."

Unknown to us, the FBI had picked up numerous community leaders, Buddhist priests, Japanese school teachers and other "dangerous aliens."

Immediately, my brother went to the police station, but was unable to see Father or get any information about his whereabouts. In the meantime, there was a call for sister Mary from the police station. Father told her he was well and would be sent south. He was allowed to speak only in English, and that was the end of the conversation.

The very next day, the *S.L.O. Telegram Tribune* [San Luis Obispo, California newspaper] ran an article about Father's arrest. Rumors in the Japanese community were rampant as to where the Issei were being detained. Several weeks passed before Mother received a letter from Mrs. Matsuura of the Guadalupe Buddhist Church, informing her that Father was in the Santa Barbara jail and was anxiously waiting to see his family.

Masaji, Toshiko and Mother hurriedly drove to see him. Nancy and I stayed at home because Mother did not want us to see Father in custody.

At the jail, the visitors were allowed three minutes each. The usually robust Father appeared drawn. My sister asked how he was. "I'm fine," he said, "but I miss the outside, the fresh air." Masaji wanted to know

what he could get for him, and Father asked for some clothes and cig-
arettes. Mother told Father, "Don't worry Papa. Everything is being
taken care of. Just take good care of yourself."

My sister and brother were informed the detainees would be transferred again, so gathering articles Father had asked for, they rushed back
to Santa Barbara. By this time, aliens were restricted from traveling, and
Mother could not go to see Father. When Toshiko and Masaji got there,
Father was already gone. If the wardens knew where he was, they
feigned not to. My sister and brother were sent to the Los Angeles FBI
office for information and, after a lot of running about, they were finally
able to locate his whereabouts: the CCC [Civilian Conservation Corps]
Camp in Tujunga . . .

We received word one day that Father was to be transferred to some-
place very cold and would need warm clothes, also that his train would
be passing the San Luis Obispo station that evening. It was Christmas
Eve, and all the stores had already closed. My sister Kofuji called Mr.
Sinsheimer, the owner of a department store and the city mayor for
twenty years, to explain our problem. Mr. Sinsheimer knew Father well,
for he had entertained many of his guests from Japan. He kindly opened
his store, and my sister came out with a bundle of warm clothes.

We waited at the train station for several hours, to no avail. Masaji
found out when the next train was due, and we waited for one too, but
Father was not on it. We waited past midnight, and when told there
would be no other trains that night, we went home despondent and
worried. We were to learn much later that Father's train had been re-
routed through Barstow, the southern route. Mother had had such high
hopes of seeing Father and had been so eager and bright at the station.
Now she looked sad, but did not let down for an instant.

Meanwhile, our phone lines had been tapped, and the road to our
farm was under surveillance. We knew this because the FBI came often
to the house and questioned us about those who had called or visited
us. Sometimes while Mother spoke on the phone, a voice would say,
"Speak English." She was cut off from all other Issei and must have felt
very much alone, though she never complained. However, Rev. Todo-
roki, a fearless Buddhist priest from the S.L.O. [San Luis Obispo] Buddhist church, visited her often to offer encouragement and strength. He
himself was eventually picked up by the FBI. . . .

The evacuation orders which first came, divided California in three
zones vertically. Zone one covered west of Highway 1 near the coast
where we lived, and we were required to move by March. Zone two
was west of Highway 99, and we were told we would probably be able
to stay there permanently. Not wanting to be too far away from home,
we joined our sister Kofuji and her husband, who had rented a farm in

Ducor, near Delano. We left Los Osos in March 1942 and slept under the stars in the open field at Ducor.... [A]bout four months later, Ducor was declared a restricted zone.... We would have to move again.

Discouraged by this latest government order, we lost the will to fight and decided to enter a government relocation camp instead of trying to relocate ourselves elsewhere. So, we boarded a train in the hot July heat for Manzanar, a camp in the California desert. My sister Toshiko, a nurse, had volunteered to work at the Manzanar hospital on the condition that our family could stay together.

Having grown up in the open spaces, we found Manzanar life oppressive and stifling. Not only were the living conditions inadequate, being thrown in with ten thousand other strangers in one square mile of desert was utterly depressing. We felt like cattle in a corral. People from our home town had gone to Arizona, and we were virtually strangers here. Mother tried to keep up our spirits by telling us how great it was that we didn't have to cook three times a day. She reminded us we should be grateful we were together as one family....

Mother received letters from Father periodically, but a large portion of the letters were cut out or blanked out in ink, censored. She was, however, grateful that father appeared to be in good health.

We were anxious to leave Manzanar. It was an abnormal way to live without a family life, as we had known it. Also, I was still in high school and wanted a legitimate diploma to continue my education.

Seven months later after our internment, we left for Payette, Idaho, where sister Alice and her husband had leased a farm. They gave us housing and work for the duration of the war. Mother cared for her son's first daughter, Lois, and also helped on the farm....

In the meantime, Father was being shifted with other internees to concentration camps in Montana, Oklahoma, Louisiana, Texas, and New Mexico. We were never sure why all this movement was taking place, except that people were continually being taken into these camps, as for example, persons of Japanese ancestry from South American countries. We wondered if the camps were getting overcrowded.

When Father was in Louisiana, Mother learned that sister Susie from an Arkansas Camp was able to visit Father with her husband, who had already been inducted in the 442nd Combat Team. My sister recalls how impressed she was at Father's understanding and compassion. "This is your country," he had said, "and I am proud my son-in-law is serving. You do your best to fight for your country. My internment should make no difference." The son-in-law was to give up his life on an Italian battlefield.

One day, Mother received an odd letter from Father, asking her opinion about the family repatriating to Japan. We thought his morale must have been very low to even ask such a question. Mother's answer was a resolute no. "The United States is our home," she said. "Our family is here, and I do not wish to leave this country."

Mother was overjoyed when Father was finally released from the New Mexico internment camp in the fall of 1944 to join his family in Payette, Idaho. The FBI was not able to charge Father with any wrongdoing. Since he was passing Boise, Idaho, where Nancy and I were going to school, we went to meet him at the train station. With a guard beside him, Father got off the train briefly to see us. I was appalled at his ashen face. Although he stood straight and tall, his clothes hung loosely on his thin body. I admired my sister, so strong and controlled, greeting Father and talking with him. I could only hold on to his sleeve and cry, happiness and sadness filling me at once.

Source: Grace Shibata, "Okaasan," in Mei T. Nakano, *Japanese American Women: Three Generations, 1890–1990* (Berkeley: Mina Press Publishers and San Francisco: National Japanese American Historical Society, 1990), pp. 88–92.

Document 8
EXCERPT FROM *MANZANAR MARTYR, AN INTERVIEW WITH HARRY Y. UENO*

Harry Yoshio Ueno was born in Paauilo, Hawaii, in 1907. When he was eight years old he was sent to Japan to live with relatives. As a Kibei, Harry returned to the United States in 1922 and worked in a number of different jobs before settling in Los Angeles. At the time of the evacuation he was married with three children and working at a fruit stand.

Ueno helped to organize the Kitchen Workers' Union at Manzanar to advocate for better working conditions for those who worked in the mess hall, and because he suspected someone was stealing from the internees' sugar and meat rations. Manzanar had numerous different groups and factions that were pro- and anti-WRA administration. Because of his work with the Kitchen Workers' Union, he was probably in greater conflict with the WRA administration and was seen as a potential agitator, disrupting the camp environment. Consequently, he was later accused in the beating of Fred Tayama, a Nisei leader, and another mess hall worker who worked closely with the Manzanar camp administration. Ueno's arrest sparked an outburst within Manzanar, which eventually led to him and others also identified as "agitators" being removed from the camp. First they were detained at the Lone Pine (Inyo County) jail, and then they were moved to Department of Justice citizen isolation camps in Leupp, Arizona, and Moab, Utah. Disillusioned with the U.S. government from his arrest and detainment, for which he was never aware of any formal charges, he decided to renounce his U.S. citizenship. Eventually, Ueno was reunited with his family at the Tule Lake Segregation Center. Later, he was represented by civil rights attorney Wayne M. Collins, and his U.S. citizenship was eventually restored.

The section presented below is excerpted from *Manzanar Martyr, An Interview with Harry Y. Ueno.* It describes in his own words what he perceived happening at Manzanar, leading up to the Manzanar riot and the death of James Ito. Another interview with Harry Ueno appears in John Tateishi's *And Justice for All* (New York: Random House, 1984).

Our district had been scheduled to go out to Santa Anita [assembly center in a horse racetrack in Los Angeles County]. But three days before we were to evacuate, they changed the notice. It said we should go to Manzanar. Then we had to hurry up and look for cheesecloth for mosquito netting. We went all over! Hollywood, Maywood, south Los Angeles near the Firestone Tire Company, all around here. Nobody had it. In some department stores they asked, "What's the matter with the Japanese? All of a sudden they are buying up all the cheesecloth." They wondered, "What's wrong?" That's the way it was in the beginning.

We were told, "Take whatever you can carry, nothing big." You couldn't take anything else, no food, no cooking utensils, stove, or anything like that. We had on hand a large 800 pound sack of rice we had bought that we had to sell to the Chinese grocery store. We took three or four suitcases, what we could carry. That's about all we could carry, you know. We left the bus from Los Angeles on May 10, 1942.

By the time we got to Manzanar, it was already dark. Then they gave us a cloth sack to make up a mattress. They said, "Go and fill up your own mattress from the pile of hay there." In the dark! "Take out the lantern and fill your mattress." Well, we could hardly sleep because of the change of place and all the excitement and the long ride on the bus. My wife is weak on any long ride like that, so she was kind of pale. But we made it. Three families were assigned to our room. There was a widow with her son, and a bachelor, and our family, all in the same room. So we put up sheets to make a partition and slept there.

. . . [I]n the same building there was one family that had been our neighbor. There were seven or eight in the family, including grandfather and grandmother. The people in the back of our place [in Los Angeles] were about four or five, with their father-in-law and mother. They were in the same building too. So we probably knew about 10 or 15 people prior to the war. We were all together in the same building.

I didn't have any strong feelings against the government or anything like that. I thought, "Well, we have to move. Maybe that's some way we could be protected from people who were stirred up by newspaper or radio propaganda. Some people wrote that it was open season for 'Jap hunting.' At least we are secure from any outside threat." Every time I had stayed in town or rode a streetcar, I always kind of feared somebody might hit my head from behind, or something. You know, the way the people were feeling; it was expressed right in the newspapers. There was always fear of a threat. Well, at least in the camp, those things were neutralized. So I didn't feel anything against the government over the Evacuation.

. . . [W]e weren't too happy about that [the camp situation] but, you know, we had had a lot of hard times during the Depression. We could overcome some hardships. We always pitched in together and worked it out, you know. A lot of people weren't happy, but we didn't care because we could overcome. We tried to make the best of the situation.

At first I went out with a group and cut the sagebrush, so I they could do a little more building on the camp. I don't mind doing hard work; I was used to it, so I just pitched in. Only there was one thing about which I was not happy. You know, in the beginning the administration wasn't sure how much they were going to pay to the people in the camp. There was a rumor that it might be seven dollars a month. The next thing we knew it was to be thirteen dollars. In the beginning, it was like that. It wasn't sixteen dollars until very late.

One day I went to the construction area and watched how the carpenters were doing. And I asked a carpenter, "How much are you getting?" That was a Caucasian carpenter. "I'm getting fourteen dollars a day," he said. My gosh, we worked one month and were getting fifteen dollars, and here he worked one day and got fourteen dollars a day! Well, it was one of those things, I figured.

When they were going to open the mess hall, they asked for volunteers to register for jobs there. So I applied for a job. I didn't know much about cooking, so I figured I would do anything, even mop the floor or wash dishes. I didn't care. But they said I was to assist the cook. . . .

Later people started complaining about the sugar. You'd go into the mess hall, and they served coffee in great big cups. The way they served is, they filled the cup from the coffee urn; then they would give only a half-teaspoon of sugar. . . . A half-teaspoon of sugar was not enough for them. They couldn't enjoy their coffee, so they started to complain. In the beginning, they had enough sugar. Eight ounces of sugar was all right for everybody because there was sugar on the table. They used to lay it on the table so people could take as much as they wanted for their coffee. But soon sugar got shorter and shorter. . . . I started checking the sugar in our mess hall. Soon I went to the next mess hall and checked and found the same condition. So I went around camp. I found out that every place was the same way.

Then I heard a lot of complaints. For instance, when we went into the camp, the administration had searched all the baggage and took all of our knives. Then they passed around the same knives to the kitchens. They never bought new ones. For feeding all those several hundred people, they needed bigger equipment, like large knives and boning knives for meat. A lot of these chiefs [chefs] had complained to the mess steward, [Joseph] Winchester, about buying some knives, but he never did. He said, "In wartime, we can't buy anything like that. They are pretty hard to buy." But when the mess hall chiefs [chefs] brought in money and ordered, this material came right away. . . . they had to do without unless they paid out of their own pockets.

There were a lot of complaints like that. When individuals went over and complained to the division head, nothing happened. They never paid attention. We figured the only way was we had to get together and organize. . . . We have to organize the mess halls. It's the only way the grievances that we have to take to the administration can be heard. . . . Individual complaints don't mean anything to the administration. So that's why we organized the union.

> Harry Ueno was first taken to Lone Pine jail in Inyo County, but
> was later brought back to Manzanar and kept in the camp jail.

The jail was just a regular barrack like those we lived in. I think that half or one-third was taken up by the police station, and the rest was for the jail purpose. . . . the window was wide open; I could have gotten out anytime I wanted to. But I didn't want to break my promise to the negotiating committee, so I stayed there. . . . About six o-clock . . . it started getting a little darker, and a lot of people filled up the open space there [in front of the jail]. They were yelling and shouting, and the wind was blowing about 35 miles an hour. You know how Manzanar is, when the wind is whipped up; it's dusty and pebbles fly. It was kind of a cold night. I think it was about a little after six that I noticed some of the MPs [military police] were shaking because so many people were out there—young fellows. Then the sergeant in charge went around and said, "Remember Pearl Harbor!" He was yelling, "Hold your ground!" because they were scared. . . . Two or three times he went around yelling "Remember Pearl Harbor! Hold your ground!" . . . Then soon they [the military police] started putting on gas masks. So I told the people in front, "You better back off, because we're going to . . . You'd better step back. Otherwise, they are going to throw the tear gas." I could see the tear gas canisters.

Then as soon as the guards put on the gas masks, they started throwing the canisters. I don't know how many—ten or twenty. . . . the smoke was so whipped up with the wind, and people started running. And you couldn't see anything; the smoke covered it up.

Then I heard five or six shots fired nearby and tommy guns or machine guns on the far east side of the police station. When the smoke was clear, I saw one man laying on the ground. I was hoping that just . . . I heard the gunshot, but I hoped that it was just a dummy bullet. I was hoping it was just to scare off the people. But I saw one man laying flat in the front of the police station. As soon as everything cleared, I saw them carry in that boy [James Ito] . . .

Source: Sue Kunitomi Embrey, Arthur A. Hansen, and Betty Kulberg Mitson, *Manzanar Martyr: An Interview with Harry Y. Ueno* (Fullerton, Calif.: The Oral History Program, California State University, Fullerton, 1986), pp. 24–6, 30–1, 56–8.

Document 9
TOM KAWAGUCHI

I was born in 1921 and was twenty when the war broke out, and turned twenty-one when I went to camp. . . . I was working for Mitsubishi until the war broke out, and I learned an awful lot about the import-export business. At the same time I learned a lot about Japanese nationals and how they conducted business. To me the Niseis [sic] were being discriminated against. They expected a lot of work out of them and gave them minimum pay. That was the philosophy then. We used to work hard, we'd go to work early, we'd go home late, but our pay didn't change. They expected this from us, and in Japan I assume this was the way of life because jobs were scarce there, and, of course, in those days jobs were scarce here too.

On December 8, 1941, I was told to go to the FBI office where they interviewed me. I said that I was just a general clerk, that I was a flunky. But they were very much aware of my movements because I used to meet Japanese ships coming and going, take down the bills of lading and trade acceptances and that sort of thing and turn them over to the purser. That's what I told the FBI. I was doing general work in accounting.

But on December 7? Let's see, I was at the public library. I was in there, and when I came out, the boys were screaming "Extra, Extra, Japs Bombed Pearl Harbor!" I wondered where in the world was Pearl Harbor? I didn't know it was in Hawaii until I started reading the paper and then . . .

I kind of got a funny feeling going home. I thought everybody and his uncle was staring at me, ready to pounce on me or something. I came back to Japantown and the place was just stone quiet. You didn't see anyone around. You felt very apprehensive and thought that something big was going to happen. You began to notice extra police cars and extra patrol cars coming into the area, and then plainclothesmen . . .

Anyway, we were in Tanforan on May 1, 1942, and then in September of 1942 we went to Topaz. I was furious. No one really knew what was happening. For example, my *Hakujin* [Caucasian/white] friends came under the scrutiny of the FBI. They were told not to become too close to Japanese families. . . .

It was just the frustration at Tanforan, that I couldn't do anything about it. Total frustration that something was happening to us and there was no way we could fight back because actually none of us had ever really been exposed to the majority culture. All of our lives we had been living in *Nihon-machi* ("Japantown"); our thinking was Nihon-machi, and we really didn't know what the real world was. . . .

When we got to Topaz [Utah] and saw the MP guards and the whole bit, we thought we were at the end of the world, a complete sense of loss. My stomach really just sank, and I thought, oh my God, I gotta get out of this place. I was going to try and get out one way or another. In due time they started coming out with the seasonal jobs—cannery workers and sugar-beet workers, and so forth. I began to do those jobs just to get out of camp life. But it didn't do anything for me. There was a lot of stoop labor. Then I began to organize the Boy Scouts and community activities for the kids. In camp this was my major concern, to keep the kids busy . . .

Then we began to hear rumors that they were going to create a Japanese combat team. Along comes Lee Tracy, a movie actor, and he starts talking about volunteers. My brother and I really talked it over and decided perhaps this is our chance to go. We didn't know it, but we both went down to volunteer. My brother said, "I'm the older one, so I'm going first." I said, "Okay, I'll stay behind but I don't think that's right. I should go and you should stay." He took his physical and he flunked because he had a heart murmur. The minute I found that he was rejected, man, I was there. When I volunteered I said I wanted to leave camp and go to New York. I had the money and had a friend I could stay with. They cleared me to leave camp and I think that delay saved my life because if I had gone in then I would have been right in the middle of Bruyeres Campaign.

I joined because I always felt very strongly about patriotism; I felt that this was my country. I didn't know any other country. When the war broke out with Japan, I was ready to fight the enemy, and I had no qualms about whether it was Japanese or German or whatever. This was my country and I wanted to defend it. It was that simple. But then I was getting this treatment, I was a little confused. I thought, wait a minute, here I want to defend my country and they lock me up. Why? Then I said, well, the opportunity has got to present itself. I've got to get out of here. And I've got to demonstrate in one form or another that I am what I am. That opportunity came, and when it came, man, I was right in there. I mean there was no second guessing.

I was a loyal American and I wanted to prove that the Japanese Americans were real Americans, just like anybody else. And this is what a lot of my friends didn't understand. When this yes-yes, no-no business took place, I was disappointed in some of them who went no-no. It took me a number of years, but I suddenly realized that a no-no answer was all part of the democratic process, that somebody else had his choice and I had my choice. We had some problems in camp because some people wanted to go as a block and say no-no. We had a considerable amount of discussion on that, because we have our own individual rights and we can express ourselves any way we want to.

There was democracy going on right in camp, in spite of the enclosure. But there were friends fighting against friends, there were brothers fighting against brothers, and it was terrible. And people asked, "Why do you want to volunteer?" I just said, "I don't understand what the argument is. Our country is being attacked and I want to defend it. It's that simple." . . .

You know when we joined the Army and when we went through basic, none of us really said anything about why we joined or anything else. We knew we had a job to do. But we never even talked about what we had to do. We were going to the best that we knew how. We never sat back and said, Here we are—the old rah-rah business. None of that happened. It seemed like all of us knew exactly why we were there and why we were going to give it our best shot. No one ever came around and told me such and such, and this is what you are going to do, and so forth . . .

. . . [A]nyway, there was a real closeness in the 442nd. We kind of felt like brothers. We really looked after each other. There was an unspoken trust between us that was evident constantly. I noticed a big difference when I left the 442nd and went with another group. In the 442nd we were like brothers under the skin, so to speak, and I knew all the fellows from San Francisco and from the Bay Area. I guess it was an extension of our life, from before camp.

What really made the 442nd a good fighting unit was that the education of most of the boys in it was above average—way above average. That was number one. Number two, they had a strong sense of pride, very strong.

And all of us were scared, no question about it. None of us felt like heroes, but we didn't want to bring shame upon our families. So we didn't want to show that we were scared, but, man, I was scared with the best of them. . . . When we went into combat, it was all the way. Once you got into the heat of battle, it was just like you were playing football or basketball. You're doing all the things naturally, but you're fighting for your life. They would point out our objectives, and we would be going toward objectives. It was really amazing, some of those kids—God, they were really gutsy guys.

I think the Japanese culture really came into play, all the things that we were taught as kids—honesty, integrity, honor. And *haji*, "not bringing shame on the family." Your upbringing and culture are there and they are not something you talk about.

A lot of people think that the 442nd was used merely as cannon fodder. I don't think so, because I've been in the Army for twenty years, and I retired as a major. You generally try to use your best troops as a spearhead to accomplish an objective, and the 442nd was good—I mean they were damn good. But as a GI, I didn't know one way or the other. Once I was commissioned, I saw things completely different—you would take your best troops and use them, and this is exactly what had happened. The 442nd was spearheading most of the attacks because they were damn good, and our casualty rates were high because we were spearheading attacks. This is where the cannon-fodder talk started, but I don't think we were really used as cannon fodder. They wanted to use us effectively, which was demonstrated in our final push when the Gothic Line fell in thirty-four minutes and we accomplished the impossible. We started climbing the hills silently at ten at night. By five the next morning, we were in position to attack. The Germans didn't even expect us. We came up right behind them.

That was the campaign where the Allies tried to break the Gothic Line for six months with three divisions—forty thousand men. Meantime, our combat team had roughly five thousand because we had some extra companies. We had our engineering company, our artillery battalion, and certain things that were a little different from the makeup of a normal regiment. . . .

It took us thirty-six minutes to take the objective, but it took us almost ten hours to climb that mountain at night. The Allied units couldn't break through, but we had some good tactical officers in our regiment. . . .

I would do the whole 442nd thing over again, because of the general thinking of a lot of my friends—they all have this American show-me attitude—and I demonstrated to them where I come from. Even today I find that I'm leading the way showing what I can do. . . . I'm constantly working toward an objective, and it surprises them that even today I have this drive in spite of the treatment I got.

So in the 442nd, a lot of us feel that this was our only chance to demonstrate our loyalty; we would never get a second chance—this was it. We saw the treatment we were getting and we wanted there to be no question about what we were and where we were going. At least that's the way I felt: give me a chance, at least to show what I can do or can't do.

Source: John Tateishi, *And Justice for All: An Oral History of the Japanese American Detention Camps* (New York: Random House, 1984), pp. 176–85.

Document 10
EXCERPT FROM *SUSPENDED: GROWING UP ASIAN IN AMERICA*

Clifford Iwao Uyeda was born in Olympia, Washington, in 1917. He was raised in Tacoma, Washington. He received a B.A. in English from the University of Wisconsin in 1940 and attended medical school at Tulane University in New Orleans. He was a captain in the U.S. Air Force and served in the Korean War from 1951 to 1953. After his military service he settled in San Francisco and worked as staff pediatrician at the Kaiser Permanente Medical Group until his retirement in 1975.

A prolific writer and former columnist for the JACL newspaper, *Pacific Citizen*, Dr. Uyeda has written about global and environmental issues and campaigned against the Navajo "relocation" from their ancestral lands. He served as the national JACL redress chairman and national president of the organization.

His memoir, *Suspended: Growing Up Asian in America*, recounts his life and experiences as a Nisei, and his family's experiences with the war. His writing is both a statement of activism and reflection of racial, environmental, and global social issues, calling for healing and understanding as human beings on the planet Earth. The following excerpt reflects on the period following the end of the war.

The ending of the war was no surprise to me. I anticipated the ending when I first heard of Pearl Harbor on December 7, 1941. It seemed that Japan had just walked right into a trap set by President Franklin Roosevelt. That the war lasted so long was due to the fanaticism of the Japanese soldiers. The Japanese military had not only sacrificed two million young men on the battlefields, but also inflicted atrocities on millions of others in Asia. The Japanese people also endured years of false hopes and hardship due to the lies told by their military government.

The war did not end because of the atomic bomb. The American leaders, both civilian and military, knew by early summer 1945 that Japan was a defeated nation and that neither atomic bomb nor an invasion of the Japanese islands were necessary for Allied victory. The Americans had broken the Japanese code even before the war had begun, and knew of Japan's request to Russia to mediate a surrender term. But Americans still quote President Harry Truman's reason for using the atomic bomb— that we saved half a million American lives. That statement has become embedded in America's memory and culture, although contrary information is accepted by many scholars. . . .

Millions of Americans in uniform were returning home. For those returning from overseas, the United States was paradise on earth, with its undamaged piers, towering skyscrapers rising in unblemished symmetry, and the rows of neat residences. The pest-holes of jungle warfare were behind them. It was time again for clean clothes and strolls without fear of ambush. Flushed with the euphoria of victory, soldiers danced down the ship's gangplanks back home to America.

Others were more cautious, and for good reason. An incident recalled by a Japanese American United States Senator from Hawaii is well known. As a much decorated veteran with one arm missing from battle casualty, Daniel Inouye was denied a haircut in San Francisco on his way home to Hawaii. He was in full uniform. That didn't stop the barber from saying to him, "We don't cut Jap hair." Other 442nd veterans returning home experienced similar treatment.

Another 442nd veteran was stopped in a shopping center in Los Angeles in December 1945, thrown into a paddy wagon by military police and put into a stockade with a remark, "We don't want Japs returning to the West Coast."

The veteran was stripped of his uniform bedecked with campaign and Purple Heart ribbons, and made to wear prison garb. Daily he was forced to scrub floors with an armed guard standing by.

"As I looked into that guard's face, I said to myself, 'So this is what I had fought for! So this is what my buddies died for!' It tore up my heart." Tears welled into his eyes. "For decades I couldn't talk about it. I was so ashamed—ashamed of the humiliation, ashamed that I didn't try to tear up that guy right there and then, and ashamed that America could be this way."

The Pacific War ended in August 1945, but the last detention camp did not close until October 1946, and the last special internment camp did not close until 1952.

For decades many Japanese Americans have questioned the real significance of the sacrifices made by the Nisei soldiers. The story of the 100th/442nd Regimental Combat Team in Europe was a symbol of the common soldier at war. It was an image of minority soldiers who had to fight prejudice at home and a foreign enemy overseas. It was an example of the willingness of citizens to make the ultimate sacrifice in order to attain for all people their rights they themselves were denied.

The 100th/442nd symbolized oppressed Americans as well as the dream possible in America.

Starting in the 1970s, Japanese Americans began making annual pilgrimages to former detention camp sites. Joined by other races, they undertook the pilgrimages to remind themselves and other Americans that freedom is not automatic; that it is extremely fragile and has to be actively pursued.

It took nearly forty years for Japanese Americans to recover from the shock caused by their incarceration experience. They had been blamed and made to feel guilty for what they did not do. Even in the 1980s, it was still too painful for most Japanese Americans to even talk about their wartime experiences. They tried to forget what had happened to them. But history could not be erased.

The struggle to recover and to repair the wounds of the exclusion and detention experience is not just a Japanese American issue. It is an American as well as a universal human rights issue. People in the United States have the right to be judged as individuals, and not merely as members of a race. We also expect individual rights to be respected not only by fellow Americans but also by our American government. Incarceration of American citizens in detention camps again? That was in 1942. It will never happen again, many would say. Those who lived through the internment experience recall vividly that in the midst of rumors of expulsion and detention, many Japanese Americans had a firm belief: "Not us. We're American citizens."

The passage of time does not lessen the injury. Some Japanese Americans proclaim that they have arrived in America, and attack those who remind them of the unpleasant past. Neither the victims nor the perpetrators have learned the lessons of history. If we ignore the violation of human rights in our own country, how are we to care about the abrogation of rights of others?

Over the years there has been suspicion among American minorities that laws exist primarily as convenient tools for the majority's exploitative uses. It is a damaging concept of America. Yet evidence abounds. There are still millions of suspended citizens living in America today. Try as they may, they are like puppets manipulated from above, their feet kicking the air inches above ground.

Our planet Earth also lies suspended in an ordinary solar system within a vast galaxy of stars. There are countless galaxies suspended in an expanding universe. Time and space exist beyond comprehension. Within the vast cosmos, the planet Earth is unique because it is abundant in life; and it is particularly precious because it possesses intelligence. If we travel back in time just a few thousand years when human knowledge and culture began their recorded history, it is noted that human life has always borne within it the responsibility not seen in other living creatures. It is our obligation and duty to consciously improve the quality of life of all living beings. The value of human life on earth is directly proportional to an involvement in rectifying injustice and restoring the joy of living to others. Ethnic, even species, differences become trivial.

During the past century, the concept of war has undergone revolutionary changes. Glorification of war is being questioned. The judgment of inevitability is in doubt. It seems that leaders are only beginning to sense that new technology has finally made wars obsolete for resolving international disputes. As the 21st century dawns, the vision and the hope of mankind lie in the realization that nothing is more precious than the concern for all living things. Survival is not only for ourselves. It is inextricably based on the concept of mutual security.

Source: Clifford I. Uyeda, *Suspended: Growing Up Asian in America* (San Francisco: National Japanese American Historical Society, 2000), pp. 229–30, 233–5.

Document 11
TESTIMONY OF WARREN FURUTANI BEFORE THE COMMISSION ON WARTIME RELOCATION AND INTERNMENT OF CIVILIANS

Warren T. Furutani was born in 1947. He has been active in the Asian Pacific American community for more than thirty years and was one of the first Asian Americans to be elected to the Los Angeles Board of Education. He describes himself as a Sansei-Yonsei, a bi-generational Japanese American whose mother and father were incarcerated at Rohwer and Jerome, Arkansas. He is currently an elected trustee for the Los Angeles Community College District and consultant to Robert Hertzberg, Speaker of the California State Assembly. The excerpt presented below is a transcription of the testimony he presented to the Commission on Wartime Relocation and Internment of Civilians in Los Angeles in 1981.

Members of the Japanese American community and dear friends that are in attendance today, members of the Commission: As stated, my name is Warren Tadashi Furutani. I am Sansei-Yonsei and I grew up in Gardena.

An issue that I would like to speak of is something that has been bothering me of late, particularly in light of the participation and some of the testimonies at the Commission hearings. What I am making reference to is that a lot of people feel that the Sansei and Yonsei—the children of parents and grandparents who were in camps—were not particularly affected or touched by the camp experience. But I think if people hold that as in fact true, then they do not understand the depth and impact of the camp experience.

I can remember growing up in Gardena in the post-war era, and going to Gardena High School, and every class I had on American history, and when we began to study the chapter on World War II. I can remember feeling very nervous any time we got to the beginning of the chapter when they talked about why the United States became involved in World War II. I remember wanting to stand up and look my classmates in the eye and say that I didn't have anything to do with it. Because when they talked about the bombing of Pearl Harbor, more often than not everybody's head would turn and look at those of us who were Japanese Americans. Because of their limited knowledge of our community, people would assume that because of a certain heritage that these things were connected.

I can remember going to any number of family gatherings, and I can go anywhere in the United States today and talk to a Nikkei or Japanese American family, and after the initial amenities are taken care of and discussions start taking place on a social level, without a doubt, they will get to the topic of the camps. Now even though I wasn't in camp, it's always a reference point for Japanese Americans. People will ask, "Were you in camp?" And of course I wasn't. That doesn't end the questioning, because then they ask if your parents were. If you tell them what camp your parents were in and if they were not themselves in that camp, then they would ask if you knew so-and-so who was in that camp. The point I am making is that the camp experience has had a direct impact on those of us who were born after the war because it is in constant reference and because it is a part of our history. And when I mean history I don't mean something that is logged in books, I don't mean something that is only studied periodically. I mean something that impacts on us as individuals and as young people today.

In wondering what this camp was, in looking to history books for information, all of us were turned away without anything. In looking for information, the only source we could begin to look to was our families and our community. And in that process I began to find out what these camps were all about. My initial reaction when I heard that my parents were herded off and put in camp was based upon being weaned on cowboy movies, being weaned on war movies and watching John Wayne. I imagined myself with guns in both hands firing away and claiming I would never be a part of that, I would never have gone to camp, and I couldn't imagine why my Nisei parents and Issei grandparents went to camp. But out of that ignorance was stirred a curiosity. With that curiosity I began to find out what the camp experience was about. Many questions began to be answered: why and under what conditions the Issei and Nisei were put in camp; and that it wasn't a matter of their having a choice, and making a choice. It was not a democratic process. It was in fact a violation of all those things that we've learned in the very same history class to be true. It was a complete violation of the constitution. I began to understand why so many Nisei fought in World War II in the heralded 100th Battalion and 442nd Regiment. It was an attempt to prove that they had the makings to be good citizens. Even though American-born, they still went in there, in my opinion, with an inferiority complex that was put upon them by the actions of the American government, to prove that they in fact were worthy of being American citizens, in fact, willing to die for them. I began to understand the true reality of the experience of the Nisei and Issei during World War II who were in the ten concentration camps and in many other jails and other compounds. Their survival was based upon a pride, an ability to endure, a tenacity, that in fact occurred.

. . . Another question that is not answered now but may be answered in the future: The impact on Sansei cannot be denied when you look at the early and untimely deaths of so many Nisei parents in the Japanese American community. It is understood that the Issei worked the hardest jobs imaginable, and that the Nisei in fact were beneficiaries of that hard work. But in that process of living a life of trying to prove that the Nisei were worthy of being Americans, a toll has been taken on their lives. And in my eye it's not been proven but will be in the future, that the Nisei that retire at sixty-two and suddenly die within ten years and are not enjoying the time of retirement that they worked so hard for because of failing health, because of getting illnesses like cancer; all of this is a direct reaction to the stress and experience that perhaps started in the camps and continued throughout their lives.

But what happened with the Sansei is that we, and I mean many of us, have been responsible for re-raising the issue of the camps. And when we did, the reaction from the Nisei community in particular was "Why? Why!" We would talk about taking a pilgrimage to Manzanar and they would go, "Why?" They would want to know why! "It's not important, we don't need to talk about it." But as we said we would do these things, their response would become more and more emotional. They began to come to meetings. They have come to the thirteen different Manzanar pilgrimages . . . And every time the stories are told, tears come to people's eyes. And the reason why it is coming out today and the reason why it will always be a part and a topic of discussion of the Japanese American experience, is because the camp experience exists in a very shallow grave. The grave is so shallow; it is very easily dug up because things have not been rectified, things have not been resolved.

In the process to understand the camp experience from the Nisei's point of view as a Sansei, what began to become clear is that the way you view the camp experience depends on the eye of the beholder. What I mean is that history is in the eyes of the beholder. One of the points of contention that has been in the media and will always be, is the term "concentration camp." But what I submit to you is that the term concentration camp is dependent upon what perspective you view the experience. If you are on the outside looking in and you are reading the public relations information from the War Relocation Authority, "relocation camp" and "assembly center" become very nice terms to deal with. But if you are on the inside looking out, I submit then, that what you are dealing with is a concentration camp. People will tell you that the reason why they object to the term concentration camp is because of its relationship to what happened to Jews in Germany. I point out to you that the Nazi regime called them concentration camps but the Jews inside the camps being killed called them death camps, not concentration camps. What you see in this effort by the Japanese American community is an attempt to bring about what is in fact justice.

I know that people have made reference to the fact that if the Japanese Americans get redress and reparations, then that means the Afro-Americans should get their 40 acres and a mule. . . . then we have to bring up the question of all the hundreds of treaties made with all the nations of Native Americans that have been broken by the United States government. And if you talk about that you'll have to talk about the broken treaty of Guadelupe Hidalgo. The point I am simply making is that the issue of the concentration camps that Japanese Americans were put in cannot be taken out of the context of American history, but must be looked at as a part of American history. In that context, you can see that it is not an exception, it is the rule.

Source: "The Commission on Wartime Relocation and Internment of Civilians: Selected Testimonies from the Los Angeles and San Francisco Hearings" in *Amerasia Journal* 8, 2 (1981): 101–5.

Glossary of Selected Terms

Assembly center. Temporary facilities used to house evacuees while the permanent relocation centers were being built. There were sixteen centers in California, Oregon, and Washington. They were on former fairgrounds, stockyards, exposition centers, and a Civilian Conservation Corps facility.

Buddhahead. Slang nickname given to Hawaiian soldiers of Japanese ancestry by mainland Japanese. Some say the term is derived from *buta* or pig. Considered derogatory.

Commission on Wartime Relocation and Internment of Civilians (CWRIC). Government commission formed in 1981 to research and investigate the causes and consequences of the World War II relocation and internment of civilians. This commission also researched the situation of Aleuts and Alaska Natives in the Pribolof Islands.

Concentration camp. Guarded facility/detention center for imprisonment or detention of groups of people for social or political reasons.

Coram nobis cases. The Supreme Court cases of Gordon Hirabayashi, Minoru Yasui, and Fred Korematsu were brought before federal court using a legal procedure called a "writ of error *coram nobis*." This can be used only for cases that have had evidence of prosecutorial misconduct or other events that previously affected the outcome of the case.

Evacuee. Term used to refer to individuals of Japanese ancestry during the period from when they left their homes to live in the assembly centers.

Executive Order 9066. Order signed by President Franklin D. Roosevelt that authorized the secretary of war or other military commander to prescribe military areas to remove "any or all persons" they felt necessary for the security of the area.

Gentlemen's Agreement. In 1907–1908, the United States and Japan came to an agreement over the immigration of Japanese laborers to the United States.

Japan would stop issuing passports to male laborers as long as the United States passed no formal laws regulating immigration from Japan. While the emigration of Japanese male laborers was curtailed, Japanese women continued to emigrate as "picture brides," wives of Japanese laborers already in America.

Go For Broke. Slogan of the 442nd Regimental Combat Team that meant "shoot the works" or "go all out" to get the job done.

Hakujin. White person, Caucasian, Japanese word.

Haole. White person, Caucasian, Hawaiian word.

Internee. Term used to refer to individuals who were living within the permanent relocation centers or internment camps. Can also be used to refer to individuals detained in Justice Department and Immigration and Naturalization Service camps.

Issei. First-generation Japanese immigrant living in America. Ineligible for citizenship until the law changed in 1952.

Japanese American Citizens League (JACL). Founded in 1929, the JACL is the oldest Asian American civil rights organization in the United States. It was the first Nisei organization that dealt with the social and political issues of the second generation. The JACL remained active throughout World War II and continues to the present day.

Kibei. Second-generation Japanese American, born in the United States, but educated in Japan.

Kotonk. Term used by Hawaiian Nisei soldiers to describe mainland Nisei soldiers. Literally, the sound of an empty coconut hitting the ground. Considered derogatory.

Military Intelligence Language School (MISLS)/Military Intelligence (MIS). Branch of the army that formed to train soldiers in the Japanese language to be used for military intelligence in the Pacific Theater.

Nikkei. Term used to describe an American citizen of Japanese ancestry.

Nisei. Second-generation Japanese American, born in the United States, a U.S. citizen. The bulk of those interned were of this generation.

Nisei soldier. Nisei men who fought in World War II in the 442nd Regimental Combat Team and the 100th Battalion (Hawaii). They also served as language specialists in the Military Intelligence Service and worked in all branches of the U.S. military.

Public Law 503. Law that made it a federal offense to violate any order issued by a designated military commander acting under the authority of E.O. 9066, effective March 21, 1942.

Redress. Compensation for a wrong or injury.

Relocation center/internment camp. The official government term was *relocation center* for the ten camps run by the WRA. They were guarded facilities for detaining both aliens and U.S. citizens. Technically, *internment camps* were the prisons run by the Department of Justice for noncitizen, suspect aliens of Japanese, German, and Italian ancestry.

Resettlement. Resettlement refers to the process through which Japanese Americans reestablished their lives, work, homes, families, and community after having been in forced detention. Time period following the close of the camps, lasting approximately through the early 1960s, although there is no definitive beginning and ending point.

Sansei. Third-generation Japanese American, born in the United States, a U.S. citizen.

Shikata ga nai. Japanese language phrase roughly translated meaning "it cannot be helped." A phrase that has been used to explain the resignation and lack of protest by Japanese as they were being moved to assembly and relocation centers.

War Relocation Authority (WRA). Civilian government agency housed within the Department of the Interior designed to administer and manage the internment centers and internee population.

Wartime Civil Control Authority (WCCA). The WCCA was the government agency supervising the evacuation of Japanese to assembly centers. Once individuals were moved to the relocation centers, the War Relocation Authority moved in to supervise the management and administration of the camps.

Yonsei. Fourth-generation Japanese American, born in the United States, a U.S. citizen.

Selected Annotated Bibliography

The list of available materials related to the Japanese American internment experience is quite extensive. This selected bibliography is divided into several parts. The first short list consists of U.S. government documents, some of which may be available at university research libraries, particularly those with collections that date back to World War II. The second list contains general books about the Japanese American experience. The third list of books are historical, sociological, and biographical materials on Japanese American history and books that focus on the Japanese American internment. Finally, there is a list of videos and films, and Internet resources.

Several excellent bibliographic essays on Japanese Americans exist. Paul Spickard's (1996: 177–85) essay details the growth and changes in the scholarship on Japanese Americans, from the early prewar studies, to historical analyses and accounts of the World War II period, to postwar studies of the Japanese American community working toward redress. Alice Yang Murray's *What Did the Internment of Japanese Americans Mean?* is intended to be a guide to teach about the history of Japanese American internment by providing classic and provocative articles and questions to guide thinking, discussion, and writing on the issue. "Suggestions for Further Reading" (Murray 2000: 153–62) in that volume provides a concise, extensive bibliographic source.

GOVERNMENT DOCUMENTS

Commission on Wartime Relocation and Internment of Civilians. *Personal Justice Denied*. Washington, D.C.: U.S. Government Printing Office, 1982. Most comprehensive report on the internment of Japanese, Aleuts, and Pribolof Islanders during World War II.
Final Report: Japanese Evacuation from the West Coast, 1942. Washington, D.C.: U.S.

Government Printing Office, 1943. Official government report of the evacuation program written by General John DeWitt.

War Relocation Authority. *WRA: A Story of Human Conservation.* Washington, D.C.: Government Printing Office, 1946. The government's account of the relocation and internment program.

GENERAL BOOKS ABOUT JAPANESE AMERICANS

Chan, Sucheng. *Asian Americans: An Interpretive History.* Boston: Twayne, 1991. History of Chinese, Japanese, Filipino, Korean, Asian Indian, and Southeast Asians in the United States.

Chuman, Frank F. *The Bamboo People: The Law and Japanese-Americans.* Del Mar, Calif.: Publishers Inc., 1976. First book on the legal history of people of Japanese ancestry in America.

Daniels, Roger. *The Politics of Prejudice.* New York: Atheneum, 1968. Focus on the time period preceding the mass evacuation and the anti-Japanese movement.

Hosokawa, Bill. *Nisei: The Quiet Americans.* New York: William Morrow, 1969. Background and history of the second-generation, American-born, Nisei, Japanese Americans.

———. *JACL In Quest of Justice: The History of the Japanese Americans Citizens League.* New York: William Morrow, 1982. History of the oldest Asian American civil rights organization in the United States, the Japanese American Citizens League.

Ichioka, Yuji. *The Issei: The World of the First Generation Japanese Immigrants 1885–1924.* New York: Free Press, 1988. Comprehensive history of the first-generation Japanese in America, their emigration and community, as well as the legal restrictions to which they were subjected.

Kitano, Harry. *Japanese Americans The Evolution of a Subculture.* Englewood Cliffs, N.J.: Prentice-Hall, 1969. Sociologist Harry Kitano and his family were interned during the war, and this is one of the first ethnic group monographs about the Japanese published after the war.

Kitano, Harry H.L. *Generations and Identity: The Japanese American.* Needham, Mass.: Ginn Press, 1993. This book builds upon Kitano's first book about Japanese Americans, focusing on the individual, group, and societal changes that have affected the Japanese American community.

Montero, Darrel. *Japanese Americans: Changing Patterns of Ethnic Affiliation over Three Generations.* Boulder: Westview Press, 1980. Sociological study of Issei, Nisei, and Sansei Japanese American ethnic identity.

Nakano, Mei. *Japanese American Women: Three Generations, 1890–1990.* San Francisco: National Japanese American Historical Society, and Berkeley: Mina Press, 1990. Historical narrative and interviews focusing on the experiences of the Issei, Nisei, and Sansei generations of Japanese American women.

Niiya, Brian (ed.) *Japanese American History: An A-to-Z Reference from 1868 to the Present.* New York: Facts on File, 1991. Comprehensive reference source about Americans of Japanese ancestry, particularly people, events, organizations, and phrases unique to Japanese American history and the World War II experience.

O'Brien, David J., and Stephen S. Fugita. *The Japanese American Experience*. Bloomington: Indiana University Press, 1991. History of the Japanese American experience through the present.

Okihiro, Gary Y. *Cane Fires: The Anti-Japanese Movement in Hawaii, 1865–1945.* Philadelphia: Temple University Press, 1991. Historical analysis of how the structure of Hawaiian plantation labor, the territorial government, and U.S. military worked to fuel the anti-Japanese movement in Hawaii.

Spickard, Paul R. *Japanese Americans: The Formation and Transformations of an Ethnic Group.* New York: Twayne, 1996. Comprehensive historical and sociological analysis of the Japanese American population with bibliographic essay.

Takaki, Ronald. *Pau Hana: Plantation Life and Labor in Hawaii, 1835–1920.* Honolulu: University of Hawaii Press, 1983. History of Japanese in Hawaii, focusing on immigrants working on the plantations.

———. *Strangers from a Different Shore.* New York: Little, Brown and Company, 1989. History of Chinese, Japanese, Filipino, Korean, Asian Indian, and Southeast Asians in the United States. Specific chapter focuses on World War II and Asian Americans.

Wilson, Robert A., and Bill Hosokawa. *East to America: A History of the Japanese in the United States.* New York: William Morrow, 1980. Documents the history of the Japanese in America until the late 1970s.

BOOKS ABOUT JAPANESE AMERICANS
DURING WORLD WAR II

Bosworth, Alan R. *America's Concentration Camps.* New York: Norton, 1967. One of the earliest postwar books that adopts the term *concentration camp* to refer to the internment and relocation centers. Documents the injustices suffered by internees.

Broom [Bloom], Leonard, and Ruth Riemer. *Removal and Return: The Socioeconomic Effects of the War on Japanese Americans.* Berkeley: University of California Press, 1949. Postwar study of property and income losses due to evacuation in the Los Angeles Japanese American community.

Chang, Thelma. *I Can Never Forget.* Honolulu: Sigi Productions, 1991. Photographs and essays that focus on the soldiers who served in the 100th Battalion and the 442nd Regimental Combat Team.

Christgau, John. *"Enemies": World War II Alien Internment.* Ames: Iowa State University Press, 1985. Includes the stories of German, Italian, and one Japanese alien who were detained in Department of Justice enemy alien internment camps.

Crost, Lyn. *Honor by Fire: Japanese Americans at War in Europe and the Pacific.* Novato, Calif.: Presidio Press, 1994. Journalist Lyn Crost reported on the 100th and 442nd during their battles in Europe.

Daniels, Roger. *Concentration Camps, U.S.A.: Japanese Americans and World War II.* New York: Holt, Rinehart and Winston, 1971. One of the first comprehensive historical and political analyses of Japanese American internment camps.

————. *Concentration Camps: North America Japanese in the United States and Canada during World War II*. Malabar, Fla.: Robert E. Krieger, 1981. Revised edition of Daniel's *Concentration Camps, U.S.A.* (New York: Holt, Rinehart, Winston, 1971). Includes updated chapters on the Japanese in Canada.

————. *Prisoners without Trial: Japanese Americans in World War II*. New York: Hill and Wang, 1993. Concise overview of the conditions before the war, during the internment, and the contemporary redress period.

Daniels, Roger, Sandra C. Taylor, and Harry H. L. Kitano (eds.). *Japanese Americans: From Relocation to Redress* (revised edition), 1991. Seattle: University of Washington Press. Comprehensive essays by more than thirty scholars and community activists examine the Japanese American experience during World War II through the redress movement of the 1980s.

Drinnon, Richard. *Keeper of Concentration Camps: Dillon S. Myer and American Racism*. Berkeley: University of California Press, 1987. Analysis of Dillon S. Myer's tenure as director of the War Relocation Authority and Commissioner of the Bureau of Indian Affairs.

Duus, Masayo Umezawa. *Unlikely Liberators: The Men of the 100th and 442nd*. Honolulu: University of Hawaii Press, 1987. Account of the Nisei soldiers of the all-Japanese American 442nd Regimental Combat Team and the 100th Infantry Battalion, focusing on their success on the battlefields of France, Germany, and Italy.

Embrey, Sue Kunitomi, Arthur A. Hansen, and Betty Kulberg Mitson. *Manzanar Martyr: An Interview with Harry Y. Ueno*. Fullerton, Calif.: Oral History Program, California State University, Fullerton, 1986. Oral history interview with Kibei activist Harry Ueno, organizer of the Kitchen Workers' Union at Manzanar, about his role in the Manzanar riots.

Fire for Effect: A Unit History of the 522 Field Artillery Battalion. Honolulu: 522nd Field Artillery Battalion Historical Album Committee, 1998. Photographs and essays by men who served in the 522nd Field Artillery Battalion, a division of the 442nd RCT.

Gardiner, C. Harvey. *Pawns in the Triangle of Hate: The Peruvian Japanese and the United States*. Seattle: University of Washington Press, 1981. An examination of the deportation of more than 2,200 people of Japanese ancestry interned at Department of Justice and Immigration and Naturalization detention centers in the United States.

Gesensway, Deborah, and Mindy Roseman. *Beyond Words: Images from America's Concentration Camps*. Ithaca, N.Y.: Cornell University Press, 1987. The discovery of a box of watercolor paintings in Ithaca, New York, led these authors to do research on the art of the concentration camps.

Girdner, Audrie, and Anne Loftis. *The Great Betrayal: The Evacuation of the Japanese-Americans during World War II*. New York: Macmillan, 1969. Historical analysis that focuses on the injustices suffered by Japanese Americans in the internment camps.

Grodzins, Morton. *Americans Betrayed: Politics of the Japanese American Evacuation*. Chicago: University of Chicago Press, 1949. Grodzins argues that the internment was caused by West Coast politicians, the media, and economic interest groups that fostered an anti-Japanese political climate.

Hansen, Arthur A., and Betty E. Mitson (eds.). *Voices Long Silent: An Oral Inquiry into the Japanese American Evacuation.* Fullerton, Calif.: The Oral History Program, California State University Fullerton, 1974. Collection of articles discussing the uses of oral history as a research tool to document the Japanese American wartime evacuation.

Hatamiya, Leslie T. *Righting a Wrong: Japanese Americans and the Passage of the Civil Liberties Act of 1988.* Stanford, Calif.: Stanford University Press, 1993. Analysis of the policy making process and factors affecting the Japanese American campaign for redress legislation.

Hill, Kimi Kodani. *Topaz Moon Chiura Obata's Art of the Internment.* Berkeley: Heyday Books, 2000. The life and work of Japanese artist Chiura Obata is documented by his granddaughter.

Hirabayashi, Lane Ryo. *The Politics of Fieldwork: Research in an American Concentration Camp.* Tucson: University of Arizona Press, 1999. Critical analysis of researcher relationships in the Japanese American Evacuation Research Study and anthropologist Dr. Tamie Tsuchiyama's in her work at the Poston (Arizona) Relocation Center.

Hohri, William Minoru. *Repairing America: An Account of the Movement for Japanese-American Redress.* Pullman: Washington State University Press, 1988. Traces the activity of one redress campaign for Japanese Americans interned during World War II.

Houston, Jeanne Wakatsuki. *Farewell to Manzanar.* Boston: Houghton Mifflin, 1973. Jeanne Wakatsuki chronicles the experience of her and her family when they were sent to the Manzanar Relocation Center in eastern California.

Ichioka, Yuji (ed.). *Views from Within: The Japanese American Evacuation and Resettlement Study.* Los Angeles: Asian American Studies Center, University of California at Los Angeles, 1989. Essays discussing the methodological and ethical issues of the Japanese American Evacuation and Resettlement Study.

Inada, Lawson (ed.) *Only What We Could Carry: The Japanese American Internment Experience.* Berkeley: Heyday Books, 2000. Literary anthology of recollections of the wartime experience, including artwork, poetry, and personal and primary source documents.

Inouye, Daniel. *Journey to Washington.* Englewood Cliffs, N.J.: Prentice Hall, 1967. Autobiography of Senator Daniel Inouye covering his life growing up in Hawaii, his service in the military during World War II, until his election to Congress.

Irons, Peter. *Justice at War: The Story of the Japanese American Internment Cases.* New York: Oxford University Press, 1983. Analysis of the original 1940s court convictions of Hirabayashi, Yasui, and Korematsu.

———. *The Courage of Their Convictions.* New York: Free Press, 1988. Discussion and analysis of U.S. Supreme Court civil rights cases, with a specific chapter on Gordon Hirabayashi.

———. *Justice Delayed: The Record of the Japanese American Internment Cases.* Middletown, Conn.: Wesleyan University Press, 1989. Edited essays and transcriptions of the *coram nobis* cases of Gordon Hirabayashi, Min Yasui, and Fred Korematsu.

James, Thomas. *Exile Within: The Schooling of Japanese Americans, 1942–1945.* Cam-

bridge: Harvard University Press, 1987. One of the very few studies analyzing the educational policies and practices within the camps.

Kessler, Lauren. *Stubborn Twig*. New York: Plume/Penguin, 1993. Lively historical biography of prominent Masuo Yasui and the Yasui family of Hood
River, Oregon.

Kikuchi, Charles. *The Kikuchi Diary: Chronicles of an American Concentration Camp*.
Urbana and Chicago: University of Illinois Press, 1973. Kikuchi's account
of his relocation and internment, and his ethnic ambivalence of being an
American-born Japanese forced into an internment camp.

Kikumura, Akemi. *Through Harsh Winters: The Life of a Japanese Immigrant Woman*.
Novato, Calif.: Chandler and Sharp, 1981. Life history of Michiko Tanaka,
including her experiences in camp, as a context for understanding the
Japanese American family.

———. *Promises Kept: The Life of an Issei Man*. Novato, Calif.: Chandler and Sharp,
1991. Life history of Akemi Kikumura's father is a companion piece to the
one about her mother.

Leighton, Alexander H. *The Governing of Men: General Principles and Recommendations Based on the Experience at a Japanese Relocation Camp*. Princeton, N.J.:
Princeton University Press, 1945. Psychologist Leighton worked for the
Bureau of Sociological Research and directed a series of community analysis research studies within the camp.

Masaoka, Mike M. *They Call Me Moses Masaoka*. New York: William Morrow,
1987. Written with Bill Hosokawa, Masaoka recalls his years growing up
in Utah, and his work with the JACL and later as a lobbyist in Washington, D.C.

Murray, Alice Yang. *What Did the Internment of Japanese Americans Mean?* Boston:
Bedford/St. Martin's, 2000. Selected readings on the Japanese American
internment with discussion questions and suggested readings.

Myer, Dillon S. *Uprooted Americans: The Japanese Americans and the War Relocation
Authority during World War II*. Tucson: University of Arizona Press, 1971.
WRA Director Dillon Myer documents the positive aspects and his per-
spective on the Japanese American internment camps.

Nagata, Donna K. *Legacy of Injustice: Exploring the Cross-Generational Impact of the
Japanese American Internment*. New York and London: Plenum Press, 1993.
First psychological study exploring the impact of the internment camps
on the Sansei, third-generation Japanese Americans.

Nishimoto, Richard. *Inside an American Concentration Camp: Japanese American Resistance at Poston, Arizona*. Selected and edited with an introduction and
afterword by Lane Ryo Hirabayashi. Tucson: University of Arizona Press,
1995. Richard Nishimoto's writings during his internment at Poston Relocation Center.

O'Brien, Robert W. *The College Nisei*. Palo Alto, Calif.: Pacific Books, 1949. Study
and report of the college Nisei and the National Japanese American Student Relocation Council.

Ogawa, Dennis M. *Kodomo no tame ni: For the Sake of the Children*. Honolulu:
University of Hawaii Press, 1978. Anthology of essays related to the Japanese experience in Hawaii, including the war.

Okada, John. *No-No Boy*. Rutherford, Vt.: Charles E. Tuttle, 1957. Reprinted by

Seattle: University of Washington Press, 1979. Novel exploring the social and psychological dilemmas of a Nisei who answered "no-no" on the loyalty questionnaire.

Okihiro, Gary Y. *Whispered Silences: Japanese Americans and World War II*. Seattle: University of Washington Press, 1996. Historical narrative on the Japanese American experience in Hawaii and the mainland accompanies this photographic essay of the internment camps.

Okubo, Mine. *Citizen 13660*. New York: Columbia University Press, 1946. Through drawings and narrative, artist Mine Okubo documents her family's experience at Tanforan Assembly Center and Topaz (Utah) Relocation Center.

Smith, Page. *Democracy on Trial: The Japanese American Evacuation and Relocation in World War II*. New York: Simon and Schuster, 1995. Historian Smith defends the WRA in their job managing a population of more than 120,000 people of Japanese ancestry during the war.

Sone, Monica. *Nisei Daughter*. Seattle: University of Washington Press, 1953. One of the early first person accounts written and published after the war examines the author's struggle for acceptance in society as a Japanese American.

Takezawa, Yasuko. *Breaking the Silence: Redress and Japanese American Ethnicity*. Ithaca, N.Y.: Cornell University Press, 1995. Sociological study of the redress movement in Seattle, Washington, and its effects upon Japanese American ethnic identity.

Tateishi, John. *And Justice for All: An Oral History of the Japanese American Detention Camps*. New York: Random House, 1984. Thirty oral history accounts of Japanese American experiences in relocation center and Department of Justice camps, as voluntary evacuees, and in the army.

Taylor, Sandra C. *Jewel of the Desert: Japanese American Internment at Topaz*. Berkeley: University of California Press, 1993. Once the fifth-largest city in Utah, Topaz internment camp was home to more than 8,000 internees who once lived in the greater San Francisco Bay area.

tenBroek, Jacobus, Edward N. Barnhart, and Floyd W. Matson. *Prejudice, War and the Constitution*. 3rd ed. Berkeley: University of California Press, 1968. The third book in the series of books based on the Japanese American Evacuation and Resettlement Study examines the internment experience from a sociopolitical perspective.

Thomas, Dorothy Swaine. *The Salvage*. Berkeley: University of California Press, 1952. Second book of the JERS project focuses on the resettlement experiences of Japanese Americans in the Midwest and East.

Thomas, Dorothy Swaine, and Richard S. Nishimoto. *The Spoilage: Japanese American Evacuation and Resettlement during World War II*. Berkeley: University of California Press, 1946. First in a series of books that were produced from the Japanese American Evacuation Research Study about the effects of evacuation and internment.

Tomita, Mary Kimoto. *Dear Miye: Letters Home from Japan 1939–1946*. Stanford, Calif.: Stanford University Press, 1995. Letters from Nisei Mary Kimoto to her friend Miye documents her time in Japan during the war.

Uchida, Yoshiko. *Journey to Topaz*. New York: Charles Scribner's Sons, 1971. First-person account of her journey from Berkeley, California, to the Tanforan Assembly Center and to the Topaz Relocation Center in Utah.

Uyeda, Clifford I. *Suspended: Growing Up Asian in America*. San Francisco: National Japanese American Historical Society, 2000. Autobiography of Nisei community activist Clifford Uyeda and his experiences before, during, and after the war.

Weglyn, Michi. *Years of Infamy*. New York: William Morrow and Co., 1976. One of the first books exposing the U.S. government's false claims of "military necessity" in the Japanese American evacuation and relocation program.

DOCUMENTARY FILMS AND VIDEO SOURCES

Children of the Camps (1999). Producer: Satsuki Ina. Examines the psychological trauma of children who were in internment camps and their lives afterward. 57 minutes. <http://www.children-of-the-camps.org> NAATA.

The Color of Honor (1988). Producer/Director: Loni Ding. Extensive documentary on the Japanese Americans who were in the Military Intelligence Service, 442nd Regimental Combat Team, 100th Infantry, and Heart Mountain Draft Resisters. 90 minutes. NAATA.

Conscience and the Constitution (2000). Producer/Director: Frank Abe. More than sixty men refused to be drafted from the Heart Mountain Relocation Center in Wyoming. They were tried and sentenced to three years in federal prison. 57 minutes.

Conversations: Before the War/After the War (1986). Director: Robert A. Nakamura. Docu-drama of three fictional Japanese American individuals who discuss their personal experiences and feelings about World War II and their internment. 29 minutes. NAATA.

Days of Waiting (1988). Director/Producer: Steven Okazaki. Documentary of Caucasian artist Estelle Ishigo, who was married to Japanese American Arthur Shigeharu Ishigo and evacuated to Pomona Assembly Center and then interned at Heart Mountain, Wyoming; won an Academy Award for Best Documentary Short. 18 minutes, color. NAATA.

A Family Gathering (1988). Director: Lise Yasui. Lise Yasui traces her family history and the story of her grandfather Masuo Yasui of Hood River, Oregon, who was arrested and detained at Department of Justice internment camps in Santa Fe and Missoula, Montana. 30 and 60 minutes, color.

Heart Mountain: Three Years in an Internment Camp (1997). A KCSM production in the New Americans Series. Consulting Producer: Dianne Fukami. Interviews former internees of the Heart Mountain (Wyoming) internment camp. 27 minutes.

Meeting at Tule Lake (1994). Director/Producer: Scott T. Tschutani for the Tule Lake Committee. Internees at the Tule Lake segregation center discuss their experiences and the issues of loyalty and their citizenship. 33 minutes. NAATA.

A Personal Matter: Gordon Hirabayashi vs. the United States (1992). Director: John de Graaf with The Constitution Project. Focuses on the life of Gordon Hirabayashi and his Supreme Court case challenging the curfew and evacuation of Japanese Americans during World War II. 30 minutes. NAATA.

Rabbit in the Moon (1999). Producer: Emiko Omori. Omori presents a controversial portrait of her family's removal and incarceration during World War II. 85 minutes. Film Library.

Starting Over: Japanese Americans After the War (1996). Producer: Dianne Fukami for KCSM television. Documentary focusing on the resettlement period after World War II and the difficulties and adjustments Japanese Americans had to make when starting their lives over after internment. 60 minutes. NAATA.

Tanforan: Race Track to Assembly Center (1995). Director: Diane Fukami for KCSM television. Documents the transformation of Tanforan racetrack in San Bruno, California, to an assembly center. 57 minutes.

Unfinished Business: The Japanese American Internment Cases (1986). Steven Okazaki, 58 minutes, color. Examines the cases of Fred Korematsu, Minoru Yasui, and Gordon Hirabayashi during World War II through the discovery of evidence of government misconduct, allowing the cases to be heard again.

Unforgettable Face (1993). Producer: Nicole Newnham. Yanina Cywinska was a sixteen-year-old imprisoned in the Dachau concentration camp. She reunites with George Oiye, a soldier in the 522nd Field Artillery Battalion, responsible for liberating prisoners of the camp in 1945. 13 minutes. NAATA.

WEB SITES AND INTERNET RESOURCES

There are numerous Web sites documenting the experience of Japanese Americans during World War II. Because Web addresses often change, those listed represent the most actively used by the Japanese American community for information pertaining to the internment during World War II. Each of these contain useful links to other Web sites on the internment experience.

Civil Liberties and Public Education Fund. <http://www.clpef.net> This site contains information about the people and projects sponsored by the Civil Liberties Public Education Fund, established by the Civil Rights Act of 1988.

Japanese American Citizens League. <http://www.jacl.org> Founded in 1929, this organization is the oldest Asian American civil rights organization in the United States.

Japanese American National Museum. <http://www. janm.org> This museum documents the experiences of Japanese Americans with an oral history and education program along with rotating exhibits about the Japanese American experience.

National Archives and Records Administration. <http://www.nara/gov> Digital photographs of the Japanese American internment can be found by using the archives database and searching the documents of the War Relocation Authority.

National Asian American Telecommunications Association. <http://www.naata net.org> Largest source of Asian and Pacific American film and video; supports and funds Asian Pacific American documentary artists.

National Japanese American Historical Society. <http://www.nikkeiheritage.org> Established in 1981 and based in San Francisco, this organization is dedicated to preserving the history of Japanese Americans in the United States.

Index

About the Author

WENDY NG is Associate Professor of Sociology at San Jose State University.